*Contemporary Approaches to Interest Measurement*

*This is a volume in the*
*Minnesota Library on Student Personnel Work*
*edited by Ralph F. Berdie*

# Contemporary Approaches to Interest Measurement

edited by
Donald G. Zytowski

University of Minnesota
Press • Minneapolis

*Library of Congress Catalog Card Number: 73-76895*

*ISBN* 0-8166-0676-5

# Foreword  1793135

IT IS APPROPRIATE that this volume be published by the University of Minnesota Press for at least two reasons. One is Minnesota's psychologists' longtime involvement in research on vocational interests and their measurement. The names of D. G. Paterson, E. G. Williamson, H. D. Carter, J. G. Darley, K. E. Clark, Leona Tyler, R. F. Berdie, and D. P. Campbell come readily to mind. The second reason is the University of Minnesota Press's history of publishing monographs and books on opinions, values, interests, and their measurement.

Significant publications of the Press have been several bulletins of the Employment Stabilization Research Institute including the Berman, Darley, and Paterson 1934 monograph, *Vocational Interest Scales*; the Rundquist and Sletto, *Minnesota Scale for the Survey of Opinions*, 1937; Strong's 1955 book, *Vocational Interests 18 Years after College*; Darley and Hagenah's book, *Vocational Interest Measurement: Theory and Practice*, 1955; Layton's *Counseling Use of the Strong Vocational Interest Blank*, 1958, and his *Strong Vocational Interest Blank: Research and Uses*, 1960; and Clark's 1961 *Vocational Interests of Nonprofessional Men*.

It is impressive that Don Zytowski has incorporated in this document papers by or about leading researchers in vocational interest measurement on the most visible interest inventories at this time. The history of research

v

on vocational interests and their measurement is dominated by two names, Strong and Kuder. Research on the instruments for the measurement of interests developed by these pioneers represents one of the most active areas of investigation in psychology in this century. It is gratifying that intensive research is being carried on currently by Campbell and Harmon on the Strong and by Zytowski on the Kuder. Equally gratifying is the development of new approaches and new instruments as presented in this volume. The Work Adjustment Project, headed by Lofquist, England, Dawis, and Weiss, and specifically the Minnesota Importance Questionnaire, described in this book by Weiss, are contributions of importance to vocational counselors. The sustained research efforts on the Minnesota Work Adjustment Project, the Clark Minnesota Vocational Interest Inventory, the Super Work Values Inventory, and the D'Costa Ohio Vocational Interest Survey represent important alternatives to the Strong and Kuder theories and instruments.

As Zytowski points out, interest inventories are useful for only a limited group — those who have access to a variety of occupations as well as those who seek to maximize their occupational satisfaction. These are persons who are work-oriented, able to anticipate differential satisfaction, and anxious to maximize satisfaction.

This book will also be found useful by only a limited group, those psychologists who are work-oriented. Vocational and counseling psychologists who study this book will be rewarded by increased satisfaction with their knowledge of contemporary approaches to interest measurement.

Wilbur L. Layton

Ames, Iowa
September 29, 1971

# Acknowledgments

THE PAPERS THAT FORM the chapters of this book grew out of several workshops on interest and work value inventories held in various parts of the country in 1968 and 1969. Since the sponsors of those workshops would not otherwise be known, I would like to acknowledge their contribution: Dr. Roy Warman, Student Counseling Service, Iowa State University; Dr. David Olsen, Student Counseling Services, Gonzaga University, Spokane, Washington; and Dr. Karl Springob, Laboratory of Psychological Studies, Stevens Institute of Technology, Hoboken, New Jersey.

At the time I proposed turning the workshop presentations into a book, Dave Campbell remarked that it always cost twice as much and took five times as long as originally expected. Were it not for the cordial, expert, and generally supportive assistance of the staff of the University of Minnesota Press, Campbell would have been right.

Donald G. Zytowski

# List of Contributors

W. Leslie Barnette, Jr.
*Professor of Psychology*
*State University of New York at Buffalo*

David P. Campbell
*Professor of Psychology*
*Director, Center for Interest Measurement Research*
*University of Minnesota*

Ayres D'Costa
*Associate Director*
*Division of Educational Measurement and Research*
*Association of American Medical Colleges*

Lenore W. Harmon
*Associate Professor*
*Department of Educational Psychology*
*University of Wisconsin — Milwaukee*

Wilbur L. Layton
*Vice-President for Student Affairs*
*Iowa State University*

Donald E. Super
*Professor of Psychology*
*Teachers College*
*Columbia University*

David J. Weiss
*Associate Professor of Psychology*
*University of Minnesota*

Donald G. Zytowski
*Professor of Psychology*
*Assistant Director, Student Counseling Service*
*Iowa State University*

# Contents

*Contemporary Approaches to Interest Measurement*

# 1

# Considerations
# in the Selection and Use
# of Interest Inventories

### Donald G. Zytowski

THE CONTEMPORARY IDEA of vocational adjustment — fitting a round peg in a round hole — requires both that the job be performed satisfactorily and that the individual find satisfaction in it (Lofquist and Dawis, 1969). The first criterion is dependent upon the job requirements and the answering abilities and resources in the person, while the second is generated by the job's attributes and the person's motivations, which are characterized by his interests or work values.

The role of motivations is increasingly important for vocational adjustment in some situations. According to Borgen (1972), motivations are important determiners of vocational adjustment among high ability persons. He summarizes evidence from several studies to show that where a wide range of abilities are present, interests are less strong influences on occupational membership than is general level of ability. For persons with high general ability, motivations are more prominent in differentiating among their vocational or career plans. Thus, persons with above-average general ability usually have more differentiated motivational structures — or interests, as we call them — which are increasingly functional in producing satisfaction.

It must be emphasized that interest inventories are useful for only a limited number of persons — those who have access to a variety of occupations and those who seek to plan ahead to maximize their occupational satisfaction. The latter group excludes persons for whom work, as it is performed in occupations, is not a meaningful or important part of their lives. Individuals who are willing to trust to accident, who are willing or even anxious to live on a marginal income, or who do not need to work would hardly concern themselves with their future occupational plans. Liking or disliking, or preference, is irrelevant for them. On the other hand, those who are work oriented and are able to anticipate differential satisfaction and take advantage of it can use information from interest inventories.

So, to practice vocational counseling, from either the employer's or the potential employee's point of view, the counselor must have adequate measures of ability and particularly of motivation. This latter variable has a fortunate, or confusing, array of measures from which the counselor may choose, depending on how well he is informed about them. There are about a dozen inventories for measuring interests in regular use today, and at least another half dozen whose popularity has faded. In the past five years a number of inventories have been significantly revised, and several new ones have been developed. One of the latter is an inventory which measures work or occupational "values" (Zytowski, 1970). The women's form of the Strong Vocational Interest Blank (SVIB) is entirely new, the men's form has had revisions and additions, and both now include basic interest scales. An expansion of the Kuder D, the Occupational Interest Survey (KOIS), which has a unique scoring system, has appeared. The Minnesota Vocational Interest Inventory (MVII) for nonprofessional occupations has been published recently as has the Ohio Vocational Interest Survey (OVIS), which is scored for a number of homogeneous scales generated from the date-people-things trichotomy of the new *Dictionary of Occupational Titles*. The Work Adjustment Project at the University of Minnesota has made available an inventory of vocational needs, scored normatively for a large number of occupations, and the Work Values Inventory (WVI) has emerged from Super's Career Pattern Study.

These inventories are the subject of this volume. Once a counselor has determined that it is appropriate to use an interest inventory, he needs to know the essential differences among the inventories available in order to select the proper one for a given kind of client. Many counselors express a preference only for information with which to interpret profiles. Interpretation, however, will proceed more skillfully if one understands how scales are formed, i.e., the nature of their content and scoring, their relation to other instruments, and the like.

4

First of all, that any interest inventory possesses adequate psychometric qualities — reliability and validity — must be established. For inventories, as compared with tests, this is not a simple matter.

Consider reliability. Two kinds must be taken into account: repeatability and internal consistency. Anyone would want a measure of interests to give the same results at two points in time. But one must realize that repeatability is complicated by the development and maturation of interests. Although an inventory ought to give the same results when repeated within a short interval, it should not be so stable as to be insensitive to changes in interests arising from maturation. Internal consistency is essential for certain kinds of scales, which will be described later, but unnecessary for others. So, depending upon the age of the client with whom the counseling psychologist is working, and what kinds of measures are employed, different levels of reliabilities may be expected and found acceptable.

Then, an interest inventory must be valid. That is, it must relate to something in the real world, or have some usefulness relative to its purpose. Clearly an ability test should predict achievement of some kind which can often be measured after a limited time. But validity for an interest measure presents a peculiar problem. While many interest inventories are intended only, or mainly, to describe, their validity must rest upon their ability to point to what the person will do, or what he is most likely to gain satisfaction from, at some future — usually fairly distant — date. Therefore the author of an interest inventory must make a considerable investment in its construction and then must wait a longer interval than he would for perhaps any other type of psychological testing instrument to discover if his inventory is valid.

Only the two prototype inventories, the SVIB and the Kuder Preference Record, have been in existence long enough to show that people do behave in accord with their scores on occupational or interest scales obtained in late adolescence or early adulthood.

Because of these problems, those who make interest inventories resort to certain alternative procedures to establish the partial or temporary validity of their instrument. In general, the goal of these procedures is to demonstrate that the inventory can differentiate between groups either in satisfaction or in occupation. This cannot be achieved with scales which overlap to any considerable degree, so the independence of scales is taken as one evidence of validity. The SVIB, since it uses a men-in-general comparison group, reports the independence of scores earned on a scale by members of the group which formed the scale (or a cross-validation group) and scores earned on that scale by the men-in-general group. Any potential scale that cannot make this discrimination is rejected. The KOIS, which is a new version of the Kuder series built on a principle similar to the SVIB, claims validity on the basis that it makes few errors-of-classification. That is, it is not likely to score persons high on an occupational scale which is not that person's real occupation.

Do not forget, though, that the final validity of an inventory is its ability to predict ultimate occupational entry and satisfaction. Even communication of results for self-clarification and definition, without predicting into the future, is based on the assumption that this prediction could be made.

If the user is satisfied that the array of interest measures available to him possess the necessary minimum of appropriate reliability and validity, then he may concern himself with their differential characteristics. Among the inventories under consideration here, the following characteristics, which distinguish one inventory from another, are the most relevant.

*Population.* Every interest measure, by virtue of several factors, is more appropriate for one group of people than for another. Sex is one such factor; the counselor must know whether the inventory is used for both sexes, or whether there are forms for each. Reading difficulty is another variable which influences utility; the lowest age level that can use the inventory is dependent upon how sophisticated its language is. Also important for those inventories which tell what occupational groups a person is similar to is the level and coverage of the occupations reported. An adolescent who seems likely to go to college will acquire little useful information from the MVII, whose occupational scales are mainly composed of skilled groups rather than the professional and semiprofessional occupations that a college graduate would usually enter.

*Items.* Although they may not be particularly important in selecting an interest inventory, details about items are sources of variability among measures. Traditionally items were generated and refined primarily by the intuition and judgment of the inventory makers. Recently, the MIQ and OVIS have drawn their items from theoretical rationales and the WVI from prior research. This may ensure that the items represent the universe of interests in some systematic way, but it does not necessarily guarantee the utility or validity of the inventory.

Inventories vary in the number of items they have. Typically there are between three and four hundred items in each inventory; the number, of course, affects the time for administration. Inventories also differ in the type of response required. Some are free choice, where the person responds either like, indifferent, or dislike to all items; others require the respondent to endorse one item one way, one another, and to leave one blank. The last form is in effect a ranking procedure.

Inventories that employ the free-response format are susceptible to a person's tendency to respond consistently in one way or another — giving socially approved answers, extremes, or many or few likes or dislikes. For inventories that test the similarity of the person responding to those in given occupations, these sets may be a part of an occupational group's typical responses, but for those that report types of interests, response sets will produce distortions in the profile. On the other hand, the forced-choice format, which reduces the influence of sets, is distasteful to some persons who do not want to reject or accept some alternatives because they may like or dislike all the alternatives given.

*Physical features.* The cost and convenience of use of different inventories may determine the selection of one over others for a given population. A primary concern is whether the materials are reusable or consumed in administration. Those which can be used more than once distribute the cost of the test booklet over many administrations; consumable booklets cost more per administration but prevent mix-ups in form matching, and do not get dirty or ragged from continued use.

*Scoring.* Interest inventories ordinarily generate more scales than any other test and consequently are more difficult or expensive to score. Most may be scored by hand but this procedure is inconvenient if more than just a few scales have to be scored. Computer scoring is available for each inventory, and is a requisite for the KOIS, whose publisher does not release keys to anyone. All scoring agencies will score from one to a few answer sheets on a quick service basis for use in counseling agencies, as well as packets of answer sheets such as a school district would produce. Costs vary chiefly on the basis of the number submitted in one batch. Not all agencies score all inventories: the user may choose his agency for some inventories, but is the captive customer for others.

Even though the form of the score output varies, all report numerical scores for each scale. Except for the KOIS and the WVI, every inventory is given on a form which permits a graphic or profiled presentation. The

7

KOIS interpretation relies not on a profiling procedure, but on a ranking system, and the scoring computer does some of the ranking for the user.

Various scoring agencies will, if it is specified in the order, produce summaries of the scores earned by a group of inventory takers in the form of frequency distributions or means and standard deviations. This is of no use to the single client who is being counseled, but may be of significant value to researchers or to administrators planning curricula.

*Scales.* The output of all interest inventories consists of scores on a number of scales. They vary in kind, reporting type of interest or similarity with persons in different occupations, and among the latter they vary in the portion of the entire range of possible occupations they cover.

Most inventories have one or more validating scales, and some have a validating index for every scale scored. These scales reflect the confidence which one may place in the entire profile or in individual scales. Moreover, any well-assembled set of items can yield scales that are not in the interest domain at all. Several inventories have such scales, which vary considerably in the information they offer regarding such factors as managerial success qualities, maturity, and similarity with college majors. Other scales have been and can be formed by a person who understands their construction. An anxiety scale has been developed for the SVIB but is not scored by any scoring service, and other scales, such as, say, one measuring leadership, could be formed for the KOIS or another inventory.

An extremely important distinction must be made when discussing interest inventory scales. This is the difference between *homogeneous* and *normative* scales. Homogeneous scales are assembled from items which are analogous in content, are strongly intercorrelated, and reflect some specific area of interest. For instance, "keep a record of traffic past a point," "sort mail," and "keep a record of community chest pledges" are all similar enough to be called clerical interests. Other items from an inventory which correlate significantly with these items would form a homogeneous scale that undoubtedly could be named "clerical." Homogeneous means that certain items have been assembled into a scale because they are closely related to each other. This is the basis of scales of the Kuder Preference Record in all its forms.

It would be expected that persons who are employed as clerks, bookkeepers, or accountants would score high on a clerical scale. But might they have some other likes or dislikes which distinguish them? The responses to interest inventory items that members of an occupation have in common constitute another kind of scale, *normative*, which was first developed with the SVIB. The items are internally consistent or homogeneous only for the occupational group which they differentiate, *not* necessarily for people-in-general. Thus, repeatability is the type of reliability which the user of normative scales most needs to concern himself with.

Normative and homogeneous scales require distinctly different means of communicating the results of scores to the inventory taker. For a normative scale, the counselor reports the degree to which the person has interests similar to those of persons in a given occupation. For homogeneous scales the person's chief or dominant *types* of interests are reported.

Hershenson (1968) differentiates between vocational and occupational counseling. The former, he maintains, is required at an earlier stage of development when self-clarification is the task and when no specific occupational plans or choices can be made. The latter is only possible when the person is sufficiently aware of his capacities and is able to engage in goal-directed activities. It seems logical to extend this distinction to say that scores on homogeneous scales of interest inventories best aid in self-clarification, but are less effective in helping one make an occupational choice, while inventories that yield information on one's similarities with various occupations do not serve the former function, but rather the latter.

Homogeneous interest inventories are frequently criticized because they are "transparent" — that is, the results can be influenced by the intention of the inventory taker: he can achieve higher scores on one or a few of the scales than represent his true interests. This may occur when the scores will be used in deciding whether or not to hire a person, or perhaps in determining who is best motivated to receive scholarship help. Youths often feel pressure to be accepted by peers, and may slant their interest inventory responses to that kind of pattern which is most esteemed by their adolescent subculture. In the appropriate situation, where a person wants to explore honestly the pattern of his interests — as in the case of a housewife who has been out of the labor force while her children have matured — the homogeneous inventory is a useful instrument.

The normatively scaled interest inventory is less susceptible to deliberate attempts to distort. This is in part because the inventory taker cannot know all the interests which might be distinctive to different occupations, especially since he is likely to overlook negative preferences or dislikes. Dislike responses figure very strongly in the building up of scores on some occupations.

9

The coverage of the scales generated in an interest inventory is an important variable in its utility. A comparison of the homogeneous scales from each inventory discussed in the book is given in Table 1.1. As can be observed, many of the same scales are repeated on all or three of the four inventories. The OVIS is distinctive in breaking down into several categories some of the scales on the other instruments. The MVII has the fewest scales, while the SVIB scales cover the broadest range.

The scope of occupational scales on a given inventory may influence the decision on whether or not it is appropriate for a given person. Table 1.2

Table 1.1. Homogeneous Scales on Four Interest Inventories

| SVIB-M | SVIB-F | MVII | OVIS |
|---|---|---|---|
| Writing | Writing | | Literary |
| | Performing arts | | Entertainment |
| Art | Art | | Artistic |
| Music | Music | | Music |
| Teaching | Teaching | | |
| Social service | Social service | | Teacher, counselor, social worker |
| | | | Training |
| | | | Skilled personal service |
| | | | Personal service |
| Medical service | Medical service | Health service | Medical |
| | | | Nursing |
| | | | Care of people and animals |
| Recreational leader | Outdoors | Outdoors | |
| | Sports | | |
| Agriculture | Biological science | | Agriculture |
| Nature | | | |
| Science | Physical science | | Applied technology |
| | | Electronics | |
| Mechanical | Mechanical | Mechanical | Machine work |
| | | Carpentry | Crafts |
| | | | Inspection-testing |
| | | | Manual |
| | Homemaking | Food service | |
| | | | Appraisal |
| Mathematics | Numbers | | Numerical |
| Office practices | Office practices | Office work | Clerical |
| Merchandising | Merchandising | | Customer services |
| Sales | Sales | Sales-office | Sales representative |
| Business management | | | Management |
| Technical supervision | | | |
| Public speaking | Public speaking | | Promotion-communication |
| Law/politics | Law/politics | | |
| Religious activities | Religious activities | | |
| Military activities | | | |
| Adventure | | | |
| | | Clean hands | |

10

shows the men's scales from the five inventories that have normative scales distributed in cells formed by Roe's fields and levels of occupations (Roe, 1956). Generally speaking, there are few scales at the highest levels, perhaps because they are by definition levels which require unusual talent. The MIQ is represented by a few scales at level II, but the bulk of this coverage is provided by the SVIB and the KOIS. Business contact or sales occupations do not receive coverage until level III, where the KOIS is especially strong. The MVII and MIQ begin to take over at level IV, which is labeled by Roe as skilled, although neither present any occupations in the fields of science or general culture. The MIQ, by reason of its many factory occupations, is very strong in the technology field at both the skilled and semiskilled levels. There is virtually no coverage at the un-

Table 1.2. Distribution of Male Occupational Scales on the SVIB, KOIS, MVII, and MIQ by Roe's Table of Fields and Levels

| Level | Service | Business Contact | Organization | Technology | Outdoor | Sciences | General Cultural | Arts and Entertainment |
|---|---|---|---|---|---|---|---|---|
| I SVIB | 1 | | | | | 6 | | |
| KOIS | 3 | | | | | 8 | | |
| MVII | | | | | | | | |
| MIQ | | | | | | | | |
| II SVIB | 2 | 1 | 8 | 1 | 1 | 5 | 7 | 4 |
| KOIS | 3 | | 4 | 5 | 1 | 6 | 8 | 1 |
| MVII | | | | | | | 1 | 1 |
| MIQ | 2 | | 1 | 3 | | 5 | 4 | |
| III SVIB | 2 | 2 | 4 | 1 | 1 | 2 | 1 | 2 |
| KOIS | 1 | 7 | 3 | 3 | 3 | 4 | 1 | |
| MVII | | 1 | | | | | | |
| MIQ | | 3 | 3 | 1 | | 2 | 3 | |
| IV SVIB | 1 | | 1 | 2 | | | | 1 |
| KOIS | 2 | | 2 | 9 | | | | |
| MVII | 1 | 1 | | 11 | | | | |
| MIQ | 8 | 1 | 6 | 12 | 1 | | | 1 |
| V SVIB | | | | | | | | |
| KOIS | 1 | | | 2 | | | | |
| MVII | 1 | | 2 | 2 | | | | |
| MIQ | 5 | | 3 | 11 | | | | 1 |
| VI SVIB | | | | | | | | |
| KOIS | | | | | | | | |
| MVII | 1 | | | | | | | |
| MIQ | 2 | | | 2 | | | | |

skilled level, probably because change from one occupation to another at this level requires no investment in particular training, and little reason to weigh whether one will enjoy the particular occupation.

Women's occupational scales on the SVIB and KOIS are compared in Table 1.3. Both inventories cover the science, general cultural, and service areas about equally well. Larger frequencies for one or the other of these inventories in a given cell are partly the result of inclusion of several settings of the same occupation. The SVIB covers fairly high-level arts and entertainment occupations well, and the KOIS goes to skilled occupations in this group as well. Neither includes occupations related to the outdoors, and technical and business contact occupations are not represented very widely. This is more likely the result of the small population of women in these fields than of oversights on the part of the inventory authors. Nevertheless, for women who are interested in exploring occupations in technical, outdoor, or sales areas, such scales would be extremely valuable and worth developing.

Table 1.4 compares the coverage of the homogeneous work value scales of the MIQ with the WVI. In actuality both sets of scales were derived from the cumulated research on what persons say they seek in their work. Differences between the two are only the consequence of

Table 1.3. Distribution of Female Occupational Scales on the SVIB and KOIS by Roe's Table of Fields and Levels

| Level | Service | Business Contact | Organization | Technology | Outdoor | Sciences | General Cultural | Arts and Entertainment |
|---|---|---|---|---|---|---|---|---|
| I SVIB ....... | | | | | | 3 | | |
| KOIS ....... | | | | | | 7 | | |
| II SVIB ....... | 3 | | 2 | 1 | | 4 | 10 | 6 |
| KOIS ....... | 7 | | 1 | 1 | | 9 | 5 | 1 |
| III SVIB ....... | 5 | 1 | 1 | | | 6 | 2 | 1 |
| KOIS ....... | | 2 | 4 | | | 4 | 4 | 1 |
| IV SVIB ....... | 2 | | 2 | | | 1 | | |
| KOIS ....... | 2 | | 5 | | | 1 | | 2 |
| V SVIB ....... | 2 | | 1 | 2 | | | | |
| KOIS ....... | | | | | | | | |
| VI SVIB ....... | | | | | | | | |
| KOIS ....... | | | | | | | | |

12

finer or coarser distinctions and of the author's ideas regarding which variables are most important. Many of the variables are identical, some are broken down into several aspects, and a few duplicate only a part of the corresponding variable. For example, the MIQ's ability utilization can be understood as an equivalent to the WVI's intellectual stimulation.

Table 1.4. Variables Measured by Two Work Values Inventories

| WVI | MIQ |
| --- | --- |
| Security | Security |
| Prestige | Social status |
| Economic returns | Compensation |
| Achievement | Achievement |
| | Advancement |
| | Recognition |
| Surroundings | Working conditions |
| | Company policy and administration |
| Associates | Co-workers |
| Management | Authority |
| Supervisory | Supervision – human relations |
| | Supervision – technical |
| Independence | Independence |
| Altruism | Social service |
| Creativity | Creativity |
| Way of life | Moral values |
| Intellectual stimulation | Ability utilization |
| Variety | Variety |
| | Responsibility |
| | Activity |

The presence of scales measuring the same or similar variables on different inventories is bound to invite comparison, particularly since counselors are apt to use more than one inventory in an attempt to be more certain of the results they obtain. There have been no formal tests of the similarities of the homogeneous scales of the inventories under consideration here. But the normative scales of the same and similar names have been scrutinized by several researchers to date.

There are three scales on the SVIB and the MVII that can be compared and fourteen scales common to the latter inventory and the KOIS. A test of their similarity (Zytowski, 1968) showed rather low correlations, ranging from −.7 for SVIB-MVII printer to .36 for KOIS-MVII truck driver. Analogous results have been obtained in comparisons of the SVIB and KOIS on twenty-seven to fifty-two scales. (The number of comparisons varies according to how similar the investigator judges the two scales ought to be.) For instance, physician is undoubtedly the same on both inventories, but some would question whether the pediatrician scale on the KOIS ought to be highly correlated with the SVIB physician. King, Norrell, and Powers (1963), comparing fourteen scales on the Kuder Form D and the SVIB, found a median correlation of .37; Wilson and Kaiser (1968), comparing twenty-seven scales on the KOIS and the SVIB, obtained a correlation of .32 for one hundred subjects; Zytowski (1968) obtained a median correlation of .25 for fifty-two comparisons of similar and same-named scales.

The reason why these relationships were lower than expected is not clear. It has been suggested that error may be introduced by the selection of different criterion groups at different times. Zytowski (1969) has shown that the new scales on the SVIB and KOIS for librarians do not differ appreciably from the original ones and that the correlation between such scales does not improve. The different scoring systems of the KOIS and the SVIB may tend to stimulate disparate results. Lefkowitz (1970) has scored engineering special keys for SVIB items by means of Strong's and Kuder's techniques, and found a slight superiority for the SVIB difference score. There seems to be some problem in the procedure, however, since Lefkowitz's lambda scores are inordinately high and invariate compared with those which are reported in the KOIS *Manual* (1966).

Kuder (1969) has suggested that correlations between scores on his inventory and others using the difference score approach are bound to be low, since the lambda score incorporates both the similarity of the inventory taker to people-in-general and the interests he has in common with the criterion group. These two components may vary independently of each other. Kuder also has contended that if the variable amounts of interests in common with people-in-general were held constant by correlating scores on the multiple pairs of scales for each person in the sample, then the relationship would be higher. Just that has been found by Zytowski (1972); the median correlation reported above rose to .57 when this approach was used. A cross-validation sample shows the same results. Still, the range of correlations obtained by this approach was wide, and some individual profiles on the SVIB and the KOIS were not significantly different from random results.

Johnson (1971) has performed a parallel analysis of twenty-one equivalent scales on the women's forms of the two inventories. The median correlation of the scales was .29. When the comparison was made by correlating the two profiles for each subject, individually, the median correlation rose to .71. Johnson was able to identify $S$s whose profile correlations were very high and very low, and compare them on certain attributes. He found that the inconsistent $S$s were significantly more careless or insincere in their responses (lower V scores), had less firm interest in their major field, and were higher on the imagination scale of a personality inventory.

From the foregoing evidence, it might be tentatively concluded that the congruent validity of the two inventories is adequate, but that some individuals who take them are unreliable.

In another study, Zytowski (1972) has obtained KOIS's and SVIB's from 290 employed men, working at and reporting satisfaction in occupations common to both inventories. The profiles were tested to determine which inventory proved superior at affirming each subject's occupation with a score that was high ranking or "worth considering," as the authors of the manuals say. Correct identifications occurred for about two-thirds of the $S$s, and neither inventory was statistically significant in superiority. But, in ranking the $S$s' occupations high, the KOIS made significantly fewer errors.

Similar tests of homogeneous scales will probably appear with similar outcomes. It seems realistic to say at this point that no inventory is demonstrably superior to any other where a lack of congruent validity is found between same-named scales. The counselor may give more than one inventory in the hope of increasing the reliability of his observations — in effect, by doubling the length of some of the scales. Those which are in agreement can be interpreted with certainty; those on which one inventory scores the person high and the other low will have to be interpreted with the admission that confidence in that scale is reserved. This should not be difficult for the counselor, who does not assume the infallibility of any of the tools he uses, but it will make problems for the client, who would like to believe that the measures made on him are utterly reliable. Suffice it to say, for the present, that perhaps some clients are unreliable, owing to the influence which different modes of responding, different samples of items, and different times of administration have on them.

*Scores.* Another matter about which the counselor should be informed is the type of scores used to express the results of taking the inventory.

Table 1.5. Various Characteristics of

| | SVIB-M | SVIB-F | MVII |
|---|---|---|---|
| Population intended for . | Males, 16 years and older for work generally requiring higher education | Females, 16 years and older, for broad range of occupational levels | Males only, non college degree oriented |
| Approximate level of readability .......... | Grade 9 | Grade 9 | Grade 9 |
| Year of latest edition ... | 1969 | 1969 | 1965 |
| Items | | | |
| Source ............. | Ad hoc | Ad hoc | Ad hoc |
| Number and format .. | 399 free choice | 398 free choice | 158 triads |
| Type of responses .... | Like, indifferent, dislike | Like, indifferent, dislike | Mark 1 like, 1 dislike, and leave 1 blank |
| Time to take .......... | 25–45 minutes | 25–45 minutes | 45 minutes |
| Costs | | | |
| Reusable test booklets. | $23/100 | $23/100 | $22/100 |
| Separate answer sheets. | $7/100 | $7/100 | $9/100 |
| Combined booklet and answer sheet ..... | Yes, but not machine scoring | Yes, but not machine scoring | No |
| Scoring | | | |
| Keys available ....... | Yes | Yes | Yes |
| Machine .......... | | | Yes |
| Group rate ........ | $.40–.75 DOQ [a] | $.40–.75 DOQ | |
| Individual service .. | $.70–1.20 DOQ | $.70–1.20 DOQ | $.33–.45 DOQ |
| Agencies .......... | TESTSCOR, NCS, MRC, Dela Data | TESTSCOR, NCS, MRC, Dela Data | NCS, MRC |
| Outputs | | | |
| Numerical .......... | Yes | Yes | Yes |
| Graphic profile ...... | Yes | Yes | Yes |
| Scales | | | |
| Validating .......... | 6 | 6 | 0 |
| Homogeneous ....... | 22 | 19 | 9 |
| Normative .......... | 54 in 11 groups | 58 in 11 groups | 21 ungrouped |
| Other informational .. | 8 | 4 | 0 |
| Type of scores used .... | T score (Raw scores for some administrative indices) | T score (Raw scores for some administrative indices) | T score |
| System report ........ | Optional/NCS only | Optional/NCS only | Optional/NCS only |
| Type of self-interpretation aids .......... | Information on back of output | Information on back of output | Information on back of profile sheet |

[a] DOQ = Depending on Quantity.

16

Seven Current Interest Inventories

| KOIS | MIQ | OVIS | WVI |
|---|---|---|---|
| Males and females, all occupational levels | Males and females, all levels except professions and self-employment | Students, grades 8 through 12 | Junior high school and older boys and girls |
| Grade 6 | Grade 6 | Grade 8 | Grade 7 |
| 1966 | 1967 | 1969 | 1970 |
| Ad hoc | Vocational needs, from Theory of Work Adjustment | People-things-data trichotomy of DOT | Job satisfaction research |
| 100 triads | 190 paired comparisons, 20 absolute judgments | 280 free choice | 45 free choice |
| Most and least preferred | "More important" in paired comparisons | 5-point LID scale | 5-point Likert |
| 30 minutes | 30 minutes | 60–90 minutes | 10–15 minutes |
| Not available | Available, apply Voc. Psych. Proj. | $9.50/35 | Not available |
| Not available | Available, apply Voc. Psych. Proj. | $4.00/35 | Not available |
| Yes, $1.20–1.50 DOQ | No | Yes, $20.00/35 | Yes, $12.00/100 |
| No | No | No | Yes |
| | | Yes | |
| Cost included in purchase of materials | Cost included in purchase of materials | $.60–.80 | $.36 |
| | | $.60–.80 | |
| SRA | Vocational Psychology Research, U. of Minn. | MRC | MRC |
| Yes | Yes | Yes | Yes (list report only) |
| Yes | Yes | Yes | No |
| 1 | 1 | 1 per scale | 0 |
| 0 | 20 | 24 | 15 |
| Male: 79 occupations, 20 college majors. Female: 56 occupations, 25 college majors | More than 100: many in development. Single scores per each of 9 clusters. | 0 | 0 |
| 8 | 0 | 1 — Student Information Questionnaire of 6 items | 0 |
| Lambda scores (see Kuder manual) | Raw scores — Homogeneous scales $D^2$ — Normative scales | Percentiles and stanines — norms grades 8–12 | Percentiles — norms grades 7–12 |
| Optional | Not available | Optional | Yes |
| Interpretative leaflet supplied | None — for counselor interpretation | Some explanation on score and profile sheet | None |

Raw scores can be used (and are used in some inventories) if information about how the person's scores compare with his other scores is all that is required. But in interest measurement each item has a basic general level of appeal or popularity, and a person's profile of interests will be considerably more meaningful if his scores are presented in terms of how he shows more than the ordinary amount of interest. This is another way of saying that his scores need to be normalized. Normalized scores also must be used to point out the person's similarity with an occupational or normative group.

The most frequently used conversion from raw scores is some variation of the T score; that is, one based on the difference between the observed score and the mean of a comparison group, expressed in fractions of the standard deviation of the group on that scale. The percentile score is also widely used. The user should understand the equivalence between scores on these two scales, but more particularly he should know what score is considered significantly high, what score low, and what range may exist between two scores before they can be considered significantly different.

*Self-interpretability.* A final matter of interest in selecting an interest inventory is the degree to which the meaning of the results may be understood by the inventory taker, without assistance from the counselor. It is correct to state that no interest inventory is completely self-interpretable, but some are, partly depending on the complexity of their scales and the age or maturity of the person who takes them. Some inventories provide instructions on the back of the profile or in an interpretive leaflet on how to interpret the report of findings. This could facilitate interpretation of the inventories to a large group of persons, who then could follow up on their individual concerns in conference with the counselor.

Table 1.5 presents data relevant to each of the variables discussed for the inventories under scrutiny in this book. Few inventories cease to change over time, so certain items of information will become obsolete at intervals. The counselor would be wise to seek information about the variations that will influence what inventory he will use and also about new developments that will modify his utilization.

# References

Borgen, F. H. Predicting career choices of able college men from occupational and basic interest scales of the Strong Vocational Interest Blank. *Journal of Counseling Psychology*, 1972, 19, 202–211.

Hershenson, D. A life stage vocational development system. *Journal of Counseling Psychology*, 1968, 15, 23–30.

Johnson, R. W. Congruence of SVIB-W and KOIS profiles. *Journal of Counseling Psychology*, 1971, 18, 450–455.

King, P., G. Norrell, and P. Powers. Relationships between twin scales on the SVIB and the Kuder. *Journal of Counseling Psychology*, 1963, 10, 395–401.

Kuder, G. F. *Occupational interest survey: General manual.* Chicago: Science Research Associates, 1966.

————. A note on the comparability of occupational scores from different interest inventories. *Measurement and Evaluation in Guidance*, 1969, 2, 94–100.

Lefkowitz, D. Comparison of the Strong Vocational Interest Blank and the Kuder Occupational Interest Survey scoring procedures. *Journal of Counseling Psychology*, 1970, 17, 357–363.

Lofquist, L. H., and R. V. Dawis. *Adjustment to work: A psychological view of man's problems in a work-oriented society.* New York: Appleton-Century-Crofts, 1969.

Roe, A. *The psychology of occupations.* New York: Wiley, 1956.

Wilson, R., and H. Kaiser. A comparison of similar scales on the SVIB and the Kuder, Form DD. *Journal of Counseling Psychology*, 1968, 15, 468–470.

Zytowski, D. G. Relationships of equivalent scales on three interest inventories. *Personnel and Guidance Journal*, 1968, 47, 44–49.

————. The concept of work values. *Vocational Guidance Quarterly*, 1970, 18, 176–186.

————. A concurrent test of accuracy-of-classification of the Strong Vocational Interest Blank and the Kuder Occupational Interest Survey. *Journal of Vocational Behavior*, 1972, 2, 245–250.

————. Equivalence of the Kuder Occupational Interest Survey and the Strong Vocational Interest Blank revisited. *Journal of Applied Psychology*, 1972, 56, 184–185.

# 2

# The Strong
# Vocational Interest Blank
# for Men

David P. Campbell

THE STRONG VOCATIONAL INTEREST BLANK (SVIB) is by no means a static instrument. As can be seen in the following outline, which summarizes the significant events in the history of the Strong Blank, this inventory has progressively changed and improved since the inception of its men's form in 1927. Because of these changes and improvements, constant study is necessary to keep up-to-date with interest measurement.

To use interest inventories most effectively in counseling, their internal workings, that is, the method of analysis necessary for generating the profile, should be understood. The basic data utilized in analyzing the SVIB are the individual's responses to items of the inventory; therefore the counselor should be aware of the kind of items used. Figure 2.1 is a list of the items from the SVIB.

An interest inventory works because there are large variations in the popularity of its items among men and women in different occupations. For instance, the first item on the Strong is actor, and the individual is asked to respond "Like," "Indifferent," or "Dislike," depending on how he feels toward the activities involved in that occupation. Among several

NOTE: The material in this chapter draws heavily from D. P. Campbell, *Handbook for the Strong Vocational Interest Blank* (Stanford, Calif.: Stanford University Press, 1971). Readers who wish more information on specific points discussed in this chapter should refer to that work. Many of the figures and tables have been taken directly from the *Handbook* and are reprinted here with the permission of the publisher, Stanford University Press.

**Part I. Occupations.** For each occupation listed below, indicate whether you would like that kind of work or not. Don't worry about whether you would be good at the job or about your lack of training for it. Forget about how much money you could make or whether you could get ahead in it. Think only about whether you would like the work done in that job.

Mark on the answer sheet in the space labeled **"L"** if you **like** that kind of work.
Mark in the space labeled **"I"** if you are **indifferent** (that is, don't care one way or another).
Mark in the space labeled **"D"** if you **dislike** that kind of work.

### Work fast. Put down the first thing that comes to mind. Answer every one.

1 Actor
2 Advertising Man
3 Architect
4 Military Officer
5 Artist

6 Astronomer
7 Athletic Director
8 Auctioneer
9 Author of novel
10 Author of technical book

11 Auto Salesman
12 Auto Racer
13 Auto Mechanic
14 Airplane Pilot
15 Bank Teller

16 Designer, Electronic Equipment
17 Building Contractor
18 Buyer of merchandise
19 Carpenter
20 Cartoonist

21 Cashier in bank
22 Electronics Technician
23 Chemist
24 Civil Engineer
25 City or State Employee

26 Minister, Priest, or Rabbi
27 College Professor
28 Foreign Service Man
29 Dentist
30 Draftsman

31 Editor
32 Electrical Engineer
33 Employment Manager
34 Geologist
35 Factory Manager

36 Income Tax Accountant
37 Farmer
38 Labor Union Official
39 Art Museum Director
40 Foreign Correspondent

41 Governor of a State
42 Hotel Manager
43 Interior Decorator
44 Interpreter
45 Inventor

46 Photographer
47 Judge
48 Labor Arbitrator
49 Laboratory Technician
50 Landscape Gardener

51 Lawyer, Criminal
52 Lawyer, Corporation
53 Librarian
54 Life Insurance Salesman
55 Locomotive Engineer

56 Machinist
57 Magazine Writer
58 Manufacturer
59 High School Principal
60 Professional Baseball Player

61 Mining Superintendent
62 Musician
63 Music Teacher
64 Psychologist
65 Office Manager

66 Orchestra Conductor
67 Pharmacist
68 Public Relations Man
69 Physician
70 Playground Director

71 Poet
72 Politician
73 Printer
74 Private Secretary
75 Radio Announcer

76 Rancher
77 Real Estate Salesman
78 Reporter, General
79 Reporter, Sports page
80 Retailer

81 Sales Manager
82 School Teacher
83 Scientific Research Worker
84 Sculptor
85 Manager, Chamber of Commerce

86 Secret Service Man
87 Computer Operator
88 Shop Foreman
89 Social Worker
90 Specialty Salesman

91 Statistician
92 Stockbroker
93 Surgeon
94 Toolmaker
95 Traveling Salesman

96 Travel Bureau Manager
97 Funeral Director
98 Watchmaker
99 Wholesaler
100 Worker in Y.M.C.A.

Figure 2.1. Items from the SVIB booklet. (Reprinted by permission of Stanford University Press, Stanford, California. Copyright 1938 by the Board of Trustees of the Leland Stanford Junior University. Copyright renewed 1965 by Margaret H. Strong. Copyright © 1945, 1964, 1965, and 1966 by the Board of Trustees of the Leland Stanford Junior University. Printed in the United States of America.)

21

An Outline of Significant Events in SVIB Revision

| Men's Form | Common | Women's Form |
|---|---|---|
| (1927–Men's SVIB initially published) | | (1933–Women's form initially published) |
| (1938–Major revision) | | (1946–Major revision) |
| 1955–60 First decisions on new revision (by Strong, R. F. Berdie, K. E. Clark) | | |
| 1. Revise booklet | | |
|   a. Keep same general format | | |
|   b. Replace undesirable items with new ones | | |
|   c. Lower reading level | | |
| 2. Use existing criterion and men-in-general samples to build new scales on unchanged items | | |
| 1958–60 First actions | | |
| 1. Data transferred from Stanford to Minnesota, and prepared for computer input | | |
| 2. Effect of revised items checked | | |
| 3. New scales built | | |
| 4. Validity and reliability checked against old form | | |
| | 1963 | |
| | 1. CIMR established at University of Minnesota | |
| | 2. All materials moved to Minnesota | |
| | 3. Death of E. K. Strong | |
| 1964 "New" revision completed, then aborted. All recently tested subjects scored high on all recently established scales | | |

| Men's Form | Common | Women's Form |
|---|---|---|
| 1965 Revision redone<br>1. New men-in-general sample<br>2. Minor changes in booklet<br>3. New scales built<br>4. Validity and reliability checked against real world | | 1965 Plans laid to revise women's form analogously to men's, but to retest all samples instead of using old data |
| 1966 "Second" new revision completed and published<br>1. New booklet<br>2. New profile groupings<br>3. Some new scales (academic achievement, occupational introversion-extroversion) | 1966–68<br>1. Basic interest scales constructed<br>2. Administrative indices developed<br>3. New MF and FM<br>4. Diversity of interests scales | 1966 Revised women's booklet ready<br>1966–68 All criterion samples retested; many new occupations added |
| 1966–67 Strong's 1930 teenager sample ($N = 650$) retested to norm Basic interest scales | | |
| 1968–69 New criterion samples tested | | |
| 1969 New profile adopted<br>1. Basic interest scales and administrative indices added<br>2. More new scales (age related, managerial orientation) | | 1969 Revision published<br>1. New booklet<br>2. New criterion samples<br>3. New profile<br>  a. Basic interest scales<br>  b. Administrative indices<br>  c. New nonprofessional occupations |
| 197– Revised profile using scales built on new samples (no change in booklet) | | |
| | 1971 Handbook for SVIB published (Stanford University Press) | |

dozen samples of men tested with the Strong, the percentages answering "Like" to this item varied from 10 among engineers to 54 among chamber of commerce executives. The percentages answering "Like" to this item are given in Table 2.1 and are presented graphically in Figure 2.2 where a better appreciation of the large spread of answers can be gained.

The distribution shown in Figure 2.2 illustrates the main kind of information used in analyzing responses to items on interest inventories. By looking at this distribution, one can immediately identify two principal characteristics of the item. First is the general level of *item popularity*, which is determined by noting where the X's pile up along the base line. For the item actor, this is at about 33 percent; that is, over the wide range of occupations covered here, approximately one-third of all men tested responded "Like" to this item. The second characteristic is *item spread*, which refers to how the X's are spread out along the base line. The best items are those which demonstrate an average popularity somewhere in the middle of the range, and those with a very large spread. Unfortunately no one knows exactly how to choose such items, and we only know we have them after we have studied the responses from a large number of persons taking the inventory.

The best item on the Strong — indicated by its spread — is college professor. Ten percent of bankers, 11 percent of carpenters, and 15 percent of real estate salesmen as compared with over 90 percent of mathematicians, psychologists, biologists, and physicists responded "Like" to this item. Figure 2.3 shows how the item looks graphically. If we had 400 items like that, we would have a very good inventory indeed.

Information theory suggests that we should have only this kind of

```
                  X   X
                  X   X
          X   X   X   X
          X   X   X   X
          X   X   X   X
          X   X   X   X   X   X   X
          X   X   X   X   X   X   X
          X   X   X   X   X   X   X
          X   X   X   X   X   X   X   X   X
      X   X   X   X   X   X   X   X   X   X
    ─────────────────────────────────────────
  0–
  5    10  15  20  25  30  35  40  45  50  55  60  65  70  75  80  85  90  95  100
```

Figure 2.2. Frequency distribution of occupational groups according to percentage of each group responding "Like" to item Number 1, actor (each X = one occupation; base line represents percentage intervals)

24

Table 2.1. Percentage of "Like" Responses to Item Number 1, Actor, for Various Occupational Groups

| Percentage Responding "Like" | Occupational Groups |
|---|---|
| 1–9 | None |
| 10 | Engineers |
| 11 | None |
| 12 | Carpenters, forest service personnel |
| 13–14 | None |
| 15 | Manufacturing presidents, physicists, policemen, bankers, farmers, purchasing agents |
| 16 | Chemists, pharmacists |
| 17–18 | None |
| 19 | Production managers, mathematicians, pilots, senior CPAs |
| 20 | Veterinary medicine, printers |
| 21 | None |
| 22 | Real estate salesmen, architects |
| 23 | Winter air force norm group |
| 24 | Dentists, office managers, school superintendents, funeral directors |
| 25 | Sales managers, math-science teachers, public administrators |
| 26 | Accountants |
| 27 | YMCA secretaries |
| 28 | Personnel, credit managers |
| 29 | Physicians |
| 30 | Osteopaths, advertising managers, YMCA physical directors, life insurance salesmen, author-journalists |
| 31 | Biologists |
| 32 | Army officers, vocational rehabilitation counselors |
| 33 | Physical therapists |
| 34 | None |
| 35 | Lawyers |
| 36 | Social science teachers |
| 37 | Business education teachers |
| 38 | Community recreation administrators |
| 39 | Artists |
| 40 | Psychiatrists |
| 41 | None |
| 42 | Psychologists |
| 43 | Ministers, social workers |
| 44 | Male librarians |
| 45 | YMCA secretaries |
| 46 | Experimental psychologists, musician performers |
| 47–51 | None |
| 52 | Musician teachers |
| 53 | None |
| 54 | Chamber of commerce members |
| 55–100 | None |

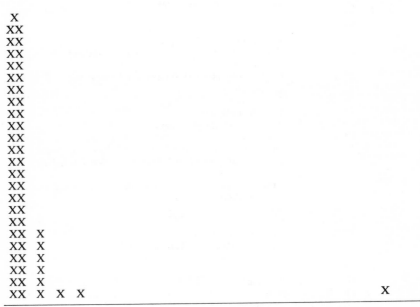

```
X
X
X
X           X                                   X           X
X   X   X                                       X           X
X   X   X           X           X   X           X           X   X
X   X   X   X   X   X   X   X   X   X       X   X   X   X       X   X
X   X   X   X   X   X   X   X   X   X   X   X   X   X   X       X   X       X
```
0–
5   10  15  20  25  30  35  40  45  50  55  60  65  70  75  80  85  90  95  100

Figure 2.3. Frequency distribution of occupational groups according to percentage of each group responding "Like" to item Number 27, college professor (each X = one occupation; base line represents percentage intervals)

```
X
XX
XX
XX
XX
XX
XX
XX
XX
XX
XX
XX
XX
XX
XX
XX
XX
XX
XX  X
XX  X
XX  X
XX  X
XX  X
XX  X   X   X                                                               X
```
0–
5   10  15  20  25  30  35  40  45  50  55  60  65  70  75  80  85  90  95  100

Figure 2.4. Frequency distribution of occupational groups according to percentage of each group responding "Like" to item Number 97, funeral director (each X = one occupation, base line represents percentage intervals)

26

Table 2.2. Base Rate Popularity for SVIB-M Occupational Items

| Item | Percentage Responding "Like" | Item | Percentage Responding "Like" |
|---|---|---|---|
| Inventor | 53 | Reporter, sports page | 26 |
| Physician | 49 | Labor arbitrator | 25 |
| College professor | 48 | Machinist | 25 |
| Scientific research worker | 48 | Playground director | 25 |
| Architect | 46 | Reporter, general | 25 |
| Surgeon | 45 | Hotel manager | 24 |
| Musician | 44 | Sculptor | 22 |
| Manufacturer | 43 | Social worker | 22 |
| Rancher | 43 | Statistician | 22 |
| Civil engineer | 42 | Laboratory technician | 21 |
| Editor | 42 | Auto mechanic | 20 |
| Author of novel | 41 | Interior decorator | 20 |
| Author of technical book | 41 | Politician | 20 |
| Airplane pilot | 40 | Wholesaler | 20 |
| Judge | 40 | Poet | 19 |
| Chemist | 38 | Retailer | 19 |
| Magazine writer | 38 | Stockbroker | 19 |
| Factory manager | 37 | Toolmaker | 19 |
| Foreign correspondent | 37 | Worker in YMCA | 19 |
| Building contractor | 36 | Cashier in bank | 18 |
| Carpenter | 36 | City or state employee | 18 |
| Employment manager | 36 | Interpreter | 18 |
| Electrical engineer | 35 | Mining superintendent | 18 |
| Landscape gardener | 35 | Minister, priest, or rabbi | 17 |
| Athletic director | 34 | Librarian | 17 |
| Governor of a state | 34 | Shop foreman | 16 |
| Schoolteacher | 34 | Pharmacist | 15 |
| Astronomer | 33 | Manager, chamber of commerce | 15 |
| Buyer of merchandise | 33 | Auto racer | 14 |
| Corporation lawyer | 33 | Real estate salesman | 14 |
| Office manager | 33 | Dentist | 13 |
| Artist | 32 | Private secretary | 13 |
| Farmer | 32 | Auto salesman | 12 |
| Advertising man | 31 | Traveling salesman | 12 |
| Secret service man | 31 | Printer | 12 |
| Criminal lawyer | 30 | Bank teller | 11 |
| Sales manager | 30 | Music teacher | 10 |
| Military officer | 29 | Specialty salesman | 10 |
| Cartoonist | 29 | Life insurance salesman | 9 |
| Actor | 28 | Watchmaker | 9 |
| Locomotive engineer | 28 | Auctioneer | 8 |
| Draftsman | 26 | Funeral director | 5 |
| Orchestra conductor | 26 | | |

item in an inventory. Intuitively, however, I think it is useful to have a few items like that illustrated in Figure 2.4. The item is mortician or, as it now reads, funeral director. The 94 percent who responded "Like" were funeral directors; the percentage of those in other occupations who responded "Like" was very low.

Table 2.2 indicates the base rate popularity for all the occupational items on the Strong. Base rate popularity means the percentage of men-in-general who respond "Like." In interest measurement, one of the issues which must be considered is whether or not it is essential to have a "men-in-general" (MIG) reference group. I think it is necessary because it is impossible to treat the item inventor, to which 53 percent of MIG responded "Like," in the same way as the item funeral director to which about 5 percent of MIG responded "Like." Something must be done to control for the effects of these items' markedly different base rate popularity. On the Strong, this is accomplished by comparing the item responses of MIG with those of each occupational sample; the items showing large differences constitute the scoring scale for that occupation. This operation of contrasting the specific occupation with the general sample is one of the most important characteristics of the SVIB scoring.

### THE SVIB PROFILE

Figure 2.5 is a copy of the SVIB profile, which gives four kinds of information, the first of which is presented in the basic interest scales (BIS). These scales are content oriented and homogeneous in nature. The second kind of information on the profile is found in the traditional occupational scales, which I spoke about earlier. Because of space limitations, the profile is in a double column format now, and scores can be plotted only from 20 to 60, though scores do occasionally range down below zero and up to 80. Since scores below 20 are all grouped at 20 and, likewise, scores above 60 are grouped at 60, plotting is sometimes a problem. Hindsight suggests that we should have used a thin middle band for the average scores, perhaps those from 25 to 45, thereby retaining more space for plotting the extremes.

The nonoccupational scales are the third source of information on the profile. I am not very satisfied with some of them, for example, the masculinity-femininity (MF) scale. The MF scale probably gives the counselor much more trouble than it is worth — it leads people to want to talk about their virility and related matters that are peripheral to vocational

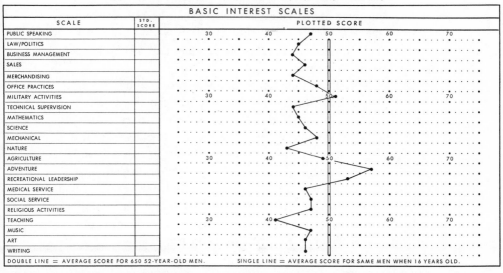

Reprinted from the *1969 Supplement* to the *Manual for the Strong Vocational Interest Blanks*,
copyrighted by the Board of Trustees of the Leland Stanford Junior University and published by Stanford University Press

Figure 2.5. Profile sheet for the SVIB for men

29

counseling. But some of our colleagues believe that the MF scale portrays the heart of the individual's personality, and thus we have retained it on the profile. There are some nonoccupational scales that I think are valuable and will be discussed later.

The last kind of information on the profile is provided by the administrative indices. Anyone who has been closely associated with any large-scale scoring enterprise will, if he is honest, be able to document scoring errors that can result from using the wrong form of booklet, keys with errors in them, the wrong keys, or some such. Although there are only four commercial scoring services, there are perhaps another dozen in universities or in other agencies that are large enough to afford their own in-house scoring, and more scoring services will surely emerge as technology provides cheaper machines. With this spread of services, we lose control over the process of scoring and cannot be sure that each service always scores the SVIB correctly. The administrative indices were added to help alleviate this problem. They provide some information on how the scoring machine and the inventory taker himself handled the answer sheet.

The first of these indices is TR — the total number of responses the machine reads from the answer sheet. The TR should be within 10 of 399 and 398, the number of items on the men's and women's forms, respectively. Actually, the number can be $\pm40$, and the profile would still be acceptably accurate. But if it is that far off, the counselor should know about it and why it has happened.

There are eighteen responses on both the men's and women's forms that are chosen by 7 percent or less of the population. These are called unpopular responses (UNP) and represent such items as "like mortician" or "dislike geography." Most people choose two or three of these unpopular responses; hardly anybody marks as many as eight. To make the index easier to interpret, we count up the person's score and subtract eight. If this results in a negative score, the person has picked considerably more of the unpopular items than does the typical person. There are two possible interpretations of a negative index: the inventory taker has a peculiar pattern of interests; or he has mishandled the response task in some way. For example, if he has marked more than 80 percent of the inventory items "Dislike," he is almost certain to trigger off the UNP index because most of the unpopular responses are dislike responses. However, if there is a negative UNP index, it is usually desirable to see if the student was given the wrong form or if he misunderstood the instructions in some way.

The third administrative index is FC — form check. This is based on item response positions where a particular item on the old form has been changed on the new form and where the new item differs a great deal in popularity. For example, item number 96 on the old men's form was typist; on the new one it is travel bureau manager. If a man responds "Like" to item number 96, it is almost certain that he was looking at travel bureau manager and not at typist. If he answers "Dislike," of course, one cannot be as sure. On both the men's and women's forms FC consists of twenty-four items on which the percentage endorsement among men-in-general differed by 40 percent or more between the old and the new item. If the person's answers to these items are summed up, one can tell with considerable certainty which form he used. If the index is negative, the probability is about .99 that he took the old form. Unless there is some definite reason for using the older form, the counselor should use the new one.

The last three indices, LP, IP, and DP, stand for percentage of "Like," "Indifferent," and "Dislike" responses to the first section of the SVIB, which contains only occupational titles as items; on the men's form, there are 100 such items, and on the women's 128. Among men- and women-in-general, these index numbers run roughly 33, 33, 33, but very wide deviations are found among individuals' responses, ranging from lows of 5 or 10 to highs of 85 or 90. I have even seen one or two answer sheets go through the scoring service with 100 percent "Like" responses. If a person has marked 100 percent of the items "Like," his test-taking strategies should be reviewed with him. Any time these percentages fall below 5 percent, or above 95 percent, the case should be studied carefully to ascertain if the profile is valid.

In one instance, for example, we received a booklet from a woman army officer with response percentages of 3, 0, and 97. Did she really dislike 97 percent of the occupations? Did she even read them? I checked through her responses and the three she marked "Like" were "be an artist," "be an interior decorator," and "be a costume designer." Because she was consistent, I was convinced that at least she had read the items, and we accepted her results as valid. However, she must have been a very unhappy army officer.

## BASIC INTEREST SCALES

We need to devote careful attention to the basic interest scales at the top of the profile because they are new and may be confusing. These scales are *content* scales, as opposed to *empirical* scales, and were constructed by finding clusters of items with high intercorrelations. Table 2.3 uses the teaching BIS as an example. Above the diagonal are item correlations based on the 1934 sample of men-in-general and below the diagonal are the same correlations based on the current MIG sample. This is a replication over thirty years and, as can be seen, the mirror images are fairly similar. The last two items are new ones that were not on the old form; we contemplated using them in the scale but chose not to. I have included them here to demonstrate the decisions involved in selecting items for a scale. The first six items became the teaching BIS, and an individual's score on this scale is based on his answers to these items. I think everyone would agree that the content is very clear and the scale could hardly be named anything other than *teaching*, or some synonym for it.

Table 2.3. Intercorrelations of Items in Men's Teaching
Basic Interest Scale

| Item Number | Item | 82 | 27 | 63 | 203 | 202 | 53 | 59 |
|---|---|---|---|---|---|---|---|---|
| 82 | School teacher ....... | | 68 | 48 | 38 | 36 | 40[a] | |
| 27 | College professor ..... | 63[b] | | 37 | 44 | 29 | 38 | |
| 63 | Music teacher ........ | 34 | 26 | | 18 | 21 | 39 | |
| 203 | Teaching adults ....... | 48 | 44 | 23 | | 45 | 18 | |
| 202 | Teaching children ..... | 38 | 22 | 24 | 53 | | 25 | |
| 53 | Librarian ........... | 40 | 34 | 35 | 18 | 17 | | |
| 59 | High school principal .. | 57 | 46 | 29 | 32 | 28 | 31 | |
| 387 | Have patience when teaching others ....... | 23 | 22 | 13 | 34 | 26 | 06 | 18 |

[a] Upper matrix based on 1934 MIG responses.
[b] Lower matrix based on 1965 MIG responses.

The basic scales are normed on a sample of fifty-two-year-old men; their mean has arbitrarily been set equal to 50. The same men, tested thirty-six years earlier, had means indicated by the jagged line. Students' scores can then be compared with either fifty-two-year-old men or the same men when they were sixteen years old. There are some fairly big differences in the two testings of the same people at different ages, and these indicate which interests change with age. A BIS score of 50 indicates the score of an "average" person; on the other hand, an occupational score of 50 on, say, the artist scale represents the score of an "average" artist. This difference between the BIS score and the occupational score should be explained carefully to the counselee.

The teaching BIS has been used to score all the occupational samples

Table 2.4. Mean Scores on the Teaching Scale for Male Occupations

| Mean Standard Score | Occupational Groups |
| --- | --- |
| 66 | Music teachers (1952)[a] |
| 65 | None |
| 64 | Music teachers (1946) |
| 63 | Elementary teachers (Minnesota), school superintendents (1969) |
| 62 | English teachers, guidance counselors (1968), ministers (1969), librarians, Danforth fellows, ministers (1965), school superintendents (1965), agricultural extension agents |
| 61 | Social science teachers (1969), teaching brothers, elementary teachers (North Dakota), school superintendents (1930), Unitarian ministers (1950), high school counselors, ministers (1927), business education teachers, student personnel workers |
| 60 | Rehabilitation counselors, social science teachers (1936), social workers (1967), mathematics-science teachers (1968) |
| 59 | Dental educators, football coaches, vocational agriculture teachers, priests (1966), sociologists, Minneapolis symphony orchestra members, community recreational directors, YMCA staff members, physiatrists, psychologists (1967), guidance counselors (1950), Unitarian ministers (1929) |
| 58 | Physical therapists (1966), psychiatrists (1967), college professors, social workers (1953), biologists, actors (1966), political scientists, mathematicians (1929), mathematics-science teachers (1936), neurological surgeons, astronomers |
| 57 | Business school professors, mathematicians (1969), psychologists (1947), psychologists (1931), pediatricians, legislators, physical therapists (1957), psychologists (1949), physicists (1968), policemen (1968) |
| 56 | Personnel directors (1969), physicians (1969), public administrators (1969), army officers (1969), YMCA secretaries, economists, psychiatrists (1949), animal husbandry professors, musicians (1952), pathologists, internists, anthropologists, chemists (1969) |
| 55 | Department store managers, medical technicians, musicians (1969), YMCA physical directors, experimental psychologists, judges, encyclopedia salesmen, optometrists, Pulitzer Prize winners, generals and admirals, navy officers, physicists (1927), orthopedic surgeons, NIAL members, interpreters |

Table 2.4 — continued

| Mean Standard Score | Occupational Groups |
|---|---|
| 54 . . . . . . . . . . . . | Salesmen (3M applicants), chamber of commerce executives, credit managers, air force officers, surgeons, computer programmers, lawyers (1949), dentists (1969), colonels, computer salesmen, newsmen, journalists (British), lawyers (1969) |
| 53 . . . . . . . . . . . . | Advertising men (1968), chiropractors, salesmen (3M), radiologists, photographers, army officers (1950), life insurance salesmen, (1966), astronauts, artists (1968) |
| 52 . . . . . . . . . . . . | Engineers (1968), food scientists, cartographers, buyers (1969), veterinarians (1966), certified public accountants (1965), urologists, personnel directors (1927), corporation presidents (1965), physicians (1949), governors, NASA scientists, pharmacists (1968), county welfare workers |
| 51 . . . . . . . . . . . . | Architects (1968), policemen (1969), life insurance salesmen (1969), sales managers (1968), purchasing agents (1969), army sergeants, foresters, public administrators (1941), chemists (1931), petroleum engineers, interior decorators, machinists |
| 50 . . . . . . . . . . . . | Investment managers, physicians (1927), steel salesmen, certified public accountants (1944), highway patrolmen, actors (1937) |
| 49 . . . . . . . . . . . . | Bankers (1969), county sheriffs, accountants, lawyers (1927), bankers (1964), osteopaths |
| 48 . . . . . . . . . . . . | Funeral directors (1969), tool and die makers, salesmen (PG&E), printers, policemen (1933), dentists (1932), veterinarians (1949) |
| 47 . . . . . . . . . . . . | Electricians, real estate salesmen (1969), skilled tradesmen, pharmacists (1947), architects (1933), office workers, life insurance salesmen (1931), production managers, advertising men (1931), authors (1931), buyers (1946) |
| 46 . . . . . . . . . . . . | Carpenters (1969), engineers (1928), corporation presidents (1935), carpenters (1936), farmers (1936), automobile salesmen, forest service men, pilots, artists (1933) |
| 45 . . . . . . . . . . . . | Sales managers (1932) |
| 44 . . . . . . . . . . . . | Funeral directors (1945), bankers (1934), farmers (1967), farmers (1968) |
| 43 . . . . . . . . . . . . | Real estate salesmen (1932), purchasing agents (1931) |

[a] Date indicates year of testing.

DAVID P. CAMPBELL

in our archives. At least one hundred and usually two or three hundred men were included in each sample. Their mean scores are shown in Table 2.4. Music teachers scored highest, averaging 66, male elementary teachers were next with 63, followed by librarians, Danforth fellows, ministers tested in 1965, and school superintendents tested in 1930. At the lowest mean, 43, were real estate salesmen, and then purchasing agents, bankers, farmers, and funeral directors. Data like these are available for each scale, and I don't think one can be a successful counselor with the SVIB unless he is willing to spend some time studying these tables.

On the teaching scale, scores of 60 and above are associated with teaching; an analogous relationship holds with all the basic scales. For example, on the art scale scores of 60 and above are associated with artistic occupations, on the mechanical scale, scores of about 60 are earned by men doing mechanical work, and so forth. Scores of 60, or even 58 and 59, are high scores, and should be treated as such.

Low scores are harder to interpret since the distributions are not symmetrical around the norm group mean of 50. Few scores are a standard deviation or two below the mean, and so a score of 40 is lower, relatively, than a score of 60 is high.

The BIS are ordered according to the similarity between them. Adjacent scales tend to have the higher intercorrelations. For example, the sales and business management scales are more highly correlated with each other than they are with the nature, art, or music scales. Art and music, in turn, are more highly correlated with each other than they are with sales and business management.

Table 2.5 shows the items on one of my favorite scales, the adventure

Table 2.5. Intercorrelations of Items in Men's Adventure
Basic Interest Scale

| Item Number | Item | 211 | 14 | 231 | 12 | 334 | 86 | 277 | 337 |
|---|---|---|---|---|---|---|---|---|---|
| 211 | Pursuing bandits in a sheriff's posse | | 24 | 26 | 37 | 23 | 44 | | |
| 14 | Airline pilot | 25 | | 27 | 37 | 16 | 22 | | |
| 231 | Climbing along edge of precipice | 23 | 12 | | 25 | 19 | 10 | | |
| 12 | Auto racer | 28 | 40 | 11 | | 22 | 32 | | |
| 334 | Taking a chance | 13 | 05 | 16 | 17 | | 11 | | |
| 86 | Secret service man | 42 | 29 | 15 | 30 | 14 | | | |
| 277 | Men who live dangerously | 21 | 22 | 20 | 25 | 16 | 27 | | |
| 337 | Thrilling, dangerous activities | 36 | 18 | 26 | 28 | 62 | 25 | 31 | |
| 321 | Airline pilot | 18 | 51 | 13 | 23 | 12 | 18 | 22 | 30 |

35

Table 2.6. Mean Scores on the Adventure Scale for Male Occupations

| Mean Standard Score | Occupational Groups |
| --- | --- |
| 66 | Astronauts |
| 65 | None |
| 64 | County sheriffs |
| 63 | None |
| 62 | None |
| 61 | Policemen (1969),[a] highway patrolmen, policemen (1968) |
| 60 | Salesmen (3M applicants), department store managers |
| 59 | Salesmen (3M), policemen (1933), computer salesmen, army officers (1969) |
| 58 | Air force officers, navy officers, sales managers (1968) |
| 57 | Investment managers, steel salesmen, pilots |
| 56 | Actors (1966), YMCA staff members, petroleum engineers, mathematics-science teachers (1968), NASA scientists, journalists (British), advertising men (1968), electricians, engineers (1968), physical therapists (1966) |
| 55 | Photographers, elementary teachers (Minnesota), community recreation directors, computer programmers, food scientists, purchasing agents (1969), foresters, tool and die makers |
| 54 | Personnel directors (1969), physicians (1969), social science teachers (1969), army sergeants, football coaches, skilled tradesmen, buyers (1969), certified public accountants (1965), army officers (1950), legislators, newsmen, life insurance salesmen (1966), social workers (1967) |
| 53 | Chamber of commerce executives, automobile salesmen, forest service men, physical therapists (1957), machinists, English teachers, funeral directors (1969), life insurance salesmen (1969), public administrators (1969), real estate salesmen (1969), cartographers, chiropractors, ministers (1969) |
| 52 | Veterinarians (1966), YMCA physical directors, optometrists, ministers (1965), orthopedic surgeons, lawyers (1969), interpreters, architects (1968), psychiatrists (1967), teaching brothers, carpenters (1969), elementary teachers (North Dakota) |
| 51 | Chemists (1969), dentists (1969), dental educators, medical technicians, musicians (1969), encyclopedia salesmen, generals and admirals, Danforth fellows, certified public accountants (1944), corporation presidents (1965), neurological surgeons, farmers (1968), psychologists (1967), guidance counselors (1950) |

36

Table 2.6 — continued

| Mean Standard Score | Occupational Groups |
|---|---|
| 50 | Business school professors, school superintendents (1969), priests (1966), sociologists, credit managers, salesmen (PG&E); printers, carpenters (1936), school superintendents (1965), physicists (1968), astronomers, college professors, vocational agriculture teachers |
| 49 | Radiologists, urologists, farmers (1936), surgeons, Minneapolis symphony orchestra members, osteopaths, mathematics-science teachers (1936), student personnel workers, buyers (1946) pharmacists (1968), actors (1937), bankers (1969), artists (1968), county welfare workers, Unitarian ministers (1929) |
| 48 | Mathematicians (1969), psychologists (1947), real estate salesmen (1932), public administrators (1941), pediatricians, chemists (1931), biologists, bankers (1964), physiatrists, business education teachers, farmers (1967), musicians (1952), anthropologists |
| 47 | Accountants, social workers (1953), psychologists (1931), office workers, Unitarian ministers (1950), economists, production managers, agricultural extension agents, experimental psychologists, personnel directors (1927), funeral directors (1945), physicians (1949), psychiatrists (1949), animal husbandry professors, artists (1933), veterinarians (1949), colonels |
| 46 | Guidance counselors (1968), pharmacists (1947), social science teachers (1936), physicians (1927), engineers (1928), purchasing agents (1931), political scientists, sales managers (1932), librarians, dentists (1932), lawyers (1949), lawyers (1927), pathologists, authors, interior decorators, governors, advertising men (1931), music teachers (1946) |
| 45 | Rehabilitation counselors, architects (1933), YMCA secretaries, life insurance salesmen (1931), high school counselors, Pulitzer Prize winners, ministers (1927), psychologists (1949), music teachers (1952), internists |
| 44 | Judges |
| 43 | Bankers (1934), corporation presidents (1935), physicists (1927) |
| 42 | None |
| 41 | School superintendents (1930) |
| 40 | Mathematicians (1929), NIAL members |

[a] Date indicates year of testing.

37

scale. Personality-type scales do not work out well on the SVIB, either because of inadequate item content or because personality items don't cluster as well as interest items, and on the adventure scale, which is more a measure of personality than of occupational interests, the item intercorrelations are lower than for the other BIS. However, there is some common content — pilot, auto racer, secret service man are indeed adventuresome activities — and the results on the scale look very reasonable. In Table 2.6, the mean scores for several occupational samples are presented; at the top are astronauts, salesmen, policemen, and army officers, and, at the bottom, artists, mathematicians, and school superintendents.

Table 2.7 gives the items in the military activities BIS, and Table 2.8 illustrates the rank-ordered means of various occupations on this scale. I have included it here to lead into one of the problems of interpretation with the SVIB. Fairly often students with a high score on a basic scale will have only average or even low scores on the related occupational scale. For example, a boy might score high on the military BIS and low on the army officer scale, an apparent inconsistency. Or a girl might score high on the mathematics BIS and low on the mathematician occupational scale. The client is going to ask for an explanation of that inconsistency and the answer, if well presented, can give him considerable insight into how his interests are distributed.

The reason for an inconsistency of this kind is that the two types of scales provide different but complementary information. The only way to score high on the military activity scale is to respond "Like" to "be an army officer," "drill a company of soldiers," and similar items. In contrast, the army officer occupational scale is based on items that differentiate military men from men-in-general and thus the item content is quite heterogeneous. Included in this scale are several different clusters of items; one concerns engineering and construction activities; another deals with

Table 2.7. Intercorrelations of Items in Men's Military Activities
Basic Interest Scale

| Item Number | Item | 4 | 123 | 151 | 210 |
|---|---|---|---|---|---|
| 4 | Military officer ............... | | 49 | 42 | 59 |
| 123 | Military drill ................. | 52 | | 66 | 68 |
| 151 | Drilling in a military company.... | 53 | 81 | | 61 |
| 210 | Drilling soldiers ............... | 59 | 68 | 74 | |
| 237 | Military men ................ | 52 | 44 | 43 | 47 |

Table 2.8. Mean Scores on the Military Activities Scale
for Male Occupations

| Mean Standard Score | Occupational Groups |
|---|---|
| 66 . . . . . . . . . . . . | Colonels |
| 65 . . . . . . . . . . . . | None |
| 64 . . . . . . . . . . . . | Army officers (1950),[a] generals and admirals, policemen (1968) |
| 63 . . . . . . . . . . . . | None |
| 62 . . . . . . . . . . . . | Army officers (1969) |
| 61 . . . . . . . . . . . . | Policemen (1933), county sheriffs |
| 60 . . . . . . . . . . . . | Air force officers |
| 59 . . . . . . . . . . . . | Army sergeants, highway patrolmen |
| 58 . . . . . . . . . . . . | YMCA physical directors, pilots, policemen (1969) |
| 57 . . . . . . . . . . . . | None |
| 56 . . . . . . . . . . . . | Navy officers, astronauts, governors |
| 55 . . . . . . . . . . . . | Football coaches, community recreational directors |
| 54 . . . . . . . . . . . . | School superintendents (1969), salesmen (3M applicants), rehabilitation counselors, public administrators (1941), credit managers, office workers, salesmen (PG&E), YMCA staff members, legislators, computer salesmen, physical therapists (1957), county welfare workers |
| 53 . . . . . . . . . . . . | Salesmen (3M), veterinarians (1966), chamber of commerce executives, engineers (1928), personnel directors (1927), automobile salesmen, optometrists, certified public accountants (1944), farmers (1967), osteopaths, veterinarians (1949), machinists, department store managers, funeral directors (1969), medical technicians, personnel directors (1969), physical therapists (1966), social science teachers (1969), purchasing agents (1969), chiropractors, elementary teachers (North Dakota) |
| 52 . . . . . . . . . . . . | Accountants, social science teachers (1936), steel salesmen, production managers, farmers (1936), purchasing agents (1931), funeral directors (1945), lawyers (1927), school superintendents (1965), bankers (1964), business education teachers, petroleum engineers, mathematics-science teachers (1936), pharmacists (1968), dental educators, engineers (1968), food scientists, sales managers (1968), cartographers, vocational agriculture teachers |
| 51 . . . . . . . . . . . . | Real estate salesmen (1932), pharmacists (1947), life insurance salesmen (1931), high school counselors, carpenters (1936), encyclopedia salesmen, elementary teachers (Minnesota), forest service men, sales managers (1932), dentists (1932), animal husbandry professors, orthopedic surgeons, |

Table 2.8 — continued

| Mean Standard Score | Occupational Groups |
|---|---|
| | advertising men (1931), buyers (1946), guidance counselors (1950), lawyers (1969), bankers (1969), dentists (1969), electricians, physicians (1969), life insurance salesmen (1969), public administrators (1969), real estate salesmen (1969), foresters, skilled tradesmen, tool and die makers |
| 50 | Architects (1933), YMCA secretaries, physicians (1927), school superintendents (1930), printers, certified public accountants (1965), urologists, bankers (1934), lawyers (1949), physicians (1949), physiatrists, life insurance salesmen (1966), music teachers (1952), student personnel workers, farmers (1968), mathematics-science teachers (1968), journalists (British), music teachers (1946), English teachers, teaching brothers, carpenters (1969), buyers (1969) |
| 49 | Advertising men (1968), judges, priests (1966), social workers (1953), chemists (1931), surgeons, computer programmers, corporation presidents (1935), newsmen, psychiatrists (1949), social workers (1967), neurological surgeons, interpreters |
| 48 | Architects (1968), ministers (1969), psychologists (1931), radiologists, biologists, experimental psychologists, ministers (1927), authors, agricultural extension agents, NASA scientists, pathologists |
| 47 | Business school professors, guidance counselors (1968), investment managers, psychologists (1947), librarians, ministers (1965), physicists (1927), psychologists (1949), musicians (1952), internists, interior decorators, actors (1937), Unitarian ministers (1929) |
| 46 | Pediatricians, Unitarian ministers (1950), economists, photographers, political scientists, Pulitzer Prize winners, artists (1933), mathematicians (1929), psychiatrists (1967), college professors |
| 45 | Musicians (1969), sociologists, corporation presidents (1965), anthropologists, psychologists (1967), astronomers, chemists (1969) |
| 44 | Minneapolis symphony orchestra members, Danforth fellows, NIAL members |
| 43 | Mathematicians (1969), physicists (1968) |
| 42 | Actors (1966), artists (1968) |

ⁿ Date indicates year of testing.

legal power and contains such items as judge, governor, lawyer; a third has items of a general managerial nature; yet another contains straight math items. Finally, a small cluster of items deals with military activities. One could respond "Dislike" to all the items on the occupational scale except those concerning military activities and score very low on the army officer scale; then, having marked "Like" to the few items on the military activities BIS, one would have a high score there and, thus, an inconsistent profile.

The inconsistency needs to be explained to the student by showing him the difference between the two types of scales. The BIS mirror the intensity of his interests in *one specific category* while the OS reflects the degree of similarity between his interests and those of men in the specified occupations — say, army officers — across a wide range of activities. Unless he has some similarities of interests with army officers across many of these categories — not just military activities — he will probably not find that a comfortable occupational environment.

## THE OCCUPATIONAL SCALES

On the bottom half of the profile are two columns of occupational scales; these were constructed by contrasting the interests of men in each occupation with a sample of men-in-general. The fifty-four occupational scales here are, for the most part, still based on the criterion samples which Strong tested in the 1930s and 1940s. In 1966, when the men's booklet was revised by dropping the poor and obsolete items, the scoring was changed slightly, as reported in greater length in the SVIB *Handbook*. But each occupation was not retested. That step was finished in 1971 with a new profile to follow in a year or two. From the counselor's standpoint, the revision won't make too much difference because the profile will remain unchanged, except that several new occupations will be added, and there will be changes in some of the groups. For example, we are adding occupations such as photographer, interior decorator, and cartographer, and are doing away with some scales that have been on the profile for a long time, for example, osteopath. More information on these changes can be found in the SVIB *Handbook*.

## THE NON-OCCUPATIONAL SCALES

At the bottom of the profile are eight non-occupational scales. Although I cannot discuss each of these scales in detail here, it is necessary to describe at least one of them in some detail to point out what the counselor should know about all of them. I shall also mention several others briefly.

*The academic achievement scale.* The first non-occupational scale on the men's profile is the academic achievement scale (AACH). It was developed by selecting items that discriminate between students with good high school and college records and those with poor records. We normed it so that graduating seniors of liberal arts colleges average about 50. The items weighted positively are concerned with art and science; those weighted negatively include business and skilled trades activities. Thus, business students will generally score low on this scale, no matter what their grades are.

The correlation of the AACH score with the MSAT (a scholastic ability test) was .38, with high school rank .58 and with cumulative grade point average .52. This fairly high correlation with GPA shrank to .36 in a cross-validation sample and to .35 in a cross-validation sample taken twenty-five years after the first sample was tested. While one cannot view this scale as a valid predictor of grades, it is a fairly good measure of persistence in school. Table 2.9 shows some mean scores of people tested in high school who were followed up several years later to determine what level of education they had achieved. Those who eventually obtained doctorates scored 62 on the AACH scale when tested in high school — a very high score. In another sample, persons who had doctorates but who were tested twenty-five years *after* they were undergraduates scored at a similar level: 58. Persons tested as high school seniors, who eventually earned bachelor's degrees averaged 39 while those who attained the same degree, but were tested twenty-five years afterward, scored nearly a standard deviation more: 47. The same gain was true for persons who did not attain a B.A.: 29 compared to 42. The age of the individual when tested influences the AACH score.

Since the SVIB has been repeated at various intervals on several differ-

Table 2.9. Men's Academic Achievement Scale Scores for Groups Attaining Various Levels of Education, Tested as High School Seniors

| Level of Attainment | N | AACH Mean |
|---|---|---|
| No degree | 75 | 29 |
| Bachelor's degree | 69 | 39 |
| Master's degree | 18 | 45 |
| Doctorate | 7 | 62 |

ent groups, there is considerable information on the temporal stability of scores for AACH (see Table 2.10). It can be seen that reliability is high even over long periods of time. The higher retest mean among the high school students illustrates that increases tend to occur with age and that the increases are greatest among those first tested early.

Table 2.10. Test-Retest Stability of the Academic Achievement Scale

| Sample | N | Retest Interval | Test-Retest Correlation | Mean Scores Test | Retest |
|--------|---|-----------------|-------------------------|------------------|--------|
| U. of M. students | 139 | Two weeks | .93 | 47 | 48 |
| Army reserve | 102 | Thirty days | .88 | 48 | 47 |
| Harvard students | 189 | Three years | .74 | 57 | 57 |
| Minn. H.S. students | 171 | Eight years | .59 | 41 | 51 |
| Stanford students | 191 | Twenty-two years | .65 | 50 | 53 |
| Minnesota bankers | 48 | Thirty years | .75 | 39 | 40 |

Recently we have been able to return to some of the settings where Strong collected data forty years ago and have tested the persons who today hold the same positions as the men tested by Strong in the 1930s. Table 2.11 gives the AACH mean scores for a number of such studies. These data demonstrate, contrary to popular belief, that the type of people in a given occupation is not changing much. However, there are a few minor changes; for example, the bankers' mean AACH score increased slightly, but their educational level has also changed and this may account for the increase.

Table 2.11. Mean Academic Achievement Scores for Persons Holding the Same Positions in a Number of Occupations at Two Points in Time

| Occupational Group | Mean Scores |
|--------------------|-------------|
| Bankers (N = 98) | |
| 1934 | 41 |
| 1964 | 43 |
| Corporation presidents (N = 25) | |
| 1935 | 45 |
| 1965 | 47 |
| Ministers (N = 98) | |
| 1927 | 52 |
| 1965 | 53 |
| School superintendents (N = 149) | |
| 1930 | 52 |
| 1965 | 53 |

Changes in mean AACH scores with age are presented in Figure 2.6. Growth takes place predominantly during the college and immediate post-graduate years when many students go on into professional and graduate schools. The scores level off at about age twenty-eight and stay constant from then on. These data suggest that increased education is associated with high scores on the scale, but it is not clear whether students who are taking graduate education develop increased AACH interests or whether students who are developing these interests seek more education.

Highest and lowest ranking occupational groups on the AACH scale are shown in the following tabulation. The order reflects the intellectual

| Group | Mean Score |
|---|---|
| Biologists | 61 |
| Mathematicians | 60 |
| Psychiatrists | 60 |
| Physicists | 59 |
| Psychologists | 58 |
| Librarians | 57 |
| Chemists | 54 |
| Physicians | 54 |
| | |
| Real estate salesmen | 36 |
| Carpenters | 36 |
| Morticians | 37 |
| Purchasing agents | 39 |
| Printers | 40 |
| Sales managers | 40 |
| Bankers | 40 |
| Farmers | 40 |

versus the business nature of the scales. Interestingly, the spread of AACH means is over a range of about three standard deviations. This is about the same range that would be found for the IQ's of these occupational samples, even though the AACH scale bears only a mild relationship to ability ($r = .30$).

It should be noted that academic achievement is only one way to succeed in our society, and this scale should not be considered a generalized measure of achievement. There are many other avenues to success and they tend to be associated with different patterns of interests. Not all

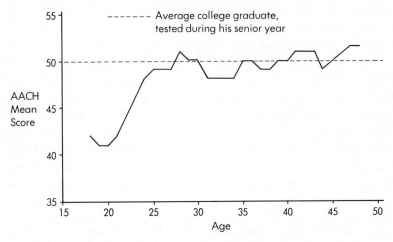

Figure 2.6. Relationship between age and scores on men's academic
achievement (AACH) scale

successful people are academically oriented and the AACH score is not
high in samples distinguished by other than intellectual accomplishment.
In Figure 2.7 are mean AACH scores for ten different samples of men
who are indisputably outstanding successes. The range is wide with, for
example, salesmen who sold two million dollars in life insurance scoring
considerably lower than Pulitzer Prize winners. A low score on AACH
does not mean a person is destined for a second-class lot in life; it only
indicates that he will not seek employment in intellectual settings.

*The diversity of interests scale.* Another scale from which we are trying to learn something new is the diversity of interests scale (DIV). A
common topic in everyday conversation is the breadth or narrowness of
an individual's interests, but this concept has been hard to deal with psychometrically for a variety of reasons. We have tried several approaches;
the first was to find people whose friends had nominated them as having
broad interests. That was a total fiasco, and the failure may tell us something about our concept of breadth of interest. Let me explain: if you
see someone coming out of the library with a book on flower arranging,
one on computer programming, a third on different kinds of steel structures, and another on gambling, you may conclude he has very broad
interests. In fact, however, he's showing interest in only one area — reading. We tend to evaluate the breadth of our friends' interests by how well

read they are and not by how experienced they are in the real world. For this reason, the peer nominations approach was not useful.

What we finally did was to construct a scale composed of items that are very diverse in character and are statistically unrelated to each other. (See the SVIB *Handbook* for the items and their intercorrelations.) Most of the correlations were near zero, indicating that there is little tendency for people who respond "Like" to a particular item to respond "Like" to any other one. The relationships were neither positive nor negative; they were simply zero. If a person claims he likes all twenty-four items, then he has said that he likes twenty-four different things; therefore he has wide interests. If, on the other hand, he maintains that he *dislikes* twenty-four different things, then he has narrow interests. This scale defines our psychometric conception of breadth and narrow-

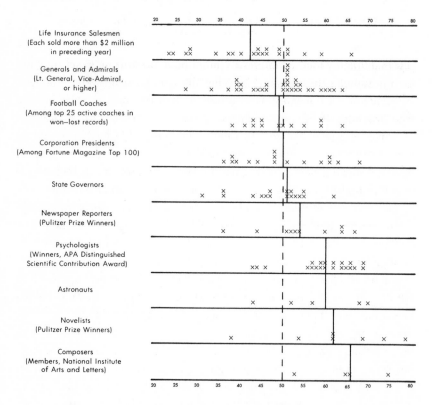

Figure 2.7. Academic achievement (AACH) scale mean scores for outstanding men in ten occupations

46

ness of interest. The scale is normed so that men-in-general average 50; on the women's version, women-in-general also average 50.

After the scale was finished, all the occupational samples in our archives were scored on it and the means were rank ordered. There were some surprises. At the top, with mean scores indicating wide interests, were computer salesmen, community recreation directors, YMCA physical directors, male elementary teachers, physical therapists, and air force officers. People in many of these occupations seem to be attracted to physical activity, and this seems to be necessary to score high on this scale. At the bottom, with "narrow" interests, were those occupations that we usually call creative: authors, artists, physicists, mathematicians, Pulitizer Prize winners, political scientists, and members of the National Institute of Arts and Letters. Creative people tend to have narrow interests, or, more likely, an intense concentration of interests. The same pattern was found among the women's occupations. Those in physically active and socially outgoing occupations scored high; those in the creative occupations — artists, authors, scientists — scored low. These results suggest that "highly focused interests" rather than "narrow interests" may be the more accurate way of describing the low-scoring occupations.

*Occupational introversion-extroversion scale.* This scale (OIE) is an empirical scale built by contrasting the responses of students who scored one standard deviation or more above the mean on the MMPI's social introversion-extroversion scale with students who scored a standard deviation or more below the mean. It is normed so that a standard score of 50 falls in the middle of these two groups; introverts score high — about 60 — and extroverts score low — about 40. This scale reflects a fairly strong tinge of social awareness, and YMCA staff members, ministers, and legislators score toward the extroverted end. Other occupational groups with extroverted scores are salesmen and chamber of commerce executives. When a score is as low as 15 or 16, that person has taken virtually every opportunity in the SVIB to say he likes to be around people. High scores are earned by introverts; some occupational groups scoring in this direction are mathematicians, farmers, and artists. This is an interesting cluster since the only interest that mathematicians, farmers, and artists have in common is that they don't like people.

*Age related scale.* The age related scale (AR) was constructed by selecting items that show sharply increasing (or decreasing) frequencies of endorsement as the individual grows older. The scores are clearly related

— on the average — to age, but just what this means psychologically, we still do not know. High scores are earned by those with advanced degrees, and low scores by those with less education and who are more business oriented. The AR was put on the profile primarily for purposes of research, and, as yet, there are not enough data available to determine how it can be used in a practical counseling setting.

*Managerial orientation scale.* This scale (MO) is composed of items that differentiate between men who were rated as superior managers and those who were rated mediocre. On this scale, the criterion group of good managers averaged a score of 50. Air force officers, personnel directors, and manufacturing presidents scored in the high 40's. At the bottom of the distribution are musicians and policemen. We have the same kind of data on the MO scale for successful people as we have on the academic achievement scale, and again it should be stressed that this scale is not a measure of any general ability to succeed in all areas. It is mainly a measure of how well an individual *likes* to manage people. People who score high on the distribution, above the criterion group, include corporation presidents, while just below the criterion group are outstanding college football coaches, three- and four-star generals and admirals, and astronauts. At the bottom of the distribution are people who are not necessarily bad managers, but who would just never want to manage anything: cartoonists, symphony members, poets, and authors.

The other non-occupational scales that appear on the profile are less important and should usually be ignored. More information on them can be found in the SVIB *Handbook.*

## THE VALIDITY OF THE SVIB

The most common question a user is apt to ask of an SVIB expert is, "How good is this test — how accurate is it?" There is no simple answer to this question and certainly no single index of validity. Nevertheless, certain information derived from administering the inventory does point to its general validity. For instance, college students were identified who scored very high on the sales occupational scales as high school seniors; ten years later 10 percent of them were selling life insurance and 32 percent were selling something else. Therefore 40 percent of them did become salesmen. Another 12 percent of them were in business-persuasion types of jobs — public relations, marketing — and 22 percent were in social service-persuasive jobs such as minister, school teacher, or lawyer. These are all people-oriented occupations. Twenty-four percent were in occupations that appeared unrelated to their profile ten years earlier. The hit rate here was about 3 to 1. This ratio appears often in the SVIB literature and suggests that, in general, about 75 percent of college students wind up in jobs that are compatible with their earlier SVIB profile.

Here is another example. A sample of high school students high on the science scales (which is the inverse pattern of high sales scores) ten years later were working in the following occupations: 37 percent of them, all of whom had engineering degrees, were employed in jobs appropriate to their training, and 41 percent were in other occupations that were clearly technical in orientation. Twenty-two percent were in occupations that did not correspond to their earlier interest in science. Again, the ratio was roughly 3 to 1. Incidentally, the overlap between these two samples was zero: there were no salesmen in science occupations and no scientists in sales.

CHANGING INTERESTS IN THE POPULATION

A vast amount of research has been done on the Strong Blank; among other things it has given evidence of changing interests in the population. A few SVIB items are slowly shifting in base rate popularity. Table 2.12 offers an example; it presents the percentage who responded "Like" to the

Table 2.12. Response Changes to Item Number 48,
Housekeeper

| Occupational Group | Percentage Responding Like |
|---|---|
| Home economics teachers | |
| 1941[a] | 60 |
| 1967 | 35 |
| Dietitians | |
| 1941 | 50 |
| 1967 | 19 |
| Social science teachers | |
| 1938 | 43 |
| 1967 | 23 |
| YWCA staff members | |
| 1934 | 42 |
| 1967 | 11 |
| Nurses | |
| 1934 | 40 |
| 1967 | 22 |

Table 2.12 — continued

| Occupational Group | Percentage Responding Like |
|---|---|
| Mathematics-science teachers | |
| 1940 | 39 |
| 1967 | 24 |
| English teachers | |
| 1934 | 38 |
| 1967 | 23 |
| Secretaries | |
| 1940 | 36 |
| 1967 | 29 |
| Occupational therapists | |
| 1942 | 35 |
| 1966 | 15 |
| Lab technicians | |
| 1941 | 35 |
| 1967 | 19 |
| Librarians | |
| 1934 | 32 |
| 1967 | 16 |
| Physical therapists | |
| 1957 | 30 |
| 1966 | 25 |
| Life insurance salesmen | |
| 1939 | 25 |
| 1967 | 13 |
| Authors | |
| 1938 | 25 |
| 1966 | 13 |
| Physical education teachers | |
| 1939 | 23 |
| 1967 | 21 |
| Physicians | |
| 1938 | 23 |
| 1967 | 13 |
| Psychologists | |
| 1942 | 23 |
| 1966 | 09 |
| Artists | |
| 1938 | 22 |
| 1967 | 11 |
| Lawyers | |
| 1938 | 20 |
| 1967 | 10 |

[a] Date indicates year of testing.

item "be a housekeeper" for a number of pairs of occupational samples. One sample in each pair was tested in the 1930s and 1940s, the other in the 1960s. Whereas 58 percent of the home economics teachers tested in 1941 responded "Like" to the item "be a housekeeper," in 1967 that number had dropped to 35 percent. The other examples in Table 2.12 show that this drop was constant over all the occupations checked. Several other items with comparable changes in the base rate have also been identified. These numerous shifts have interesting cultural implications, of course, and massive psychometric implications. They mean, for instance, that the percentage used from women-in-general as base rate data for the item housekeeper in the 1930s can no longer be used in the 1960s. Such shifts are true of both men and women and affect about 15 percent of the items. This is one of the reasons why the inventories had to be revised.

From a practical standpoint these shifts probably mean that interest inventories should be renewed every fifteen to twenty years. But I know that because the cost of revising an interest inventory is too great for any single person or company to absorb, major revisions will not be undertaken that often. Publishers simply cannot afford the $300,000 or so needed to revise the inventories they have published. Fortunately, the majority of items show substantial robustness over time.

SOME ILLUSTRATIVE PROFILES

To illustrate various aspects of the Strong Blank a discussion of a few profiles would be helpful. Figure 2.8 shows two profiles for Joe, an army sergeant who filled in the SVIB twice within a two- or three-week period. He was a subject in a new criterion sample; and when he returned his completed form, he asked for a second one. When he returned the second one, it became clear why he wanted to take the inventory twice. Although an army sergeant, Joe did not like the army, and intended to retire and sell real estate. He had been selling real estate for the previous four or five years on the side and felt that he enjoyed this work; nevertheless, he desired some kind of confirmation from the Strong Blank. From the biographical data recorded on the two booklets, it was evident that he had filled them in with different sets. On the first he reported all his military experiences and clearly filled in the booklet thinking, "I'm a sergeant, I'm a sergeant, I'm a sergeant." On the second booklet, he listed his real estate experience, and now was thinking, "I'm a realtor, I'm a realtor, I'm a realtor." Probably he expected to receive profiles that differed considerably from each other.

This is a fairly common occurrence. Most people consider their answers to the items on the SVIB to be will-o-wispy — subject to change with their whims of the moment. Frequently they say, "Oh, I know if I were to take that test next week when I'm in a different mood that I'd come out differently."

Joe's results demonstrate how wrong this assertion usually is. Although he assumed a real estate sales set, and although there were a few mild differences on some of the scales, the profiles were quite similar. His score on the sales scale did go up the second time, but it was already high enough on the first testing to be one of his highest scores. Note that his score on the military activities scale was low on both inventories. Basically, his responses were consistent from one time to the next.

The average person completing the inventory twice in thirty days alters his responses to approximately 25 percent of the items, but his changes tend to cancel each other out. People do not change their responses to the items that they feel strongest about, and it is these items that cluster together and create the extreme scores on the profile. I have seen a few profiles change drastically over a six- or eight-month period, but this doesn't happen very often.

On Joe's profile, the high scores are in sales and advertising. He scored quite low on technical supervision and production management, and on the army and air force officer scales. Obviously he is not happy with the army and probably should get out. He marked 25 percent of the items "Like" the first time and 23 percent the second time, which is quite stable, considering the two different sets he was working from. He scored low on the academic achievement scale (34) and fairly high on the managerial orientation scale (47). This latter score is in that part of the distribution populated by people in managerial-type occupations. On OIE he scored 42 on one testing and 48 on the other; these scores are toward the extroverted end, but are not as high as those of the "average" salesman.

The general theme of the profile is as follows: high sales, high business administration, low military, low mathematics, low mechanical, low technical leadership, high in adventure (as noted earlier salesmen are high on this scale), and very high in writing, which is unusual for army sergeants. (The writing scale contains such items as "I like to write reports," "I'd like to be an author," "I'd like to be a poet," "I like to read literature.")

Reprinted from the *1969 Supplement* to the *Manual for the Strong Vocational Interest Blanks*,
copyrighted by the Board of Trustees of the Leland Stanford Junior University and published by Stanford University Press

## BASIC INTEREST SCALES

| SCALE | RES | SGT* STD. SCORE | PLOTTED SCORE |
|---|---|---|---|
| PUBLIC SPEAKING | 56 | 61 | |
| LAW/POLITICS | 61 | 53 | |
| BUSINESS MANAGEMENT | 65 | 67 | |
| SALES | 73 | 65 | |
| MERCHANDISING | 59 | 59 | |
| OFFICE PRACTICES | 45 | 45 | |
| MILITARY ACTIVITIES | 37 | 37 | |
| TECHNICAL SUPERVISION | 44 | 49 | |
| MATHEMATICS | 37 | 37 | |
| SCIENCE | 43 | 50 | |
| MECHANICAL | 36 | 39 | |
| NATURE | 42 | 42 | |
| AGRICULTURE | 53 | 56 | |
| ADVENTURE | 53 | 59 | |
| RECREATIONAL LEADERSHIP | 30 | 34 | |
| MEDICAL SERVICE | 38 | 35 | |
| SOCIAL SERVICE | 30 | 37 | |
| RELIGIOUS ACTIVITIES | 32 | 35 | |
| TEACHING | 45 | 34 | |
| MUSIC | 34 | 34 | |
| ART | 47 | 53 | |
| WRITING | 58 | 53 | |

DOUBLE LINE = AVERAGE SCORE FOR 650 52-YEAR-OLD MEN.     SINGLE LINE = AVERAGE SCORE FOR SAME MEN WHEN 16 YEARS OLD.

## OCCUPATIONAL SCALES

| | OCCUPATION | RES | SGT* STD. SCORE | | OCCUPATION | RES STD. SCORE | SGT* |
|---|---|---|---|---|---|---|---|
| I | DENTIST | 23 | 25 | VI | LIBRARIAN | 29 | 28 |
| | OSTEOPATH | 23 | 19 | | ARTIST | 31 | 32 |
| | VETERINARIAN | 24 | 29 | | MUSICIAN PERFORMER | 30 | 25 |
| | PHYSICIAN | 23 | 22 | | MUSIC TEACHER | 28 | 21 |
| | PSYCHIATRIST | 12 | 11 | VII | C.P.A. OWNER | 32 | 41 |
| | PSYCHOLOGIST | 26 | 26 | VIII | SENIOR C.P.A. | 13 | 20 |
| | BIOLOGIST | 17 | 28 | | ACCOUNTANT | 15 | 28 |
| II | ARCHITECT | 29 | 37 | | OFFICEWORKER | 22 | 27 |
| | MATHEMATICIAN | 18 | 19 | | PURCHASING AGENT | 34 | 40 |
| | PHYSICIST | 13 | 19 | | BANKER | 28 | 33 |
| | CHEMIST | 10 | 21 | | PHARMACIST | 31 | 34 |
| | ENGINEER | 27 | 34 | | FUNERAL DIRECTOR | 34 | 36 |
| III | PRODUCTION | 18 | 34 | IX | SALES MANAGER | 49 | 47 |
| | ARMY OFFICER | 16 | 17 | | REAL ESTATE SALESMAN | 53 | 52 |
| | AIR FORCE OFFICER | 19 | 25 | | LIFE INS. SALESMAN | 50 | 46 |
| IV | CARPENTER | 14 | 21 | X | ADVERTISING MAN | 49 | 51 |
| | FOREST SERVICE MAN | 20 | 22 | | LAWYER | 39 | 39 |
| | FARMER | 32 | 37 | | AUTHOR-JOURNALIST | 42 | 42 |
| | MATH-SCIENCE TEACHER | 7 | 5 | XI | PRESIDENT-MFG. | 45 | 50 |
| | PRINTER | 25 | 27 | | | | |
| | POLICEMAN | 7 | 7 | | | | |

### SUPP. OCCUPATIONAL SCALES

| | OCCUPATION | RES | SGT* STD. SCORE | | OCCUPATION | RES STD. SCORE | SGT* |
|---|---|---|---|---|---|---|---|
| V | PERSONNEL DIRECTOR | 36 | 37 | | CREDIT MANAGER | 30 | 26 |
| | PUBLIC ADMINISTRATOR | 37 | 38 | | CHAMBER OF COM. EXEC. | 48 | 45 |
| | REHABILITATION COUNS. | 39 | 30 | | PHYSICAL THERAPIST | 10 | 1 |
| | YMCA STAFF MEMBER | 26 | 19 | | COMPUTER PROGRAMMER | 21 | 24 |
| | SOCIAL WORKER | 29 | 20 | | BUSINESS ED. TEACHER | 42 | 37 |
| | SOCIAL SCIENCE TEACHER | 29 | 22 | | COMMUNITY REC. ADMIN. | 36 | 27 |
| | SCHOOL SUPERINTENDENT | 26 | 17 | | | | |
| | MINISTER | 20 | 13 | | | | |

## NON-OCCUPATIONAL SCALES

| | | | | | | | |
|---|---|---|---|---|---|---|---|
| 35 | 43 | 35 | 55 | 47 | 42 | 71 | 28 |
| 34 | 46 | 32 | 59 | 47 | 48 | 72 | 33 |
| AACH | AR | DIV | MFII | MO | OIE | OL | SL |

RES / SGT

## ADMINISTRATIVE INDICES

| | | | | | |
|---|---|---|---|---|---|
| RES 383 | 6 | 8 | 25 | 23 | 52 |
| SGT 382 | 5 | 7 | 23 | 22 | 55 |
| TR | UNP | FC | LP | IP | DP |

Figure 2.8. Joe's SVIB profile

53

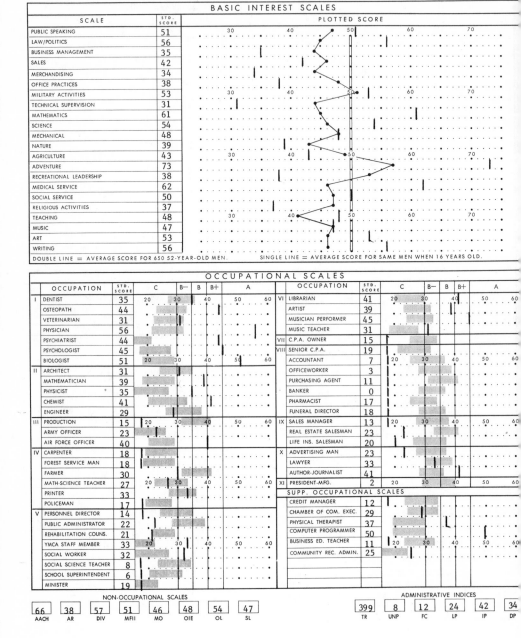

Figure 2.9. Ted's SVIB profile

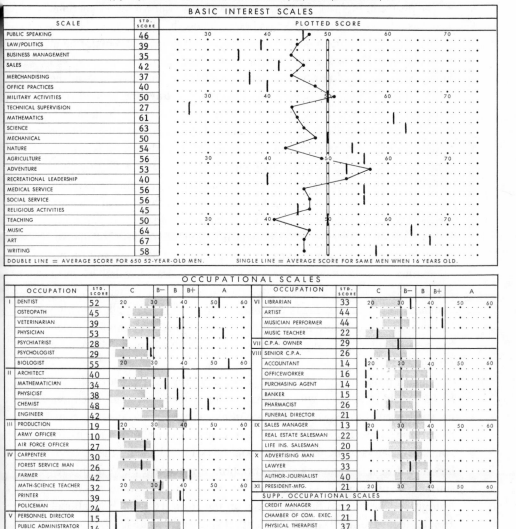

## BASIC INTEREST SCALES

| SCALE | STD. SCORE | PLOTTED SCORE |
|---|---|---|
| PUBLIC SPEAKING | 46 | |
| LAW/POLITICS | 39 | |
| BUSINESS MANAGEMENT | 35 | |
| SALES | 42 | |
| MERCHANDISING | 37 | |
| OFFICE PRACTICES | 40 | |
| MILITARY ACTIVITIES | 50 | |
| TECHNICAL SUPERVISION | 27 | |
| MATHEMATICS | 61 | |
| SCIENCE | 63 | |
| MECHANICAL | 50 | |
| NATURE | 54 | |
| AGRICULTURE | 56 | |
| ADVENTURE | 53 | |
| RECREATIONAL LEADERSHIP | 40 | |
| MEDICAL SERVICE | 56 | |
| SOCIAL SERVICE | 56 | |
| RELIGIOUS ACTIVITIES | 45 | |
| TEACHING | 50 | |
| MUSIC | 64 | |
| ART | 67 | |
| WRITING | 58 | |

DOUBLE LINE = AVERAGE SCORE FOR 650 52-YEAR-OLD MEN.   SINGLE LINE = AVERAGE SCORE FOR SAME MEN WHEN 16 YEARS OLD.

## OCCUPATIONAL SCALES

| | OCCUPATION | STD. SCORE | | OCCUPATION | STD. SCORE |
|---|---|---|---|---|---|
| I | DENTIST | 52 | VI | LIBRARIAN | 33 |
| | OSTEOPATH | 45 | | ARTIST | 44 |
| | VETERINARIAN | 39 | | MUSICIAN PERFORMER | 44 |
| | PHYSICIAN | 53 | | MUSIC TEACHER | 22 |
| | PSYCHIATRIST | 28 | VII | C.P.A. OWNER | 29 |
| | PSYCHOLOGIST | 29 | VIII | SENIOR C.P.A. | 26 |
| | BIOLOGIST | 55 | | ACCOUNTANT | 14 |
| II | ARCHITECT | 40 | | OFFICEWORKER | 16 |
| | MATHEMATICIAN | 34 | | PURCHASING AGENT | 14 |
| | PHYSICIST | 38 | | BANKER | 15 |
| | CHEMIST | 48 | | PHARMACIST | 26 |
| | ENGINEER | 42 | | FUNERAL DIRECTOR | 21 |
| III | PRODUCTION | 19 | IX | SALES MANAGER | 13 |
| | ARMY OFFICER | 10 | | REAL ESTATE SALESMAN | 22 |
| | AIR FORCE OFFICER | 27 | | LIFE INS. SALESMAN | 20 |
| IV | CARPENTER | 30 | X | ADVERTISING MAN | 35 |
| | FOREST SERVICE MAN | 26 | | LAWYER | 33 |
| | FARMER | 42 | | AUTHOR-JOURNALIST | 40 |
| | MATH-SCIENCE TEACHER | 32 | XI | PRESIDENT-MFG. | 21 |
| | PRINTER | 39 | | | |
| | POLICEMAN | 24 | | | |

### SUPP. OCCUPATIONAL SCALES

| OCCUPATION | STD. SCORE |
|---|---|
| CREDIT MANAGER | 12 |
| CHAMBER OF COM. EXEC. | 21 |
| PHYSICAL THERAPIST | 37 |
| COMPUTER PROGRAMMER | 33 |
| BUSINESS ED. TEACHER | 15 |
| COMMUNITY REC. ADMIN. | 9 |

V PERSONNEL DIRECTOR 15
PUBLIC ADMINISTRATOR 14
REHABILITATION COUNS. 14
YMCA STAFF MEMBER 15
SOCIAL WORKER 11
SOCIAL SCIENCE TEACHER 6
SCHOOL SUPERINTENDENT 5
MINISTER 22

### NON-OCCUPATIONAL SCALES

| 66 | 46 | 55 | 46 | 25 | 53 | 54 | 43 |
|---|---|---|---|---|---|---|---|
| AACH | AR | DIV | MFII | MO | OIE | OL | SL |

### ADMINISTRATIVE INDICES

| 396 | 8 | 4 | 22 | 30 | 48 |
|---|---|---|---|---|---|
| TR | UNP | FC | LP | IP | DP |

Figure 2.10. Lowell's SVIB profile

The profile in Figure 2.9 belongs to a man I have known for a long time. Ted was a long-haired hippie years before it was the thing to do. He was in one of my classes in about 1961–62 and at that time he was majoring in anthropology. He was a very bright, but mixed-up kid from a broken home. Since I have known him, he has traveled extensively, was in the Peace Corps, existed for several months in Africa traveling around on a motorcycle, wrecked that, and then hitchhiked across the Sahara. Although Ted's life-style is somewhat unusual, he is not at all rebellious against society, and he is not into heavy drinking or drugs; he is a kind, gentle, completely nonviolent individual.

Ted's high scores on the SVIB occupational scales were on the psychologist and physician scales — in general, the biological and social sciences. He scored very low in the business and accounting areas. This pattern of high science–low business is fairly typical among liberal arts college students. On the academic achievement scale he scored 68 once and 66 the other time or considerably above the average score recorded by most Ph.D.'s. His academic goal is a doctorate in anthropology, with a strong emphasis on linguistics. He is well on his way to that goal and, assuming he can continue to submit himself to the rigors of graduate school — which has been a problem for him in the past — I think he will probably achieve that goal.

The last profile is that of a ten-year-old boy (Fig. 2.10). Normally the SVIB shouldn't be used with students under sixteen years old, but there are some special cases where, if the counselor is careful and uses his common sense, some interesting knowledge can be gained and some useful counseling can be done. If a ten-year-old boy can understand the vocabulary and if he has some vague appreciation of the world of work, his results can be meaningful. Lowell happened to be very bright; he was in the fifth grade when tested but his scores on the Iowa Tests of Educational Development averaged around the tenth- to eleventh-grade level.

His scores on the SVIB reflect strong interests in art, writing, science, and math, and he scored 66 on the academic achievement scale — above the average Ph.D. His scores on the business scales, both the basic and occupational scales, show that, at the ripe age of ten, he has already rejected business as a potential career. He will almost certainly enter college and go on to graduate school. But to make such plans now would be premature, and would ignore the fact that he is still a little boy and should be allowed

56

several years to fool around, as little boys are wont to do. There is time later for academic endeavors.

The main reason for giving Lowell the SVIB was simply curiosity, on his part and his parents'. They had interesting conversations about the results, but there was no attempt to treat the inventory as anything other than a parlor game, which only incidentally concerned the world of work.

This discussion has been a brief overview of the Strong Blank; by necessity the coverage has been shallow, and only the most important points have been dealt with. For a more thorough treatment of the points above, and for more empirical information on the entire system, the *Handbook for the SVIB* (Stanford University Press, 1971) should be consulted.

## References

Campbell, D. P. *Manual for the Strong Vocational Interest Blanks for men and women.* Stanford: Stanford University Press, 1966.

———. Stability of interests within an occupation over thirty years. *Journal of Applied Psychology,* 1966, 50, 51–56.

———. The stability of vocational interests within occupations over long time spans. *Personnel and Guidance Journal,* 1966, 44, 1012–19.

———. The 1966 revision of the Strong Vocational Interest Blank. *Personnel and Guidance Journal,* 1966, 44, 744–749.

———. The development of the SVIB: 1927–1967. In Paul McReynolds (ed.), *Advances in psychological assessment,* vol. 1. Palo Alto: Science and Behavior Books, 1968, 105–130.

———. Changing patterns of interests within the American society. *Measurement and Evaluation in Guidance,* 1968, 1, No. 1, 36–49.

———. The problems in revising an established psychological test. Paper presented at the Third Annual MMPI Symposium, Minneapolis, Minnesota, April 1969.

———. Some desirable characteristics of interest inventories. Paper presented at the meetings of the American Personnel and Guidance Association, Las Vegas, April 1969.

———. *Strong Vocational Interest Blanks Manual — 1969 Supplement.* Stanford: Stanford University Press, 1969.

———. *Handbook for the Strong Vocational Interest Blank.* Stanford: Stanford University Press, 1971.

———, F. H. Borgen, S. H. Eastes, C. B. Johansson, and R. A. Peterson. A set of basic interest scales for the Strong Vocational Interest Blank for men. *Journal of Applied Psychology,* 1968, 52, No. 6, Pt. 2.

Campbell, D. P., and L. W. Harmon. Vocational interests of non-professional women. Final report of Project No. 6-1820, Grant DEG 3-6-061820-0755. Office of Education, Department of Health, Education, and Welfare, December 1968.

Strong, E. K., Jr. Good and poor interest items. *Journal of Applied Psychology,* 1962, 46, 269–275.

———. Reworded versus new interest items. *Journal of Applied Psychology,* 1963, 47, 111–116.

———, D. P. Campbell, R. F. Berdie, and K. E. Clark. Proposed scoring changes for the SVIB. *Journal of Applied Psychology,* 1964, 48, 75–80.

# 3

# The 1969 Revision of the Strong Vocational Interest Blank for Women

Lenore W. Harmon

THE STRONG VOCATIONAL INTEREST BLANK is the oldest vocational interest inventory still in general use. Including it in a book on new interest inventories therefore requires some explanation. The women's form was first introduced in 1933 and revised in 1946. The "new" women's SVIB is a second revision which utilizes the knowledge gained from over thirty-five years of research on and use of both the men's and women's forms of the inventory. This revision contains much that is new, such as a complete set of basic interest scales and occupational scales for many new occupations.

The word *revision* is a curious one to use in describing a psychological instrument. Although I know that an author who revises a book has changed, deleted, and/or added some words, I don't know exactly what the author of an interest inventory has done when he says he has completed a revision. What he has done depends on how the test was first developed. If he originally developed his items and scales by the "armchair" method, his revision probably reflects some new, if untested, ideas. If he originally developed his scales by factor analysis, then his revision may be a result of a new factor analysis.

## SVIB METHODOLOGY

The method of measuring vocational interests that is described below was used in the 1933 edition and the 1946 and 1969 revisions, although the

58

basic scales of the current revision were developed by a different procedure.

First a set of items is presented to members of a number of occupational groups such as artists, physicians, accountants, executive housekeepers, and airline stewardesses. Second, some set of occupational groups is designated as a women-in-general (WIG) group. In practice, the WIG group usually includes representatives of whatever occupational groups are available for testing. Its composition is very important because it is used as a reference group against which the occupational groups are compared. Third, the percentage of each occupational group responding "Like," "Indifferent," and "Dislike" to each SVIB item is compared with the response percentage for WIG. For example, on the basis of such a comparison, the item foreign correspondent is weighted positively on the stewardess scale and negatively on the executive housekeeper scale. In practice, the size of the weights applied and the size of the difference which is weighted have varied over the years.

Fourth, occupational scales are developed from the individual items that differentiate occupational groups from WIG. The following example presents which of the first forty-two items of the revised SVIB appear on the executive housekeeper and stewardess scales. Comparing the two short sets of items gives one an idea of the interests of women in these occupations. Most of the housekeepers in the group tested worked in hospitals and the items that differentiate them from WIG suggest this orientation.

| Executive Housekeeper Scale (first 9 items) | Stewardess Scale (first 9 items) |
|---|---|
| 13. Bacteriologist | 2. Dental assistant |
| 14. Bookkeeper | 4. Advertiser |
| 18. Buyer | 7. Artist's model |
| 19. Cartoonist (−) | 12. Airplane pilot |
| 24. College professor (−) | 18. Buyer of merchandise |
| 31. Dietitian | 26. Children's clothes designer |
| 37. Employment manager | 28. Costume designer |
| 41. Florist | 37. Employment manager |
| 42. Foreign correspondent (−) | 42. Foreign correspondent |

Finally, all scales developed in this manner are drawn together into a profile which can be used to report the scores of individuals who complete the inventory.

This is basically the way the SVIB was developed in 1933, and the same steps were followed in preparing the 1969 revision. But at each step changes were made in the items themselves, the occupational groupings, and the profiling.

WHAT'S NEW IN THE 1969 REVISION

*Items.* The 1933 edition of the women's SVIB had 410 items. In the 1946 edition the ten least effective items were dropped so that the blank could be scored by machine. (IBM scoring equipment at that time had a maximum capacity of 400 items.)

In the 1969 edition 111 items were changed. Some, such as those referring to confectioner and the *American* magazine, were completely replaced because they were outdated. Other items were updated: "Aviatrix" became airplane pilot; manikin became fashion model. Ineffective items were replaced. For instance, proofreader was deleted because virtually everyone responded "Dislike," and items that everyone responds to in the same way do not differentiate between groups (Strong, 1962). Items objectionable to some people, for example, Negro and people with physical disabilities, were replaced. Other items were made simpler and easier to read without altering substantially their meanings. For instance, people who are unconventional was changed to nonconformists.

The new items that replaced outdated, ineffectual, and objectionable items were chosen (1) to increase the numbers of items overlapping with the men's form (*Popular Mechanics* magazine replaced musical comedy); (2) to augment the occupational flavor of the items (be married versus single was changed to be married to a research scientist versus a sales executive); (3) to represent lower level occupations more adequately (dental assistant, electronics technician, and nurses aide replaced ineffectual occupational names); (4) to increase specificity (formal affairs became formal dress affairs); and (5) to increase the diversity of the item pool (computer programmer and policewoman were added).

The 1969 revision contains only 398 items to avoid confusion with the 1946 edition, which is still used for some purposes, and with the men's form, which has 399 items.

To illustrate how the items work, a set of tables and figures will be used to show the percentage of each occupational group responding "Like" to various items. In general, the appropriate occupational groups respond positively. Table 3.1 gives the percentage of each occupational group that responded "Like" to the item artist's model. Stewardesses, entertainers,

60

and beauticians responded "Like" most frequently while women chemists, physicians, and medical technologists rarely did. Figure 3.1 graphically illustrates the distribution of the occupational groups according to the percentage of each group that responded "Like" to this item. As can be seen, most groups do not like the occupation, but a few do. The item will probably appear on their scales. The distribution for the item college professor is much broader (see Table 3.2 and Fig. 3.2) indicating that opinion about the occupation varies considerably among the groups. The groups

Table 3.1. Percentage of "Like" Responses to Item Number 7, Artist Model, for Various Women's Occupational Groups

| Percentage Responding "Like" | Occupational Groups |
|---|---|
| 1 | Chemists |
| 2–4 | None |
| 5 | Physicians, medical technologists |
| 6 | Mathematicians, army officers, math-science teachers, executive housekeepers |
| 7 | Army enlisted personnel, physical therapists, librarians |
| 8 | Interior decorators, wives of animal husbandry professors, navy officers, translators, social science teachers, lawyers |
| 9 | Elementary teachers, licensed practical nurses, psychologists, navy enlisted personnel, sewing machine operators, home economics teachers, business education teachers, artists |
| 10 | Instrument assemblers, life insurance underwriters, directors of Christian education, physical education teachers, dietitians |
| 11 | Occupational therapists, newswomen |
| 12 | YWCA staff members, registered nurses, language teachers |
| 13 | Saleswomen, telephone operators, photographers, wives of physicists, guidance counselors |
| 14 | None |
| 15 | English teachers |
| 16 | Art teachers |
| 17 | None |
| 18 | Dental assistants, wives of social workers |
| 19 | Radiologic technologists |
| 20 | Secretaries |
| 21–28 | None |
| 29 | Beauticians |
| 30–39 | None |
| 40 | Entertainers |
| 41–51 | None |
| 52 | Airline stewardesses |
| 53–100 | None |

61

Table 3.2. Percentage of "Like" Responses to Item Number 24, College Professor, for Various Women's Occupational Groups

| Percentage Responding "Like" | Occupational Groups |
|---|---|
| 1–9 | None |
| 10 | Beauticians |
| 11–14 | None |
| 15 | Sewing machine operators |
| 16–18 | None |
| 19 | Saleswomen, telephone operators, instrument assemblers |
| 20–24 | None |
| 25 | Licensed practical nurses |
| 26–27 | None |
| 28 | Navy enlisted personnel, radiologic technologists, executive housekeepers |
| 29 | None |
| 30 | Dental assistants |
| 31 | None |
| 32 | Secretaries |
| 33 | Army enlisted personnel |
| 34 | None |
| 35 | Interior decorators |
| 36 | None |
| 37 | Entertainers |
| 38 | None |
| 39 | Life insurance underwriters |
| 40–44 | None |
| 45 | Airline stewardesses |
| 46 | None |
| 47 | Photographers, physical therapists |
| 48 | Elementary teachers |
| 49 | Medical technologists |
| 50–51 | None |
| 52 | Registered nurses |
| 53 | None |
| 54 | Wives of social workers |
| 55 | Wives of animal husbandry professors |
| 56 | Home economics teachers |
| 57–58 | None |
| 59 | Navy officers, artists |
| 60 | None |
| 61 | Occupational therapists, newswomen, dietitians |
| 62–63 | None |
| 64 | High school physical education teachers, math-science teachers, business education teachers |
| 65 | Wives of physicists, army officers |
| 66–70 | None |
| 71 | YWCA staff members, lawyers |
| 72 | Translators, physicians |
| 73 | None |
| 74 | Directors of Christian education |

Table 3.2 — continued

| Percentage Responding "Like" | Occupational Groups |
|---|---|
| 75–76 . . . . . . . . . | None |
| 77 . . . . . . . . . . . | Social science teachers |
| 78 . . . . . . . . . . . | English teachers |
| 79 . . . . . . . . . . . | None |
| 80 . . . . . . . . . . . | Language teachers, librarians |
| 81 . . . . . . . . . . . | None |
| 82 . . . . . . . . . . . | Art teachers |
| 83–84 . . . . . . . . . | None |
| 85 . . . . . . . . . . . | Guidance counselors |
| 86–90 . . . . . . . . . | None |
| 91 . . . . . . . . . . . | Chemists |
| 92 . . . . . . . . . . . | None |
| 93 . . . . . . . . . . . | Psychologists |
| 94–96 . . . . . . . . . | None |
| 97 . . . . . . . . . . . | Mathematicians |
| 98–100 . . . . . . . . | None |

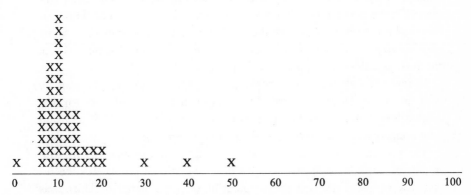

Figure 3.1. Frequency distribution of occupational groups according to percentage of each group responding "Like" to item Number 7, artist's model (each X = one occupation; base line represents percentage intervals)

Figure 3.2. Frequency distribution of occupational groups according to percentage of each group responding "Like" to item Number 24, college professor (each X = one occupation; base line represents percentage intervals)

that endorse it highly include educators and scientists in fields requiring graduate degrees; the groups that do not are those with the least education.

*Occupational groups.* For the 1969 revision fifty-two occupational groups were tested between 1964 and 1968. SVIB scales for thirty-three of these groups had never been developed before; nineteen of the groups had been tested previously. Only six occupational groups that were represented on previous editions were used again without being retested. The major additions are in esthetic occupations (art teacher, interior decorator), linguistic occupations (language teacher, translator), highly trained theoretical occupations (mathematician, chemist), business occupations (accountant, bankwoman), and nonprofessional occupations in the paramedical, industrial, clerical, and military areas.

Nearly 25,000 women were asked to complete the SVIB in the course of preparing the revision. About 10,000 of these did not do so or were eliminated from the criterion groups because they were not currently employed in the occupation, they were not satisfied with the occupation, or they had not been employed in the job for the minimum number of years necessary to be considered a member of that occupational group. Hence the average criterion group includes 285 women.

In contrast, only fifteen occupational groups were tested for the original women's SVIB. However, most of the scoring and statistical work for that edition was done by hand. It goes without saying that the 1969 revision could hardly have been accomplished without electronic data processing.

The procedure for testing women in occupational groups begins with finding a source of subjects. Most of the occupational groups for the revision were tested through the cooperation of professional organizations or employers. Some groups cooperated freely; others wanted some assurances. For instance, the airlines wanted to be certain that the data would not be used to force them to hire older women as stewardesses. Some people declined to cooperate altogether. One employer refused because she felt that a separate pink form of the SVIB was discriminatory against women — that they should be tested with the same form used for men. Testing each occupational group was a study in itself. Valuable insights into occupations and into the women who are employed in them were one of the by-products of the revision.

Tables 3.3 through 3.8 and Figure 3.3 illustrate what the study of one group, executive housekeepers, revealed. Table 3.3 suggests that there are no really young executive housekeepers. Apparently the housekeeping of a large hospital or hotel is never entrusted to anyone under thirty. The most typical educational level for an executive housekeeper is graduation from high school, although some have finished only the eighth grade and others have done graduate work. Figure 3.3 demonstrates that the typical

Table 3.3. Age and Education of Executive Housekeeper Sample

| Age [a] | N | Education [b] | N |
|---------|---|---------------|---|
| 31–35 | 3 | Eighth grade | 14 |
| 36–40 | 13 | Some high school | 51 |
| 41–45 | 22 | High school graduate | 138 |
| 46–50 | 55 | Some college | 51 |
| 51–55 | 78 | B.A. degree | 12 |
| 56–60 | 74 | Graduate work | 4 |
| 61–65 | 23 | Total | 270 |
| 66–70 | 4 | | |
| 71–75 | 1 | | |
| Total | 273 | | |

[a] Mean age = 52.8 years; [b] S.D. = 6.8 years.

Table 3.4. Likes and Dislikes of Executive Housekeepers
for Selected Occupations as Compared with WIG

| | Percentage Responding | |
|---|---|---|
| Item | Executive Housekeepers | WIG |
| *"Like" Responses* | | |
| Housekeeper | 95 | 26 |
| Interior decorator | 85 | 69 |
| Buyer of merchandise | 75 | 50 |
| Hotel manager | 68 | 27 |
| Employment manager | 67 | 31 |
| Florist | 66 | 47 |
| Church worker | 62 | 37 |
| Musician | 61 | 60 |
| *"Dislike" Responses* | | |
| Dentist | 6 | 9 |
| Artist's model | 6 | 14 |
| Life insurance saleswoman | 8 | 6 |
| Scientific illustrator | 10 | 17 |
| Criminal lawyer | 12 | 26 |
| Politician | 12 | 19 |
| Waitress | 12 | 8 |
| Electronics technician | 12 | 11 |

executive housekeeper rates her job as one which requires working with others and supervising many others. On the SVIB occupational items executive housekeepers respond "Like" to items having to do with housekeeping, decorating, buying, and managing, and "Dislike" to those dealing with business or science (Table 3.4). Their dislikes are not too different from those of most women. On the items concerning certain selected activities, their interests in homemaking, organizing, and managing are also apparent (Table 3.5).

Table 3.5. Likes of Executive Housekeepers
for Selected Activities as Compared with WIG

| | Percentage Responding "Like" | |
| Activity | Executive Housekeepers | WIG |
| --- | --- | --- |
| Decorating a room with flowers ............ | 88 | 75 |
| Meeting and directing people .............. | 76 | 58 |
| Organizing cupboards and closets ........... | 71 | 52 |
| Giving "first-aid" assistance .............. | 71 | 52 |
| Preparing dinner for guests ................ | 69 | 68 |
| Sewing ................................. | 68 | 54 |
| Adjusting difficulties of others ............. | 59 | 52 |
| Doing research work ..................... | 51 | 46 |
| Displaying merchandise in a store .......... | 43 | 37 |
| Writing reports .......................... | 37 | 25 |
| Taping a bruised ankle ................... | 33 | 29 |
| Making a speech ........................ | 25 | 31 |
| Repairing electrical wiring ................. | 20 | 17 |
| Arguments ............................. | 13 | 21 |
| Acting as cheerleader .................... | 10 | 22 |

Table 3.6. Preference of Executive Housekeepers
for Ten Positions as Compared with WIG

| | Percentage Responding "Like" | |
| Position | Executive Housekeepers | WIG |
| --- | --- | --- |
| Owner-manager of chain of women's shops .. | 65 | 37 |
| Author of best-selling novel ............... | 46 | 50 |
| Prominent artist ......................... | 39 | 40 |
| President, women's college ................ | 37 | 36 |
| World-renowned scientist ................. | 26 | 31 |
| Supreme court justice .................... | 25 | 21 |
| Tennis champion ........................ | 16 | 22 |
| Famous actress .......................... | 16 | 28 |
| Outstanding opera singer ................. | 14 | 16 |
| Wife of U.S. president ................... | 12 | 19 |

Table 3.7. Executive Housekeepers' Self-Reported Talents

| | Percentage Responding "Yes" | |
|---|---|---|
| Talent | Executive Housekeepers | WIG |
| Able to meet emergencies quickly and effectively | 88 | 70 |
| Am always on time with my work | 79 | 67 |
| Usually get other people to do what I want done | 77 | 53 |
| Can correct others without giving offense | 73 | 50 |
| Plan my work in detail | 71 | 49 |
| Can smooth out tangles and disagreements between people | 70 | 45 |
| Win friends easily | 69 | 68 |
| Stimulate the ambition of my associates | 66 | 37 |
| Can write a concise, well-organized report | 56 | 61 |
| Usually start activities of my group | 51 | 48 |
| Keep detailed records of expenses | 49 | 28 |
| Usually liven up the group on a dull day | 35 | 36 |
| Have mechanical ingenuity (inventiveness) | 31 | 30 |
| Have more than my share of novel ideas | 30 | 39 |
| Remember faces, names, and incidents better than the average person | 25 | 37 |
| Can prepare successful advertisements | 13 | 16 |

Table 3.8. Job Characteristics Important to Executive Housekeepers as Compared with Those Important to WIG

| | Percentage Responding "Like" | |
|---|---|---|
| Job Characteristic | Executive Housekeepers | WIG |
| Opportunity to make use of all of one's knowledge and experience | 51 | 63 |
| Co-workers — congenial, competent, and adequate in number | 43 | 45 |
| Steadiness and permanence of work | 40 | 21 |
| Freedom in working out one's own methods of doing work | 34 | 55 |
| Opportunity for promotion | 33 | 21 |
| Courteous treatment from superiors | 29 | 20 |
| Salary received for work | 25 | 33 |
| Opportunity to ask questions and to consult about difficulties | 16 | 18 |
| Opportunity to understand just how one's superior expects work to be done | 16 | 7 |
| Certainty one's work will be judged by fair standards | 14 | 17 |

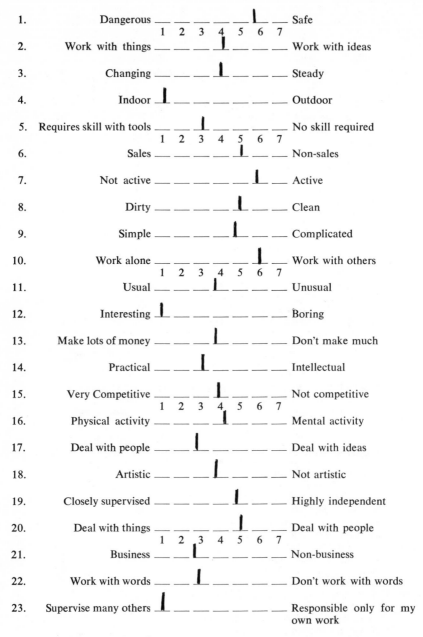

1. Dangerous ___ ___ ___ ___ ___ |___ ___ Safe
               1  2  3  4  5  6  7

2. Work with things ___ ___ ___ |___ ___ ___ ___ Work with ideas

3. Changing ___ ___ ___ |___ ___ ___ ___ Steady

4. Indoor |___ ___ ___ ___ ___ ___ ___ Outdoor

5. Requires skill with tools ___ ___ |___ ___ ___ ___ ___ No skill required
                        1  2  3  4  5  6  7

6. Sales ___ ___ ___ ___ |___ ___ ___ Non-sales

7. Not active ___ ___ ___ ___ ___ |___ ___ Active

8. Dirty ___ ___ ___ ___ |___ ___ ___ Clean

9. Simple ___ ___ ___ |___ ___ ___ ___ Complicated

10. Work alone ___ ___ ___ ___ ___ |___ ___ Work with others
             1  2  3  4  5  6  7

11. Usual ___ ___ ___ |___ ___ ___ ___ Unusual

12. Interesting |___ ___ ___ ___ ___ ___ ___ Boring

13. Make lots of money ___ ___ ___ |___ ___ ___ ___ Don't make much

14. Practical ___ ___ |___ ___ ___ ___ ___ Intellectual

15. Very Competitive ___ ___ ___ |___ ___ ___ ___ Not competitive
               1  2  3  4  5  6  7

16. Physical activity ___ ___ ___ |___ ___ ___ ___ Mental activity

17. Deal with people ___ ___ |___ ___ ___ ___ ___ Deal with ideas

18. Artistic ___ ___ ___ |___ ___ ___ ___ Not artistic

19. Closely supervised ___ ___ ___ ___ |___ ___ ___ Highly independent

20. Deal with things ___ ___ ___ ___ |___ ___ ___ Deal with people
             1  2  3  4  5  6  7

21. Business ___ ___ |___ ___ ___ ___ ___ Non-business

22. Work with words ___ ___ |___ ___ ___ ___ ___ Don't work with words

23. Supervise many others |___ ___ ___ ___ ___ ___ ___ Responsible only for my own work

Figure 3.3. How the typical executive housekeeper rates her job

68

In one set of items SVIB respondents are asked to pick three out of ten positions that they would most like to have. The only one executive house-keepers chose more often than WIG was owner-manager of a chain of women's shops (Table 3.6). When reporting their talents, the executive housekeepers felt that they were competent, well organized, and well able to direct others (Table 3.7). It is interesting that when indicating what job characteristics were important to them, they placed "steadiness of work" and "co-workers" above "freedom to work out one's own methods" (Table 3.8).

The typical executive housekeeper emerges as a middle-aged high school graduate who likes homemaking tasks, is well organized and able to supervise many others efficiently, but is not resentful of being super-vised herself.

Examining all the data for each occupational group sampled for the 1969 revision would provide the counselor with a wealth of occupational information.

*Women-in-general.* Once most of the occupational groups had been tested, representatives from each of forty-two groups were selected ran-domly. Then, some wives and high school students were added to form a WIG group of 1000 women. Strong's 1946 WIG sample included nearly 8000 women from twenty-six different groups combined so that each group was represented equally (Strong, 1943).

The biggest differences between the new and old WIG groups are the greater occupational breadth of the new group and its temporal narrow-ness. All the women in the latest WIG group were tested after 1963. Campbell (1970) has concluded that an in-general group works best if it includes people tested over a long time span. The 1969 WIG group does not. New scales developed in 1980 or 1985 that use it might measure cul-tural change rather than occupational characteristics.

Because WIG response percentages to SVIB items are used in scale building, the composition of the WIG group does affect the scales. Just who should be in this group is an interesting if unanswerable question. A partial answer is that a large, broad group is a better representation of women-in-general than a small, narrow one.

*Scales.* A comparison of newly tested occupational groups with a new WIG group necessarily results in new scales, although the old and new occupational scales included in earlier editions overlap to some extent.

The old system of selecting items resulted in the inclusion of some items that differentiated between occupational groups and WIG by as little as 6 percent. The new system selects and weights only the most valid items, usually those which differentiate by 15 percent or more. The new occupational scales utilize a $\pm 1$ item weighting system instead of the $\pm 4$ system previously used, which simplifies scoring without sacrificing reliability or validity (Strong, Campbell, Berdie, and Clark, 1964).

One of the completely "new" features on the revised SVIB is a set of basic scales. These are relatively short scales that represent a single content area. They were developed by intercorrelating the responses of women-in-general to most of the SVIB items and by gathering related items into scales. Several thousand intercorrelations were generated. Items in part V, Order of Preference of Activities, were not intercorrelated because they require forced-choice responses. Items to which any response, "Like," "Indifferent," or "Dislike," was less than 15 percent were not intercorrelated either (Campbell, Borgen, Eastes, Johansson, and Peterson, 1967).

The result was nineteen relatively short, reliable scales, each of which measured one dominant interest theme. They have mean scores of 50 and standard deviations of 10. Table 3.9 shows, as an example, the items on the public speaking basic scale. Item 160, which is set apart at the bottom of the table, is one of the new items. It is separate because there are actually two sets of basic scales: the first is based on items common to the 1946 and 1969 forms; the second utilizes all the items in the 1969 revision. The latter scales are longer and better and should be used in most situations. The table also shows the intercorrelations between the items on the scale. The correlation coefficients above the diagonal are based on Strong's WIG group tested in the 1930s and 1940s. Those below the diagonal are based on the new WIG group.

Actually, only 5 percent of the pairs of items in the total matrix correlated at .25 or above, and only 1 percent correlated at .35 or above (Campbell et al., 1967). Items that correlated with other items in the group at .20 or above were chosen for basic scales unless they were unreasonable and would have made the scale difficult to interpret. For instance, if the item "preparing a meal" had, for some reason, correlated at .20 or above with all the items on the public speaking scale, it would have been left out to avoid "muddying" the interpretive waters. A few items that correlated at less than .20 with some of the other items in the cluster were retained because they seemed to make sense.

70

Table 3.9. Intercorrelations of Items in Public Speaking Basic Interest Scale

| Item Number | Item | 24 | 33 | 81 | 91 | 92 | 172 | 173 | 181 | 182 | 184 | 195 | 394 |
|---|---|---|---|---|---|---|---|---|---|---|---|---|---|
| 24 | College professor | | 22 | 17 | 28 | 21 | 23 | 08 | 18 | 16 | 29 | 17 | 23 |
| 33 | Dramatist | 35 | | 17 | 37 | 42 | 14 | 16 | 17 | 18 | 25 | 08 | 32 |
| 81 | Politician | 28 | 31 | | 30 | 26 | 33 | 34 | 19 | 26 | 30 | 16 | 32 |
| 91 | Radio announcer | 19 | 28 | 22 | | 57 | 32 | 18 | 25 | 25 | 43 | 32 | 46 |
| 92 | Radio program director | 23 | 27 | 31 | 61 | | 31 | 21 | 26 | 24 | 30 | 23 | 35 |
| 172 | Being head of a civic improvement program | 26 | 24 | 37 | 28 | 36 | | 39 | 34 | 41 | 41 | 36 | 38 |
| 173 | Expressing judgments publicly, regardless of what others say | 24 | 17 | 33 | 20 | 17 | 37 | | 27 | 28 | 33 | 23 | 36 |
| 181 | Interviewing men for a job | 27 | 23 | 30 | 18 | 27 | 38 | 27 | | 64 | 30 | 34 | 30 |
| 182 | Interviewing clients | 24 | 18 | 24 | 20 | 28 | 32 | 24 | 66 | | 35 | 40 | 30 |
| 184 | Making a speech | 25 | 26 | 32 | 24 | 22 | 37 | 30 | 22 | 26 | | 35 | 67 |
| 195 | Meeting and directing people | 21 | 20 | 26 | 19 | 24 | 39 | 27 | 38 | 39 | 37 | | 29 |
| 394 | Public speaking | 24 | 29 | 27 | 28 | 24 | 37 | 23 | 23 | 24 | 63 | 34 | |
| 160 | Electioneering for office | 24 | 27 | 62 | 26 | 25 | 39 | 33 | 31 | 28 | 36 | 24 | 28 |

SOURCE: Reprinted with permission of the publisher from *Handbook for the Strong Vocational Interest Blank* by David P. Campbell (Stanford: Stanford University Press, 1971), p. 164.

Table 3.10 shows how various occupational groups score on the public speaking scale. The high and low scoring groups are particularly interesting and seem reasonable when one considers what YWCA staff members, lawyers, speech pathologists, lab technicians, and sewing machine operators do. An understanding of what items are on the basic scales and what occupations score high on them is the best tool available for interpreting them.

The basic scale profile (Fig. 3.4) of executive housekeepers complements what we already know about them. The basic scales are helpful in determining the general interest areas of individuals. They are not as specific as the occupational scales, and thus they allow for more generalization in interpretation.

The 1969 revision of the women's form also includes some new non-occupational scales. The diversity of interest scale has already been discussed in chapter 2. In a way it is opposite to the basic scales because the items are statistically unrelated. The average score on the diversity of interest scale is 50; 57 is high; 43 is low. Stewardesses score highest (56), while authors (43) and artists (42) score low. A study by Anastasi and Schaefer (1969) suggests that adolescent girls who are creative in art and in writing have "manifested an absorbing interest in the field since child-

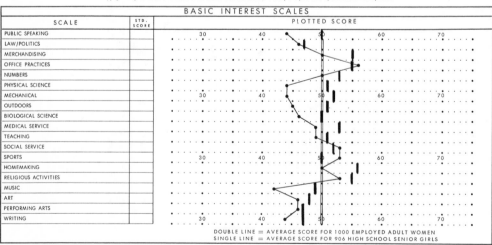

Figure 3.4. Basic interest scale profile for executive housekeepers

Table 3.10. Mean Scores on the Women's Public Speaking Scale
for Selected Women's Occupations

| Mean Standard Score | Occupational Groups |
|---|---|
| 58 | YWCA staff members (1967)[a] |
| 57 | Speech pathologists, lawyers (1934), lawyers (1967) |
| 56 | Guidance counselors, life insurance underwriters, psychologists (1966), army officers |
| 55 | Directors of Christian education |
| 54 | County welfare workers, English teachers (1967), stewardesses, life insurance saleswomen (1937), music teachers, newswomen, social workers, social science teachers (1967), psychologists (1942) |
| 53 | YWCA staff members (1934), models, translators |
| 52 | Musicians, navy officers, interior decorators, language teachers, librarians (1967), entertainers, graduates, army enlisted personnel, art teachers, engineers |
| 51 | Nongraduates, social science teachers (1934), college physical education teachers (1968), accountants |
| 50 | College physical education teachers (1954), occupational therapists (1966), dietitians (1967), high school physical education teachers (1939), executive housekeepers, photographers, authors, wives of social workers, business education teachers (1967), visiting nurses, bankwomen |
| 49 | English teachers (1934), chemists, physicians (1967), dietitians (1941), wives of physicists, registered nurses, buyers, physical therapists (1957), home economics teachers (1967) |
| 48 | Home economics teachers (1941), public health nurses, physicians (Western Reserve), high school physical education teachers (1967), nun-teachers, physicians (1934), elementary teachers, saleswomen, secretaries (1934), wives of animal husbandry professors, secretaries (1967) |
| 47 | Mathematicians, physical therapists (1966), dental assistants, housewives, librarians (1934), occupational therapists |
| 46 | Navy enlisted personnel, artists (1967), office workers, mathematics-science teachers (1967), licensed practical nurses, dentists, nurses (1934), telephone operators, radiologic technologists, mathematics-science teachers (1934) |
| 45 | Medical technologists |
| 44 | Artists (1934), instrument assemblers, beauticians |
| 43 | None |
| 42 | Sewing machine operators |

SOURCE: Adapted with permission of the publisher from *Handbook for the Strong Vocational Interest Blank* by David P. Campbell (Stanford: Stanford University Press, 1971), p. 187.
    [a] Date indicates year of testing.

hood." Such absorbing interests may well preclude excursions into other areas of interest.

The occupational introversion-extroversion scale, another new addition, is made up of items that differentiate introverts from extroverts as defined by scores on the MMPI social introversion-extroversion scale. It was standardized so that introverts score about 60 and extroverts about 40. When occupational groups are scored on the scale, nonprofessional and scientific groups score high while life insurance underwriters, YWCA staff members, and guidance counselors score low (see Table 3.11). Women with high scores on this scale seem to like being in the spotlight

Table 3.11. Mean Scores on the Occupational Introversion-Extroversion Scale for Selected Women's Occupations

| Mean Standard Score | Occupational Groups |
|---|---|
| 62 | Sewing machine operators |
| 61 | None |
| 60 | None |
| 59 | None |
| 58 | None |
| 57 | Beauticians, instrument assemblers |
| 56 | Mathematicians, mathematics-science teachers, medical technologists |
| 55 | Telephone operators |
| 54 | Artists, licensed practical nurses, radiologic technologists, navy enlisted personnel |
| 53 | Physical therapists |
| 52 | Chemists, dental assistants, elementary teachers |
| 51 | High school physical education teachers, physicians, saleswomen, secretaries |
| 50 | Business education teachers, home economics teachers, registered nurses, photographers |
| 49 | Dietitians, executive housekeepers, translators |
| 48 | Art teachers, language teachers, librarians, occupational therapists, army enlisted personnel |
| 47 | Entertainers |
| 46 | Interior decorators, navy officers |
| 45 | English teachers |
| 44 | Newswomen |
| 43 | Directors of Christian education, psychologists, social science teachers |
| 42 | Stewardesses, lawyers, army officers |
| 41 | Guidance counselors |
| 40 | Life insurance underwriters, YWCA staff members |

SOURCE: Adapted with permission of the publisher from *Handbook for the Strong Vocational Interest Blank* by David P. Campbell (Stanford: Stanford University Press, 1971), p. 241.

Table 3.12. Mean Scores on the Women's Academic Achievement
Scale for Selected Occupational Groups

| Mean Standard Score | Occupational Groups |
|---|---|
| 62 | Chemists |
| 61 | None |
| 60 | Mathematicians, psychologists |
| 59 | None |
| 58 | None |
| 57 | Translators, psychologists |
| 56 | Physicians |
| 55 | Mathematics-science teachers, engineers |
| 54 | English teachers |
| 53 | Librarians |
| 52 | Artists, lawyers, medical technologists, photographers, authors, librarians, social science teachers, YWCA secretaries, lawyers, speech pathologists |
| 51 | Language teachers, mathematics-science teachers, army officers, artists, physical education teachers (college), dentists, laboratory technicians |
| 50 | Art teachers, English teachers, newswomen, social workers |
| 49 | Guidance counselors, occupational therapists, social science teachers, music teachers, physical therapists |
| 48 | Accountants, dietitians, directors of Christian education, physical therapists, navy officers, YWCA staff members, music performers, nurses |
| 47 | Nurses, life insurance saleswomen, dietitians, occupational therapists |
| 46 | Interior decorators, home economics teachers |
| 45 | Elementary teachers, army enlisted personnel, business education teachers, high school physical education teachers |
| 44 | Entertainers, licensed practical nurses, life insurance underwriters, radiologic technologists, housewives |
| 43 | Business education teachers, executive housekeepers, home economics teachers, high school physical education teachers, navy enlisted personnel, stenographer-secretaries |
| 42 | Bankwomen, office workers |
| 41 | Models, buyers |
| 40 | Stewardesses, dental assistants, secretaries |
| 39 | None |
| 38 | Saleswomen, telephone operators |
| 37 | Instrument assemblers |
| 36 | None |
| 35 | Sewing machine operators |
| 34 | None |
| 33 | None |
| 32 | Beauticians |

SOURCE: Adapted with permission of the publisher from *Handbook for the Strong Vocational Interest Blank* by David P. Campbell (Stanford: Stanford University Press, 1971), p. 206.

75

and originating or leading group activities, and generally they enjoy people.

The academic achievement scale, introduced in 1966 by David Campbell, was developed by contrasting the item responses of women who got high grades with those who got low grades in college. It was normed so that 50 is the average score for college graduates. People who earn M.A.'s score about 55; those with Ph.D.'s about 60. College dropouts and those who do not enter college score well below 50. Table 3.12 shows how the occupational groups score on this scale. In general, scientific and technical groups score high; nonprofessional groups score low. Among the professional occupations businesswomen score lowest.

The masculinity-femininity scale has appeared on the profile since the 1930s. However, it has been recently revised. The 250+ items common to both the men's and women's forms were inspected to find those that differentiated between men and women in the eighteen occupations for which both a men's and a women's sample were available. The FMII and MFII scales were normed separately. Thus, 50 is the average score for women on the FMII scale, but it is not equivalent to a score of 50 on the MFII scale for men. Table 3.13 gives the scores on the MFII and FMII scales of both sexes employed in various occupations. It is important to note that the high end of the FMII scale represents greater occupational *femininity* than does the low end, while the high end on the MFII scale represents greater occupational *masculinity* than does the low end. Therefore, the threatening scores for both sexes are at the low end of the scale.

Although the case of the young man who is concerned about his feminine interests has been recognized for a long time, the case of the woman who is afraid of her masculine interests has not. Lately I have found it very helpful in counseling women to make a distinction between femininity and sexuality. Far too many women limit their roles to feminine stereotypes because they fear for their sexuality. One of my clients hates being intelligent, creative, competent, and independent. She is also afraid she may be a homosexual. She was originally a math major and could easily have earned a graduate degree in math or science, but she has changed her major to English education where she is doing equally well — and feels more comfortable about herself as a woman.

*The profile.* Many of the modifications in the women's SVIB are not necessarily apparent when one looks at the profile, but the profile (Fig. 3.5) has changed.

76

Table 3.13. Means and Standard Deviations on MFII and FMII
Scales for MF Validation Samples
(Mean for All Groups for Each Sex = 50, S.D. = 10)

| Occupation | Male Samples (MFII Standard Scores) | | | Female Samples (FMII Standard Scores) | | |
|---|---|---|---|---|---|---|
| | N | Mean | S.D. | N | Mean | S.D. |
| Artist ................... | 218 | 39.6 | 8.8 | 388 | 57.3 | 8.5 |
| Author-journalist ........... | 242 | 43.3 | 9.8 | 387 | 56.4 | 9.4 |
| Business education teacher .... | 322 | 54.6 | 10.9 | 249 | 46.0 | 10.6 |
| Dentist ................... | 235 | 53.6 | 9.1 | 188 | 44.7 | 10.6 |
| Engineer ................. | 511 | 53.7 | 9.7 | 322 | 42.0 | 11.1 |
| Lawyer ................. | 249 | 51.8 | 10.1 | 370 | 47.1 | 9.9 |
| Librarian ................ | 425 | 39.3 | 9.9 | 420 | 57.0 | 8.7 |
| Life insurance salesman ...... | 310 | 53.6 | 9.6 | 201 | 48.3 | 10.1 |
| Math-science teacher ........ | 288 | 56.1 | 9.4 | 466 | 47.8 | 10.4 |
| Musician performer ......... | 441 | 45.1 | 10.6 | 287 | 55.0 | 9.4 |
| Music teacher ............. | 490 | 44.0 | 10.7 | 444 | 54.0 | 9.1 |
| Office worker .............. | 316 | 53.2 | 9.8 | 425 | 46.5 | 10.7 |
| Physical therapist ........... | 348 | 56.1 | 10.4 | 399 | 46.0 | 10.6 |
| Physician ................. | 532 | 53.4 | 10.5 | 413 | 47.3 | 11.2 |
| Psychologist ............... | 1045 | 51.4 | 10.6 | 378 | 48.8 | 10.7 |
| Social science teacher ........ | 217 | 54.1 | 10.2 | 392 | 52.8 | 9.5 |
| Social worker ............. | 400 | 50.3 | 10.5 | 464 | 50.7 | 9.8 |
| YMCA-YWCA staff member . | 113 | 47.6 | 9.2 | 197 | 54.9 | 9.1 |

SOURCE: Adapted with permission of the publisher from *Handbook for the Strong Vocational Interest Blank* by David P. Campbell (Stanford: Stanford University Press, 1971), p. 233.

The basic interest scales appear at the top of the profile. The double line represents the average score for women-in-general; the jagged line represents the average score for 906 high school seniors. An interest in office practices, for example, seems to decrease with age, while interests in music and physical science increase with age. Like scores on the diversity of interest scales, scores over 57 on the basic scales are considered high; scores under 43 are considered low. They represent, respectively, the top and bottom 25 percent of WIG. In reviewing an individual's scores, the counselor should make allowances for the age of his client.

The occupational scales which appear below the basic scales have been regrouped. Until 1966, the women's profile was simply a listing of the scales available; groups were not separated as they were on the men's profile. In 1966 the scales available were classified on the basis of scale intercorrelations. With the addition of new scales, based on different occupational groups, new intercorrelations were generated. Scales with high correlations (.65 or above) and scales for groups that score 40 or above on

Reprinted from the 1969 Supplement to the Manual for the Strong Vocational Interest Blanks,
copyrighted by the Board of Trustees of the Leland Stanford Junior University and published by Stanford University Press.

## BASIC INTEREST SCALES

| SCALE | STD. SCORE | PLOTTED SCORE |
|---|---|---|
| PUBLIC SPEAKING | | |
| LAW/POLITICS | | |
| MERCHANDISING | | |
| OFFICE PRACTICES | | |
| NUMBERS | | |
| PHYSICAL SCIENCE | | |
| MECHANICAL | | |
| OUTDOORS | | |
| BIOLOGICAL SCIENCE | | |
| MEDICAL SERVICE | | |
| TEACHING | | |
| SOCIAL SERVICE | | |
| SPORTS | | |
| HOMEMAKING | | |
| RELIGIOUS ACTIVITIES | | |
| MUSIC | | |
| ART | | |
| PERFORMING ARTS | | |
| WRITING | | |

DOUBLE LINE = AVERAGE SCORE FOR 1000 EMPLOYED ADULT WOMEN
SINGLE LINE = AVERAGE SCORE FOR 906 HIGH SCHOOL SENIOR GIRLS

## OCCUPATIONAL SCALES

| | OCCUPATION | STD. SCORE | C | B— | B | B+ | A | | OCCUPATION | STD. SCORE | C | B— | B | B+ | A |
|---|---|---|---|---|---|---|---|---|---|---|---|---|---|---|---|
| I | MUSIC TEACHER | | | | | | | VII | ARMY—ENLISTED | | | | | | |
| | ENTERTAINER | | | | | | | | NAVY—ENLISTED | | | | | | |
| | MUSICIAN PERFORMER | | | | | | | | ARMY—OFFICER | | | | | | |
| | MODEL | | | | | | | | NAVY—OFFICER | | | | | | |
| II | ART TEACHER | | | | | | | VIII | LAWYER | | | | | | |
| | ARTIST | | | | | | | | ACCOUNTANT | | | | | | |
| | INTERIOR DECORATOR | | | | | | | | BANKWOMAN | | | | | | |
| III | NEWSWOMAN | | | | | | | | LIFE INS. UNDERWRITER | | | | | | |
| | ENGLISH TEACHER | | | | | | | | BUYER | | | | | | |
| | LANGUAGE TEACHER | | | | | | | | BUSINESS ED. TEACHER | | | | | | |
| IV | YWCA STAFF MEMBER | | | | | | | IX | HOME ECON. TEACHER | | | | | | |
| | RECREATION LEADER | | | | | | | | DIETITIAN | | | | | | |
| | DIRECTOR, CHRISTIAN ED. | | | | | | | X | PHYSICAL ED. TEACHER | | | | | | |
| | NUN-TEACHER | | | | | | | | OCCUPATIONAL THERAPIST | | | | | | |
| | GUIDANCE COUNSELOR | | | | | | | | PHYSICAL THERAPIST | | | | | | |
| | SOCIAL SCIENCE TEACHER | | | | | | | | PUBLIC HEALTH NURSE | | | | | | |
| | SOCIAL WORKER | | | | | | | | REGISTERED NURSE | | | | | | |
| V | SPEECH PATHOLOGIST | | | | | | | | LIC. PRACTICAL NURSE | | | | | | |
| | PSYCHOLOGIST | | | | | | | | RADIOLOGIC TECHNOLOGIST | | | | | | |
| | LIBRARIAN | | | | | | | | DENTAL ASSISTANT | | | | | | |
| | TRANSLATOR | | | | | | | XI | EXECUTIVE HOUSEKEEPER | | | | | | |
| VI | PHYSICIAN | | | | | | | | ELEMENTARY TEACHER | | | | | | |
| | DENTIST | | | | | | | | SECRETARY | | | | | | |
| | MEDICAL TECHNOLOGIST | | | | | | | | SALESWOMAN | | | | | | |
| | CHEMIST | | | | | | | | TELEPHONE OPERATOR | | | | | | |
| | MATHEMATICIAN | | | | | | | | INSTRUMENT ASSEMBLER | | | | | | |
| | COMPUTER PROGRAMMER | | | | | | | | SEWING MACHINE OPERATOR | | | | | | |
| | MATH-SCIENCE TEACHER | | | | | | | | BEAUTICIAN | | | | | | |
| | ENGINEER | | | | | | | | AIRLINE STEWARDESS | | | | | | |

NON-OCCUPATIONAL SCALES

AACH    DIV    FMII    OIE

ADMINISTRATIVE INDICES

TR    UNP    FC    LP    IP    DP

Figure 3.5. Profile sheet for the SVIB for women

78

scales other than their own were placed together. Obviously, there were some exceptions, since one scale might correlate with two scales which in turn do not correlate with each other. For instance, occupational therapist correlates highly with art teacher, but not with artist or interior decorator with which art teacher does correlate. At the same time art teacher does not correlate highly with the medical occupations with which occupational therapist correlates. The profile offers no way to show the relation between the art teacher and occupational therapist scales, although counselors who work with the Strong have known for a long time that women who score high on the occupational therapist scale usually have an interest in arts and crafts. Thus, the profile grouping is somewhat arbitrary and should not be regarded as the only possible way to organize the occupations.

For descriptive purposes the eleven groups of occupational scales have been titled as follows: (I) music-performing; (II) art; (III) verbal-linguistics; (IV) social service; (V) verbal-scientific; (VI) scientific; (VII) military-managerial; (VIII) business; (IX) home economics; (X) health-related services; (XI) nonprofessional. These scales have been normed so that the average score of the occupational group on which the scale is based is a standard score of 50 with a standard deviation of 10. As in the past, letter grades have been assigned to the scores. An A corresponds to standard scores of 45 and above, B+ to scores of 40 to 44, B to scores of 35 to 39, B— to scores of 30 to 34. The C+ letter grade has been dropped, and C corresponds to any standard score below 30. Thus, 84 percent of the occupational group on which a scale is based earns an A or a B+. Such scores are usually considered to represent a high degree of similarity of interests among women in the occupation.

Previous profiles allowed for the graphic presentation of any standard score on an occupational scale from —10 to 75. The range of exact graphic presentation on the new profile has been restricted to that from 20 to 60, although the standard score column still has the exact standard score in it.

The shaded areas on Figure 3.5 represent the scores of the middle third of the WIG group (Campbell, 1963). They can be used to determine how different an individual taking the inventory or the whole occupational group is from WIG on a given scale. For instance, chemists and WIG are well separated by the chemist scale, while elementary teachers and WIG are not as well separated by the elementary teacher scale. A woman who scores 45 on both scales has a more significant score on the chemist scale because she has to answer less like WIG to achieve it than she did to get her elementary teacher score.

Beneath the occupational scales are boxes for the non-occupational scales and the administrative indices, which are discussed in chapter 2. They are not clearly identified, so the counselor may elect not to talk about them with his client at all if he wishes.

VALIDITY

The most important question one can ask about a vocational interest test is how well it can predict what people actually do vocationally. Data to answer this question are not yet available for the revision of the women's form because not enough time has elapsed since it was published to produce any studies of predictive validity. None of the thousands of women who have taken the SVIB in the past are suitable subjects for follow-up studies because the new scales include items that were not on the inventories they completed. For a few years the best data on the validity of the women's SVIB will be of the concurrent type. Concurrent validity is established if women currently in a given occupation or curriculum have scores which are appropriate to their occupation or curriculum.

Since this revision is the first of the women's Strong Blank to include scales for some high-level business occupations, I was interested in how college women going into business occupations would score on it. Figure 3.6 represents the SVIB mean scores of the total membership of one chapter of Phi Chi Theta, a professional "fraternity" for women business students. The N was 10, which gives a good indication of the popularity of business as a major for women in a university of 16,000 students. On the basic scales these women scored high on law/politics, merchandising, numbers, and public speaking; low on biological science and medical service. On the occupational scales their high scores were concentrated in groups VII (military-managerial) and VIII (business); they also had high scores on the secretary, stewardess, YWCA staff member, and social science teacher scales. The lowest scores were recorded for group VI (scientific), although within it the computer programmer and math-science teacher scales were moderately high.

Like men in business occupations, the academic achievement scores of these women business students were low. Their FMII scores tended toward the masculine end of the scale, and their OIE scores presented

Reprinted from the *1969 Supplement to the Manual for the Strong Vocational Interest Blanks*,
copyrighted by the Board of Trustees of the Leland Stanford Junior University and published by Stanford University Press.

## BASIC INTEREST SCALES

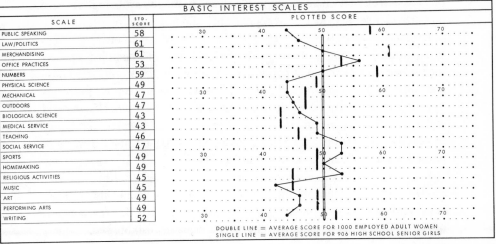

| SCALE | STD. SCORE |
|---|---|
| PUBLIC SPEAKING | 58 |
| LAW/POLITICS | 61 |
| MERCHANDISING | 61 |
| OFFICE PRACTICES | 53 |
| NUMBERS | 59 |
| PHYSICAL SCIENCE | 49 |
| MECHANICAL | 47 |
| OUTDOORS | 47 |
| BIOLOGICAL SCIENCE | 43 |
| MEDICAL SERVICE | 43 |
| TEACHING | 46 |
| SOCIAL SERVICE | 47 |
| SPORTS | 49 |
| HOMEMAKING | 49 |
| RELIGIOUS ACTIVITIES | 45 |
| MUSIC | 45 |
| ART | 49 |
| PERFORMING ARTS | 49 |
| WRITING | 52 |

DOUBLE LINE = AVERAGE SCORE FOR 1000 EMPLOYED ADULT WOMEN
SINGLE LINE = AVERAGE SCORE FOR 906 HIGH SCHOOL SENIOR GIRLS

## OCCUPATIONAL SCALES

| | OCCUPATION | STD. SCORE | | OCCUPATION | STD. SCORE |
|---|---|---|---|---|---|
| I | MUSIC TEACHER | 18 | VII | ARMY–ENLISTED | 39 |
| | ENTERTAINER | 24 | | NAVY–ENLISTED | 34 |
| | MUSICIAN PERFORMER | 21 | | ARMY–OFFICER | 40 |
| | MODEL | 33 | | NAVY–OFFICER | 43 |
| II | ART TEACHER | 12 | VIII | LAWYER | 38 |
| | ARTIST | 20 | | ACCOUNTANT | 43 |
| | INTERIOR DECORATOR | 23 | | BANKWOMAN | 41 |
| III | NEWSWOMAN | 29 | | LIFE INS. UNDERWRITER | 42 |
| | ENGLISH TEACHER | 31 | | BUYER | 33 |
| | LANGUAGE TEACHER | 33 | | BUSINESS ED. TEACHER | 34 |
| IV | YWCA STAFF MEMBER | 40 | IX | HOME ECON. TEACHER | 28 |
| | RECREATION LEADER | 39 | | DIETITIAN | 35 |
| | DIRECTOR, CHRISTIAN ED. | 19 | X | PHYSICAL ED. TEACHER | 23 |
| | NUN-TEACHER | 05 | | OCCUPATIONAL THERAPIST | 26 |
| | GUIDANCE COUNSELOR | 32 | | PHYSICAL THERAPIST | 27 |
| | SOCIAL SCIENCE TEACHER | 40 | | PUBLIC HEALTH NURSE | 22 |
| | SOCIAL WORKER | 24 | | REGISTERED NURSE | 21 |
| V | SPEECH PATHOLOGIST | 27 | | LIC. PRACTICAL NURSE | 20 |
| | PSYCHOLOGIST | 18 | | RADIOLOGIC TECHNOLOGIST | 23 |
| | LIBRARIAN | 32 | | DENTAL ASSISTANT | 28 |
| | TRANSLATOR | 26 | XI | EXECUTIVE HOUSEKEEPER | 33 |
| VI | PHYSICIAN | 17 | | ELEMENTARY TEACHER | 41 |
| | DENTIST | 17 | | SECRETARY | 32 |
| | MEDICAL TECHNOLOGIST | 23 | | SALESWOMAN | 27 |
| | CHEMIST | 04 | | TELEPHONE OPERATOR | 16 |
| | MATHEMATICIAN | 10 | | INSTRUMENT ASSEMBLER | 28 |
| | COMPUTER PROGRAMMER | 30 | | SEWING MACHINE OPERATOR | 27 |
| | MATH-SCIENCE TEACHER | 32 | | BEAUTICIAN | 38 |
| | ENGINEER | 27 | | AIRLINE STEWARDESS | 40 |

NON-OCCUPATIONAL SCALES

| 40 | 54 | 42 | 41 |
|---|---|---|---|
| AACH | DIV | FMII | OIE |

ADMINISTRATIVE INDICES

TR  UNP  FC  LP  IP  DP

Figure 3.6. Profile for ten members of a professional honorary for
women in business

81

them as extroverts. Their mean profile seems to make psychological sense and provides some evidence of concurrent validity for the revision.

Evidence such as this will continue to be collected in counseling offices throughout the country. Most likely the evidence will demonstrate that the women's revision makes psychological sense, since it profits from having followed the men's revision by three years. Some potential problems were ironed out then. And the item content of the empirically derived scales, the reliabilities, and the percentage of overlap between the scores of occupational groups and WIG (Campbell, 1970) all point toward an interest inventory that has concurrent validity.

Predictive validity has never been well established for the women's SVIB or for any other interest inventory for women. It has always been easier and more important to study men. It is hoped that this revision will be the first on which predictive validity is adequately established.

COUNSELING WOMEN
USING THE NEW SVIB FOR WOMEN

Interest inventories have always been useful in counseling because they confirm vocational choices, suggest others, and point up conflicts which need to be resolved before occupational decisions can be made. This revision of the women's form not only can accomplish these things, but it can do so better than its forerunner since it more adequately covers the domain of vocational choices. It allows an individual to compare herself with women in thirty-three *new* fields including artistic, scientific, linguistic, military, business, and nonprofessional occupations. It also enables her to compare her interests in the basic occupational activities (represented by the basic scales) with those of a group of employed women. This is helpful since most occupational scales are based on a mixture of occupational themes. An example mentioned previously will serve to make this point clear. The occupational therapist scale seems to include elements that reflect an interest in both art and medical service. To know whether one or the other predominates in a given woman's interest is sometimes more helpful than knowing that she is similar to occupational therapists.

The new revision of the women's SVIB is the result of many years of research. Although the revision is probably the best instrument we now have for measuring women's interests, it is by no means definitive; like its predecessors, it will someday have to be revised again or replaced as interests and occupations change. To give some indication of what lies ahead for the SVIB women's form — as well as all interest inventories — a brief history of attempts to measure women's interests will prove helpful.

In the 1920s women could vote in every state in the union. They were needed in an expanding business economy and were welcomed in colleges and universities. The first effort to differentiate the interests of women in various occupations was made by Hogg in 1928, one year after the men's SVIB was first published. She was successful, but the results were disappointing because the differentiation between women's occupational groups was not as good as between men's groups. She concluded, "Women in various occupations are alike: their interests are similar in that they all want to do something, they are in the particular occupations which offered the least resistance for them to enter to satisfy the desire to do something; to be modern women."

In 1931 Manson attempted to differentiate the interests of teachers, nurses, sales proprietors, salesladies, and women in several business occupations. Again, the result was not as good as had been hoped. Manson's inquiries led her to contend that there may be a genuine sex difference in occupational interest such that men's interests are stronger and more specific, whereas women's are weaker and more general.

A decade after E. K. Strong introduced the SVIB for women, he asserted that there was no essential difference in differentiating among women's occupations and differentiating among men's occupations (Strong, 1943). He explained the problem observed by Hogg and Manson in this way: "At the present time far too many women enter an occupation as a stop-gap until marriage. Consequently, they take a job because it is convenient, not because they intend to continue in it indefinitely. The result is that most occupations contain a considerable number of women who would not be there if they had selected an occupational career as men do. Any sampling of such occupations gives a rather heterogeneous group of women. Occupational scales based on such criterion groups cannot be expected to differentiate very well." He therefore studied professional occupations to avoid the most heterogeneous groups.

The problems of measuring women's interests have been solved by the careful selection of occupation criterion group members and by good item selection techniques. We now have suitable SVIB scales for nonprofessional occupations such as sewing machine operators, which Strong would not have attempted to measure (Campbell and Harmon, 1968). But many of the women we *counsel* are *very* adequately described by Strong's statement.

In 1962 when I began counseling, I found that my women clients got few high scores on the SVIB and that their attitudes toward the high scores they did achieve were often unenthusiastic. For example, a college junior with an A on the steno-secretary scales and B+'s on the housewife and office worker scales felt somehow that her college education should qualify her for something more. On the other hand, the college junior who got an A on the lawyer or physician scales demurred, "I couldn't do that, it's too competitive," or "I really don't want to go to school that long."

Using typical feminine logic, I decided that the problem was with the SVIB. David Campbell was beginning to revise the men's SVIB at that time, so I started agitating early for doing "something" about the women's form as well.

Later on I did a study using the 1946 revision which showed that the SVIB predicts eventual career areas quite accurately for women who are already committed to careers (Harmon, 1969). A further study suggested that career commitment occurs relatively late for women (Harmon, 1970). I was forced to recognize that the women's SVIB did as well as could be expected given some facts about women.

Many women in our society grow up believing that their major accomplishment, satisfaction, and source of identity in life will be marriage. As children, they played house while their brothers played going to work. They define themselves in relation to their potential husband and not as individuals. Some girls say to me, "What I do will depend on the man I marry," not "The man I choose to marry will depend on what I do." They do not recognize the variety of life plans, many including work at some time after marriage, which are open to them. At the age when they appear for counseling they simply cannot see beyond a few years of work and a happy marriage. In actuality, over 50 percent of all women between the age of forty-five and fifty-four worked in 1964 (United States Department of Labor, 1965), and the rate has gone up since then. Hill and Campbell (1969) pointed out that the desire of women in various occupations for challenging, independent activities has increased over the last thirty years. This finding, however, was not based on young or unemployed women. We can only hope the same changes are taking place in these groups.

84

I am not implying that all women should choose careers either in addition to or in place of marriage. I am suggesting that they should make choices about such things as marriage and careers on the basis of mature knowledge about themselves and their society, and not on the basis of romanticized stereotypes.

Another group of women who present problems in counseling are those who are returning to work after the age of thirty-five. Many of them made no plans for this eventuality when they were younger. Now they lack skills and have family responsibilities which make skill attainment a very complicated undertaking. An eighteen-year-old can spend eighteen hours a day on campus with little difficulty; the busy mother of three children is lucky if she can arrange to spend a couple of hours three times a week on campus.

The existence of a revised SVIB for women does not change the social facts. Only insofar as it reflects a wide spectrum of the occupations available and accents potential areas of conflict can it contribute to counseling women about their individual choices.

## SOME ILLUSTRATIVE PROFILES

I have chosen some cases that will serve to illustrate the use of the new SVIB in counseling women. It would be best if I could present completed cases, including a follow-up study several years after counseling. Unfortunately, I cannot do that and still illustrate the use of an inventory published so recently.

The first profile is that of Claudia, one of the officers of the business fraternity Phi Chi Theta (see Fig. 3.7). It is fairly typical of the group with high scores on the basic scales for law/politics and merchandising and on the occupational scales in groups VII and VIII.

Claudia, a senior in merchandising, is very pretty in a delicate, fragile way. Her high school faculty rated her outstanding on every personal characteristic except leadership, where the consensus was that she led only occasionally and in minor affairs. Upon graduating from high school she enrolled in elementary education. After two years she decided to change to business even if it meant spending an extra year in school and amassing a surplus of credits.

Today Claudia is looking forward to a career in merchandising. Her decision to enter the world of business was not easy; it is a choice few women make. She arrived at it after trying some more traditional roles for

Reprinted from the *1969 Supplement* to the *Manual for the Strong Vocational Interest Blanks*,
copyrighted by the Board of Trustees of the Leland Stanford Junior University and published by Stanford University Press.

## BASIC INTEREST SCALES

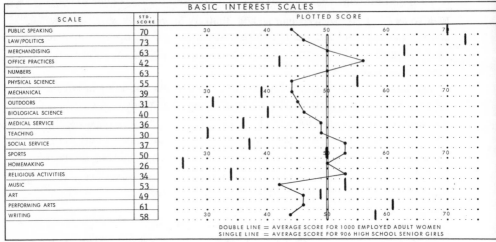

| SCALE | STD. SCORE |
|---|---|
| PUBLIC SPEAKING | 70 |
| LAW/POLITICS | 73 |
| MERCHANDISING | 63 |
| OFFICE PRACTICES | 42 |
| NUMBERS | 63 |
| PHYSICAL SCIENCE | 55 |
| MECHANICAL | 39 |
| OUTDOORS | 31 |
| BIOLOGICAL SCIENCE | 40 |
| MEDICAL SERVICE | 36 |
| TEACHING | 30 |
| SOCIAL SERVICE | 37 |
| SPORTS | 50 |
| HOMEMAKING | 26 |
| RELIGIOUS ACTIVITIES | 34 |
| MUSIC | 53 |
| ART | 49 |
| PERFORMING ARTS | 61 |
| WRITING | 58 |

DOUBLE LINE = AVERAGE SCORE FOR 1000 EMPLOYED ADULT WOMEN
SINGLE LINE = AVERAGE SCORE FOR 906 HIGH SCHOOL SENIOR GIRLS

## OCCUPATIONAL SCALES

| | OCCUPATION | STD. SCORE | | OCCUPATION | STD. SCORE |
|---|---|---|---|---|---|
| I | MUSIC TEACHER | 26 | VII | ARMY−ENLISTED | 42 |
| | ENTERTAINER | 43 | | NAVY−ENLISTED | 26 |
| | MUSICIAN PERFORMER | 33 | | ARMY−OFFICER | 59 |
| | MODEL | 50 | | NAVY−OFFICER | 60 |
| II | ART TEACHER | 17 | VIII | LAWYER | 65 |
| | ARTIST | 30 | | ACCOUNTANT | 51 |
| | INTERIOR DECORATOR | 41 | | BANKWOMAN | 40 |
| III | NEWSWOMAN | 44 | | LIFE INS. UNDERWRITER | 66 |
| | ENGLISH TEACHER | 43 | | BUYER | 40 |
| | LANGUAGE TEACHER | 48 | | BUSINESS ED. TEACHER | 33 |
| IV | YWCA STAFF MEMBER | 56 | IX | HOME ECON. TEACHER | 11 |
| | RECREATION LEADER | 45 | | DIETITIAN | 27 |
| | DIRECTOR, CHRISTIAN ED. | 17 | X | PHYSICAL ED. TEACHER | 13 |
| | NUN-TEACHER | -2 | | OCCUPATIONAL THERAPIST | 11 |
| | GUIDANCE COUNSELOR | 40 | | PHYSICAL THERAPIST | 19 |
| | SOCIAL SCIENCE TEACHER | 53 | | PUBLIC HEALTH NURSE | 12 |
| | SOCIAL WORKER | 30 | | REGISTERED NURSE | 08 |
| V | SPEECH PATHOLOGIST | 49 | | LIC. PRACTICAL NURSE | 04 |
| | PSYCHOLOGIST | 34 | | RADIOLOGIC TECHNOLOGIST | 17 |
| | LIBRARIAN | 45 | | DENTAL ASSISTANT | 12 |
| | TRANSLATOR | 43 | XI | EXECUTIVE HOUSEKEEPER | 20 |
| VI | PHYSICIAN | 31 | | ELEMENTARY TEACHER | 05 |
| | DENTIST | 17 | | SECRETARY | 28 |
| | MEDICAL TECHNOLOGIST | 16 | | SALESWOMAN | 20 |
| | CHEMIST | 06 | | TELEPHONE OPERATOR | 02 |
| | MATHEMATICIAN | 11 | | INSTRUMENT ASSEMBLER | 09 |
| | COMPUTER PROGRAMMER | 27 | | SEWING MACHINE OPERATOR | -5 |
| | MATH-SCIENCE TEACHER | 18 | | BEAUTICIAN | 22 |
| | ENGINEER | 35 | | AIRLINE STEWARDESS | 49 |

NON-OCCUPATIONAL SCALES

| 52 | 51 | 46 | 23 |
|---|---|---|---|
| AACH | DIV | FMII | OIE |

ADMINISTRATIVE INDICES

| 398 | 6 | 18 | 39 | 18 | 43 |
|---|---|---|---|---|---|
| TR | UNP | FC | LP | IP | DP |

Figure 3.7. Claudia's SVIB profile

women and finding that they did not suit her. She has developed, since high school, into a girl who can lead in matters of major importance and who enjoys being a leader. Claudia has not rejected marriage as a possibility for her, but she does plan to get established in her career before considering marriage seriously.

The second profile is that of a twenty-six-year-old woman, Lori, who is returning to school after six years as a housewife. As can be seen in Figure 3.8, her scientific interests are quite clear-cut. Lori was a National Merit Scholar who was in the honors program of the arts college. She was majoring in chemistry when she dropped out of school at the end of her sophomore year to get married. In her last semester her grades had dropped sharply.

When she came in for counseling, she said that she did not intend to go back into chemistry because she did not believe she was capable of learning advanced chemistry. She was considering teaching English as a career. She agreed to take the SVIB, and did so, but she did not return to see the counselor for over six months. When she did return, her attitude had changed considerably. She had enrolled in an English course but had come to realize that she had limited interest in the field, although she was doing well. She had faced some situations that had forced her to make a sort of personal declaration of independence from her husband. Her position as a wife was unchanged, but she was more independent, more confident of her abilities, and more free to make unusual choices than she had been previously.

As she looked at her SVIB profile, the fear over her ability seemed to disappear. Lori noted that her one bad semester was probably more closely related to her personal problems at that time than to her abilities. She decided to enroll in a zoology course the next semester and began to investigate the medical technology program. It appealed to her because jobs in the field do not require an advanced degree. Since she is a part-time student with full family responsibilities, even two more years of schooling will take a long time, and she is anxious to get into a career in science and to become more independent.

The profile presented in Figure 3.9 appears to belong to a woman with wide interests, including social and medical service occupations, teaching, and positions of power. Actually Diane is a senior in English education, who has never considered any career other than teaching. As a child the

Reprinted from the *1969 Supplement* to the *Manual for the Strong Vocational Interest Blanks*,
copyrighted by the Board of Trustees of the Leland Stanford Junior University and published by Stanford University Press.

### BASIC INTEREST SCALES

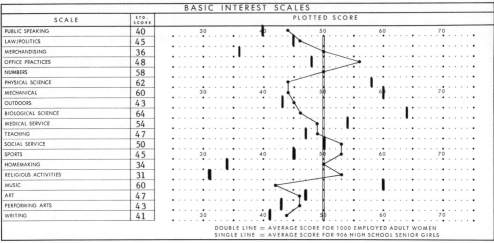

| SCALE | STD. SCORE |
|---|---|
| PUBLIC SPEAKING | 40 |
| LAW/POLITICS | 45 |
| MERCHANDISING | 36 |
| OFFICE PRACTICES | 48 |
| NUMBERS | 58 |
| PHYSICAL SCIENCE | 62 |
| MECHANICAL | 60 |
| OUTDOORS | 43 |
| BIOLOGICAL SCIENCE | 64 |
| MEDICAL SERVICE | 54 |
| TEACHING | 47 |
| SOCIAL SERVICE | 50 |
| SPORTS | 45 |
| HOMEMAKING | 34 |
| RELIGIOUS ACTIVITIES | 31 |
| MUSIC | 60 |
| ART | 47 |
| PERFORMING ARTS | 43 |
| WRITING | 41 |

DOUBLE LINE = AVERAGE SCORE FOR 1000 EMPLOYED ADULT WOMEN
SINGLE LINE = AVERAGE SCORE FOR 906 HIGH SCHOOL SENIOR GIRLS

### OCCUPATIONAL SCALES

| | OCCUPATION | STD. SCORE | | OCCUPATION | STD. SCORE |
|---|---|---|---|---|---|
| I | MUSIC TEACHER | 17 | VII | ARMY–ENLISTED | 29 |
| | ENTERTAINER | 25 | | NAVY–ENLISTED | 36 |
| | MUSICIAN PERFORMER | 27 | | ARMY–OFFICER | 20 |
| | MODEL | 18 | | NAVY–OFFICER | 36 |
| II | ART TEACHER | 12 | VIII | LAWYER | 28 |
| | ARTIST | 36 | | ACCOUNTANT | 31 |
| | INTERIOR DECORATOR | 15 | | BANKWOMAN | 30 |
| III | NEWSWOMAN | 22 | | LIFE INS. UNDERWRITER | 13 |
| | ENGLISH TEACHER | 18 | | BUYER | 18 |
| | LANGUAGE TEACHER | 17 | | BUSINESS ED. TEACHER | 21 |
| IV | YWCA STAFF MEMBER | 17 | IX | HOME ECON. TEACHER | 9 |
| | RECREATION LEADER | 18 | | DIETITIAN | 30 |
| | DIRECTOR, CHRISTIAN ED. | 3 | X | PHYSICAL ED. TEACHER | 26 |
| | NUN-TEACHER | 23 | | OCCUPATIONAL THERAPIST | 39 |
| | GUIDANCE COUNSELOR | 18 | | PHYSICAL THERAPIST | 53 |
| | SOCIAL SCIENCE TEACHER | 22 | | PUBLIC HEALTH NURSE | 32 |
| | SOCIAL WORKER | 18 | | REGISTERED NURSE | 29 |
| V | SPEECH PATHOLOGIST | 26 | | LIC. PRACTICAL NURSE | 33 |
| | PSYCHOLOGIST | 40 | | RADIOLOGIC TECHNOLOGIST | 48 |
| | LIBRARIAN | 35 | | DENTAL ASSISTANT | 28 |
| | TRANSLATOR | 44 | XI | EXECUTIVE HOUSEKEEPER | 20 |
| VI | PHYSICIAN | 53 | | ELEMENTARY TEACHER | 31 |
| | DENTIST | 53 | | SECRETARY | 26 |
| | MEDICAL TECHNOLOGIST | 57 | | SALESWOMAN | 17 |
| | CHEMIST | 37 | | TELEPHONE OPERATOR | 24 |
| | MATHEMATICIAN | 45 | | INSTRUMENT ASSEMBLER | 35 |
| | COMPUTER PROGRAMMER | 44 | | SEWING MACHINE OPERATOR | 25 |
| | MATH-SCIENCE TEACHER | 46 | | BEAUTICIAN | 25 |
| | ENGINEER | 43 | | AIRLINE STEWARDESS | 6 |

NON-OCCUPATIONAL SCALES

| 49 | 53 | 48 | 68 |
|---|---|---|---|
| AACH | DIV | FMII | OIE |

ADMINISTRATIVE INDICES

| 398 | 4 | 11 | 27 | 27 | 47 |
|---|---|---|---|---|---|
| TR | UNP | FC | LP | IP | DP |

Figure 3.8. Lori's SVIB profile

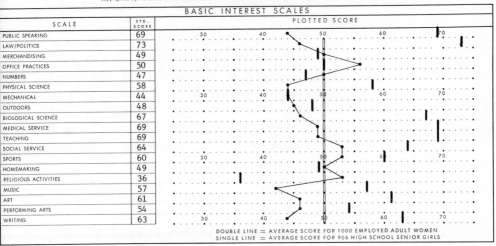

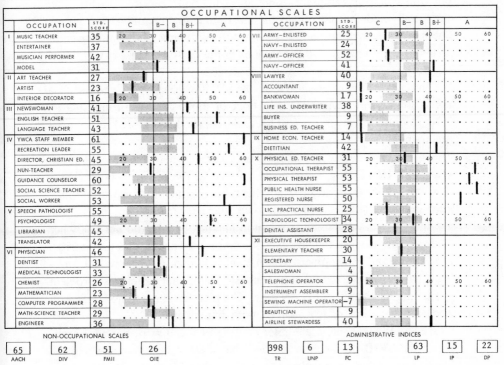

Figure 3.9. Diane's SVIB profile

only career women she knew were teachers. Her occupational choice is deceptively traditional.

Diane originally planned to teach science and did very well in her science courses. However, she felt that teaching science was not as good a vehicle for molding young people as teaching English. She is extremely interested in social issues and has, in the past, been quite an activist. In the last year, she has decided that she would rather change the world through education than through protesting. She has enthusiastically accepted a position that will allow her to teach social issues in literature to high school students next year.

Schoolteachers do not usually wield much power, but Diane may well be the exception. She realizes that she is intellectually gifted and creative. Because of a slight speech impediment, she has learned to offer her innovative ideas to others who are perceived as leaders. In a group she is not one who stands up and presents her ideas, but her ideas *are* presented and she usually finds herself one of the most influential members of a group. She has been a behind-the-scenes innovator in many of the student-initiated curricular changes on the campus in the last two years. It will be interesting to follow her career as an educator.

Cindy, a senior in nursing, took the SVIB after she was referred to a counselor by the adviser in the school of nursing. (See profile in Fig. 3.10.) Before the inventory had been scored, she had decided to drop out of nursing.

She had first considered nursing as a career when she was about ten years old. Her family had seemed pleased at the prospect of having a daughter who was a nurse. Lately, they had assumed that she would take a job in the hospital in their small town after her graduation.

Cindy was an outstanding student in nursing, but she did not enjoy her studies or her work in the hospital. She considered her studies too narrowly scientific and her contacts with patients too focused on physical problems. On leaving the school of nursing, she found that her biggest problem was telling her family of her decision. The fact that she had not settled on another occupation made it an even more difficult ordeal.

She had thought she might enter the field of social work but after looking at the SVIB profile, she realized that there were other alternatives. She had never before considered the whole area of language skills because her brother is talented in writing and she was afraid to compete with him. In one counseling session, she began to recall how much she did like Eng-

Reprinted from the 1969 Supplement to the Manual for the Strong Vocational Interest Blanks,
copyrighted by the Board of Trustees of the Leland Stanford Junior University and published by Stanford University Press.

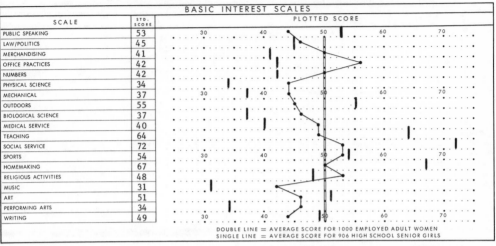

## BASIC INTEREST SCALES

| SCALE | STD. SCORE |
|---|---|
| PUBLIC SPEAKING | 53 |
| LAW/POLITICS | 45 |
| MERCHANDISING | 41 |
| OFFICE PRACTICES | 42 |
| NUMBERS | 42 |
| PHYSICAL SCIENCE | 34 |
| MECHANICAL | 37 |
| OUTDOORS | 55 |
| BIOLOGICAL SCIENCE | 37 |
| MEDICAL SERVICE | 40 |
| TEACHING | 64 |
| SOCIAL SERVICE | 72 |
| SPORTS | 54 |
| HOMEMAKING | 67 |
| RELIGIOUS ACTIVITIES | 48 |
| MUSIC | 31 |
| ART | 51 |
| PERFORMING ARTS | 34 |
| WRITING | 49 |

DOUBLE LINE = AVERAGE SCORE FOR 1000 EMPLOYED ADULT WOMEN
SINGLE LINE = AVERAGE SCORE FOR 906 HIGH SCHOOL SENIOR GIRLS

## OCCUPATIONAL SCALES

| | OCCUPATION | STD. SCORE | | OCCUPATION | STD. SCORE |
|---|---|---|---|---|---|
| I | MUSIC TEACHER | 22 | VII | ARMY–ENLISTED | 17 |
| | ENTERTAINER | 27 | | NAVY–ENLISTED | 24 |
| | MUSICIAN PERFORMER | 23 | | ARMY–OFFICER | 23 |
| | MODEL | 32 | | NAVY–OFFICER | 35 |
| II | ART TEACHER | 31 | VIII | LAWYER | 18 |
| | ARTIST | 30 | | ACCOUNTANT | 5 |
| | INTERIOR DECORATOR | 24 | | BANKWOMAN | 18 |
| III | NEWSWOMAN | 41 | | LIFE INS. UNDERWRITER | 31 |
| | ENGLISH TEACHER | 40 | | BUYER | 17 |
| | LANGUAGE TEACHER | 42 | | BUSINESS ED. TEACHER | 22 |
| IV | YWCA STAFF MEMBER | 48 | IX | HOME ECON. TEACHER | 39 |
| | RECREATION LEADER | 47 | | DIETITIAN | 27 |
| | DIRECTOR, CHRISTIAN ED. | 39 | X | PHYSICAL ED. TEACHER | 36 |
| | NUN-TEACHER | 6 | | OCCUPATIONAL THERAPIST | 37 |
| | GUIDANCE COUNSELOR | 36 | | PHYSICAL THERAPIST | 26 |
| | SOCIAL SCIENCE TEACHER | 36 | | PUBLIC HEALTH NURSE | 50 |
| | SOCIAL WORKER | 26 | | REGISTERED NURSE | 41 |
| V | SPEECH PATHOLOGIST | 25 | | LIC. PRACTICAL NURSE | 15 |
| | PSYCHOLOGIST | 12 | | RADIOLOGIC TECHNOLOGIST | 18 |
| | LIBRARIAN | 26 | | DENTAL ASSISTANT | 19 |
| | TRANSLATOR | 19 | XI | EXECUTIVE HOUSEKEEPER | 24 |
| VI | PHYSICIAN | 16 | | ELEMENTARY TEACHER | 33 |
| | DENTIST | 3 | | SECRETARY | 40 |
| | MEDICAL TECHNOLOGIST | 6 | | SALESWOMAN | 17 |
| | CHEMIST | -13 | | TELEPHONE OPERATOR | 15 |
| | MATHEMATICIAN | -1 | | INSTRUMENT ASSEMBLER | 21 |
| | COMPUTER PROGRAMMER | 14 | | SEWING MACHINE OPERATOR | 10 |
| | MATH-SCIENCE TEACHER | 21 | | BEAUTICIAN | 44 |
| | ENGINEER | -3 | | AIRLINE STEWARDESS | 40 |

NON-OCCUPATIONAL SCALES

| 30 | 60 | 39 | 44 |
|---|---|---|---|
| AACH | DIV | FMII | OIE |

ADMINISTRATIVE INDICES

| 398 | 7 | 8 | 34 | 5 | 62 |
|---|---|---|---|---|---|
| TR | UNP | FC | LP | IP | DP |

Figure 3.10. Cindy's SVIB profile

Reprinted from the *1969 Supplement to the Manual for the Strong Vocational Interest Blanks*,
copyrighted by the Board of Trustees of the Leland Stanford Junior University and published by Stanford University Press.

## BASIC INTEREST SCALES

| SCALE | STD. SCORE |
|---|---|
| PUBLIC SPEAKING | 43 |
| LAW/POLITICS | 49 |
| MERCHANDISING | 44 |
| OFFICE PRACTICES | 42 |
| NUMBERS | 45 |
| PHYSICAL SCIENCE | 49 |
| MECHANICAL | 38 |
| OUTDOORS | 46 |
| BIOLOGICAL SCIENCE | 45 |
| MEDICAL SERVICE | 43 |
| TEACHING | 47 |
| SOCIAL SERVICE | 45 |
| SPORTS | 35 |
| HOMEMAKING | 45 |
| RELIGIOUS ACTIVITIES | 34 |
| MUSIC | 50 |
| ART | 51 |
| PERFORMING ARTS | 39 |
| WRITING | 39 |

DOUBLE LINE = AVERAGE SCORE FOR 1000 EMPLOYED ADULT WOMEN
SINGLE LINE = AVERAGE SCORE FOR 906 HIGH SCHOOL SENIOR GIRLS

## OCCUPATIONAL SCALES

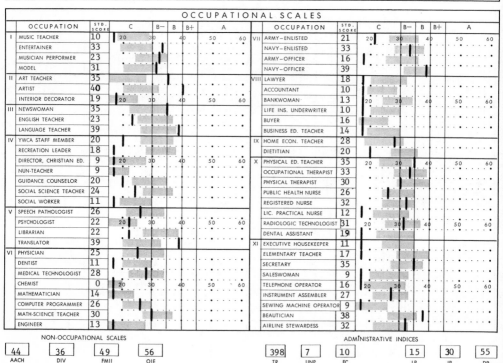

| | OCCUPATION | STD. SCORE | | OCCUPATION | STD. SCORE |
|---|---|---|---|---|---|
| I | MUSIC TEACHER | 10 | VII | ARMY – ENLISTED | 21 |
| | ENTERTAINER | 33 | | NAVY – ENLISTED | 33 |
| | MUSICIAN PERFORMER | 23 | | ARMY – OFFICER | 16 |
| | MODEL | 31 | | NAVY – OFFICER | 39 |
| II | ART TEACHER | 35 | VIII | LAWYER | 18 |
| | ARTIST | 40 | | ACCOUNTANT | 10 |
| | INTERIOR DECORATOR | 19 | | BANKWOMAN | 13 |
| III | NEWSWOMAN | 35 | | LIFE INS. UNDERWRITER | 10 |
| | ENGLISH TEACHER | 23 | | BUYER | 16 |
| | LANGUAGE TEACHER | 39 | | BUSINESS ED. TEACHER | 14 |
| IV | YWCA STAFF MEMBER | 20 | IX | HOME ECON. TEACHER | 28 |
| | RECREATION LEADER | 18 | | DIETITIAN | 20 |
| | DIRECTOR, CHRISTIAN ED. | 9 | X | PHYSICAL ED. TEACHER | 35 |
| | NUN-TEACHER | 9 | | OCCUPATIONAL THERAPIST | 33 |
| | GUIDANCE COUNSELOR | 20 | | PHYSICAL THERAPIST | 30 |
| | SOCIAL SCIENCE TEACHER | 24 | | PUBLIC HEALTH NURSE | 26 |
| | SOCIAL WORKER | 11 | | REGISTERED NURSE | 32 |
| V | SPEECH PATHOLOGIST | 26 | | LIC. PRACTICAL NURSE | 12 |
| | PSYCHOLOGIST | 22 | | RADIOLOGIC TECHNOLOGIST | 31 |
| | LIBRARIAN | 22 | | DENTAL ASSISTANT | 19 |
| | TRANSLATOR | 39 | XI | EXECUTIVE HOUSEKEEPER | 11 |
| VI | PHYSICIAN | 25 | | ELEMENTARY TEACHER | 17 |
| | DENTIST | 11 | | SECRETARY | 35 |
| | MEDICAL TECHNOLOGIST | 28 | | SALESWOMAN | 9 |
| | CHEMIST | 0 | | TELEPHONE OPERATOR | 16 |
| | MATHEMATICIAN | 14 | | INSTRUMENT ASSEMBLER | 27 |
| | COMPUTER PROGRAMMER | 26 | | SEWING MACHINE OPERATOR | 9 |
| | MATH-SCIENCE TEACHER | 30 | | BEAUTICIAN | 38 |
| | ENGINEER | 13 | | AIRLINE STEWARDESS | 32 |

NON-OCCUPATIONAL SCALES

| 44 | 36 | 49 | 56 |
|---|---|---|---|
| AACH | DIV | FMII | OIE |

ADMINISTRATIVE INDICES

| 398 | 7 | 10 | 15 | 30 | 55 |
|---|---|---|---|---|---|
| TR | UNP | FC | LP | IP | DP |

Figure 3.11. Rosemary's SVIB profile

92

lish and creative writing in high school. Cindy was also enthusiastic about activity-centered types of social service like recreation leadership. In fact, she had been planning to take a job at a summer camp. She had practically no experience in sports or camping because until she was a senior in high school she weighed over two hundred pounds. At present, she is attractive and very slim. Having shed both her extra pounds and a vocational choice made too permanently and too soon (and which unfortunately became associated with her parents' side in her struggle for independence), Cindy decided to explore occupations in recreation and in teaching English.

The fifth profile is remarkable in that it seems to show a lack of interests (see Fig. 3.11). Rosemary is a freshman student who is considering entering elementary education. She is the oldest child in a very large family. Her mother has just realized that she herself would like to have a career but has no skills. Therefore, she is strongly encouraging her daughter to make a practical career choice.

Rosemary actually is somewhat talented in art and spends much time drawing and painting. Since her family sees art as a completely impractical career, she does not feel free to pursue it. She seemed relieved when the conflict between practicality and art was discussed in counseling. She is still planning to major in education but she understands that her choice is based more on expedience than on interest.

Rosemary intends to marry a young member of a symphony orchestra in the near future. It will be interesting to see whether her plans change and whether her SVIB profile shows more significant scores as she matures and becomes more independent.

## COUNSELING AND WOMEN'S INTERESTS

The assumptions counselors make about women will determine how they use the new SVIB. Friedersdorf (1969) has concluded that male high school counselors expect college-bound women to like and to be interested in traditionally feminine rather than traditionally male occupations. She pointed out that such attitudes influence how women are counseled. It may take only one negative reaction, verbal or nonverbal, to a high score on the chemistry or the engineering scale to dissuade a young woman from considering careers in science.

If the counselor assumes that young women's interests are unimportant or nonexistent — even though evidence suggests that many women do work after marriage and that their interests develop later than those of men — he may allow his clients to waste the best or only years they will have for education and training. The most sound advice to give a woman who is being counseled seems to be, "Consider every suggestion, every high score seriously. A woman can decide not to use her education or training, but she cannot decide to use education or training which she does not have."

The new SVIB for women is designed to give the counselor and his counselee a maximum of information for discussion and planning. The counselor can negate its breadth by refusing to discuss high scores in unusual occupations or potential conflicts between marriage and career.

PROBLEMS

There are some problems and questions that have arisen concerning the revised women's form that should be dealt with here.

1. There has been some question about the relation of the scores on the 1946 form to those on the new revision. Comparable scales are correlated but the possibility of some large shifts in individual scale scores does exist. Since all interest measurement of the type outlined here is relative to the occupational groups, WIG groups, and item selection techniques used, the best measurement results from the best subjects and procedures. Until long-term predictive studies are completed, there is really no way to compare the predictive validity of the old and new scales. Strong used the best subjects and procedures available in the 1930s. Campbell used the best procedures he could devise in the 1960s. There is no way to tell today whether an old score of 50 or a new score of 40 on the physical therapist scale is the truer approximation of an individual's interest in physical therapy. We must wait and compare the scores with what the individual does.

2. There seem to be a number of cases in which the basic scales and the occupational scales do not support each other. For instance, in one case a girl had high scores on the occupational scales for social worker and guidance counselor, but she scored 50 on the basic scale for social service. It is easy to speculate on the reasons for this discrepancy, but it is difficult to decide whether to place less weight on high scores not supported by basic scales than on others that are supported by the basic scales.

3. The whole area of how the percentage of "Like," "Indifferent," and "Dislike" scores is related to the basic scales is interesting. Since most

items on the basic scales have "Like" scored in the positive direction, a response set for "Dislike" may preclude any high scores on the basic scales.

4. The problem of the cultural bias of the SVIB has gone unexplored. Obviously, the jobs available in a given society reflect some things about that society. For example, we have no scale for women truck drivers. In other countries or in the United States at some future time, a scale for women truck drivers might be appropriate. A good interest inventory is one that reflects society and its needs.

However, I believe that the culturally disadvantaged groups in our country are quite immature in their vocational thinking and planning. Whether or not the new women's SVIB, even with its nonprofessional scales, will be useful in working with young women from impoverished backgrounds remains to be seen. Perhaps as a group they will get no high scores, or perhaps measurement of their interests will turn out to be considerably less reliable than it is for more advantaged women because their rate of vocational development is slower.

As the inventory is used other problems will probably show up, but in the meantime research will attempt to solve some of the ones I have pointed out. Thus, it remains to be seen how effective the revised women's form of the SVIB actually is.

## References

Anastasi, A., and C. E. Schaefer. Biographical correlates of artistic and literary creativity in adolescent girls. *Journal of Applied Psychology*, 1969, 53, 267–273.

Campbell, D. P. Chance on SVIB: Dice or men? *Journal of Applied Psychology*, 1963, 47, 127–129.

———. *Manual for the Strong Vocational Interest Blanks for men and women.* (Revised from E. K. Strong, Jr.) Stanford: Stanford University Press, 1966.

———. *Strong Vocational Interest Blanks Manual — 1969 supplement.* Stanford: Stanford University Press, 1969.

———. *Handbook for the Strong Vocational Interest Blank.* Stanford: Stanford University Press, 1971.

———, F. H. Borgen, S. H. Eastes, C. B. Johansson, and R. A. Peterson. A set of basic interest scales for the SVIB for men. *Journal of Applied Psychology*, 1968, 52, Part 2.

Campbell, D. P., and L. W. Harmon. Vocational interests of non-professional women. Final report of Project No. 6-1820, Grant OEG 3-6-061820-0755. Office of Education, Department of Health, Education, and Welfare, December 1968.

Friedersdorf, N. W. A comparative study of counseling attitudes toward the further educational and vocational plans of high school girls. Ph.D. dissertation. Purdue University, 1969.

Harmon, L. W. The predictive power over ten years of measured social service and scientific interests among college women. *Journal of Applied Psychology*, 1969, 53, 193–198.

———. The anatomy of career commitment in women. *Journal of Counseling Psychology*, 1970, 17, 77–80.

Hill, D. S., and D. P. Campbell. The changing interests of women. Paper read at Midwestern Psychological Association Convention, Chicago, Illinois, May 1969.

Hogg, M. I. Occupational interests of women. *Personnel Journal*, 1928, 6, 331–337.

Manson, G. E. Occupational interests and personality requirements of women in business and the professions. *Michigan Business Studies*, 1931, 3, No. 5.

Strong, E. K., Jr. *Vocational interests of men and women*. Stanford: Stanford University Press, 1943.

———. Good and poor interest items. *Journal of Applied Psychology*, 1962, 46, 269–275.

———, D. P. Campbell, R. F. Berdie, and K. E. Clark. Proposed scoring changes for the Strong Vocational Interest Blank. *Journal of Applied Psychology*, 1964, 48, 75–80.

United States Department of Labor. *1965 handbook on women workers*. Women's Bureau Bulletin No. 290. Washington, D.C.: United States Government Printing Office, 1966.

# 4

# The Minnesota Vocational Interest Inventory

## W. Leslie Barnette, Jr.

THE MINNESOTA VOCATIONAL INTEREST INVENTORY (MVII) provides systematic information about the interest patterns of men in nonprofessional occupations, mostly skilled trades. The inventory is the result of research undertaken to extend the Strong Blank and the Kuder Occupational Interest Survey, neither of which is well suited for lower level occupations.

### ORIGIN AND FORMAT

The inventory originated from Kenneth E. Clark's experiences as a research psychologist for the navy during World War II. He became concerned about the haphazard assignment of recruits to naval trade schools; he noted such assignments were often made on irrelevant grounds. Because some military jargon was unfamiliar to new naval recruits (for example, what is the work of an aviation boatswain's mate?), their ability to make correct choices tended to be limited.

As a result, Clark developed an inventory that would facilitate assigning recruits to suitable jobs and that could be used for individual counseling. The early items were written in 1946–47. After that time, and until the MVII was published by the Psychological Corporation in 1965, data were collected from almost 30,000 civilian workers and some 20,000 naval personnel. Two forms were developed: a navy and a civilian form. This chapter will be concerned solely with the civilian form.

The published version of the MVII (Clark and Campbell, 1965) consists of 474 statements grouped into 138 triads to which the inventory taker responds. The format is forced choice — the person being tested must indicate the activities he likes most and those he likes least. The individual items are arranged in haphazard fashion. Time to complete the MVII varies from 45 minutes to 1½ hours. Both hand-scoring and machine-scoring forms of the inventory are available. Campbell (1966) has published a comprehensive review.

SCALES

The MVII includes two types of scales — occupational and area. There are twenty-one occupational scales (as for baker, printer, plumber, electrician) which were constructed empirically in a manner similar to SVIB scale construction. Each scale was developed by comparing the responses of workers in a specific occupation with those of a tradesmen-in-general (TIG) group (a reference group of skilled tradesmen in fourteen different occupations). Wherever possible, each occupational key was cross-validated. Norms were developed by scoring each criterion group on its own occupational scale and here the mean was set at 50 with a standard deviation of 10. A subject's score on any of these scales indicates the degree of similarity between his expressed interests as inventoried by the MVII and those of successfully employed men making up the criterion group. Clark and Campbell (1965) report that about seven out of ten men working in a given occupation score above 45 on their own scale; any score above 45 indicates interests clearly in common with men in that occupation. A score between 35 and 45 is in the borderline area, much as is a B— rating on the SVIB. Scores below 25 definitely show lack of compatibility with men in that occupation.

The area or homogeneous scales are composed of items that cluster closely together, i.e., are highly intercorrelated. They are more "pure" measures of independent traits and are more meaningful psychologically. Looking for clusters (or items highly intercorrelated) would have been an overwhelming task if done for all MVII items: the inventory contains 1140 items, and about 650,000 correlations would be necessary. The task was reduced by taking only "Like" items from the first half of the inventory or 288 items from the first edition of the MVII (which meant about

41,000 covariance measures). The scales were named after the item content was reviewed. There are nine of these scales (for example, mechanical, office work, health service, clean hands, outdoors), and they provide measurement for broader interest areas than do the occupational scales. Interpretation of these scales involves an orientation toward a person rather than toward an occupation. Such scales can clarify the typical interests of men within a single occupation. For example, high correlations are found between the occupational scale for milk wagon driver and certain of the homogeneous scales. That is, men who score high on this particular occupational scale (delivery men who drive milk trucks making retail rather than bulk deliveries) tend also to score high on the clerical and low on the mechanical area scales; this indicates that such drivers are sales clerks operating from vehicles. Like the occupational scales, the nine area scales have a mean of 50 and a standard deviation of 10.

VALIDITY AND RELIABILITY

To test the validity of the occupational scales, Clark again adopted the procedure used by Strong. He checked the degree to which each occupational scale separates workers in that vocation from the TIG reference group. Tilton's percentage overlap (the percentage of persons in one distribution whose scores may be matched by scores in other distributions) was the index employed (Tilton, 1937). Perfect separation of two groups would occur when the overlap was zero; no separation at all would produce an overlap of 100. The higher the percentage of overlap, the lower the validity of that scale. The average overlap for these scales is 41 percent, with the range extending from a low of 27 percent for the radio/TV repairman scale to a high of 63 percent for the stock clerk scale. However, even for this latter scale, the means of the criterion and the reference group (TIG) are one standard deviation apart.

To determine the validity of the area scales is a different matter since these were not designed to separate occupational groups. Here the authors try to demonstrate construct validity. For such a purpose, two types of information are relevant: the item content of each of these scales; and the patterns of scores earned on these scales by different occupational groups.

Test-retest reliability for all scales was determined for ninety-eight students at the Dunwoody Industrial Institute in Minneapolis with a thirty-day interval between testings (Bradley, 1958). Only five of the occupational scales and two of the area scales produced coefficients of less than .75 indicating, in general, satisfactory indices for these scales.

A second study on the reliability of the MVII has appeared. Olson and Johnson (1968) administered the inventory twice to ninety-seven volunteer psychiatric patients at a two-week interval. They found the median test-retest $r$ to be .83 for the occupational scales and .84 for the area scales. The profiles derived from both these scales are thus shown to be remarkably stable.

## MVII RESEARCH

Clark began working on the MVII in 1946, but his first report was not published until 1949. Here he described the various sources for his 570 inventory items and how he enlisted the cooperation he received from business and industrial organizations and union representatives in the Minneapolis–St. Paul area. He discussed many difficulties he encountered, especially in trying to have subjects complete the inventory either at union meetings or at their place of employment. Although some 3500 inventories were distributed at union meetings and union members voted his program "hearty support," he obtained a mere 129 usable returns (Clark, 1949). Mailed questionnaires, in the end, proved to be the most effective source of data. Inventories mailed to 320 electricians in the Twin Cities, with one follow-up letter, produced 201 returns or 63 percent. Eight AFL unions in St. Paul produced 55–75 percent returns with a final N of 1143 used for key construction (Clark, 1949). The geographical bias in developing the MVII is freely admitted by Clark, but he feels this does not interfere with his principal aim of finding differences between trade groups. Scoring keys were developed for these eight trades.

Examination of these eight occupational keys disclosed clusters. Workers in three unions related to the building trades (electricians, sheet metal workers, plumbers) tended to have related interests that differed markedly from workers in service occupations (bakers, milk wagon drivers who were also shown to have related interests). Skilled trade groups may thus be ordered into families of occupations with similar interests. This led to the development of homogeneous or area scales, extensively discussed in Clark's 1961 publication and largely based on the doctoral dissertation of Gee (1955).

Clark's second publication examines various methods of developing scoring keys for the MVII (Clark and Gee, 1954). The effects of differing numbers of items in a scale on overlap were studied on workers from various labor unions in the Minneapolis–St. Paul area. Similarly, the effects of differing scale lengths on reliability were also tested, using data from the Dunwoody Institute students. In general, this work showed that large numbers of items were not needed to form scales: adequate validity, as represented by occupational scales which overlapped least with the men-in-general group, and reliability coefficients in the low 80s were obtained from scales containing as little as fifteen items, as well as from those with sixty to seventy items.

The use of varying bands of differences between the rates of endorsement of items by the occupational group and the men-in-general group was also studied in terms of its influence on reliability. A key consisting of items which showed only 6 percent or more difference between the criterion and men-in-general groups was formed. In the same way, 7 percent, 8 percent, 9 percent, and up to 26 percent keys were constructed. It was demonstrated that very little was lost in the way of test-retest reliability by radically reducing the number of items in any one scoring key. For example, the 6 percent key with 580 items produced a reliability coefficient of .84, while the 26 percent key with only twenty-one items had a reliability of .78. Earlier the arbitrary decision was made to employ an 11 percent key; for the electrician scale, such a key consisted of 234 items and showed a reliability coefficient of .80 (Clark, 1949).

Bradley (1958) utilized the MVII, along with a variety of other aptitude tests, in an attempt to arrive at prediction equations for the trade and technical courses taught at the Dunwoody Industrial Institute. Two groups of students were involved. One sample consisted of male students whose average age was twenty-two and who had completed 11.5 years of schooling before registering at Dunwoody for the 1953–54 academic year. A second group of 319 students in the 1954–55 school year was used for cross-validation purposes. The following aptitude tests were employed: AGCT, Bennett Mechanical Form AA, Revised Minnesota Paper Form Board. The 1953–54 group was administered the Kuder Vocational Preference Record and the 1954–55 group was tested with the MVII. The criterion was student scholastic achievement in four areas as graded at Dunwoody: shopwork, trade and job knowledge, applied subjects, and general subjects. Prediction equations established on the earlier group were cross-validated on the second group. The latter group was a rather superior one, with mean aptitude test scores slightly below those given in the manuals for engineering college freshmen. The best predictor of school grades was the AGCT (the average correlation with all seventeen courses at Dunwoody was .68), followed by the Bennett Mechanical (.52) and, lastly, the Minnesota Paper Form Board (.35). For specific courses, like carpentry, auto mechanic, and electrical, the $r$ for grades was .70, .65, and .75, respectively. When individual MVII scoring keys are employed, the results are highly variable. Here are samples of the findings:

The MVII printer key correlated −.07 with printing grades (N = 13). The MVII machinist key correlated .72 with mechanical drafting grades, but only .38 with machine shop grades (N = 38). The MVII electrical key correlated .15 with electrical grades (N = 30). The MVII baker key correlated .14 with bakery grades (N = 42).

Whereas the Kuder failed to discriminate among the Dunwoody courses, the MVII successfully worked when applied to the cross-validation group. On several of the MVII scales, the mean scores of the Dunwoody students were equal to those of men actually working in the trade. Bradley in his conclusion reports, "Observation of its [MVII] value in this study suggests that it will be as valuable in measuring the interests of nonprofessional men as the SVIB has been in measuring the interests of professional men" (Bradley, 1958).

There are a few findings that demonstrate a relationship between job satisfaction and MVII scores. Perry (1960) studied a group of navy clerical workers, examining their personnel data sheets to see whether they had indicated that they would choose the same career were they to start over again at age eighteen. He thus secured an occupationally satisfied and dissatisfied group, and discovered that MVII scores on relevant keys were significantly higher for the satisfied group. Perry also used data based on civilians and civilian occupations. The MVII stock clerk key was originally constructed on a St. Paul sample. When tried out on a Minneapolis sample, it did not satisfactorily cross-validate. To confuse things even more, the key based on this Minneapolis sample did not cross-validate on the St. Paul sample. But the St. Paul key did work well on the navy clerical group. Further investigation showed that 91 percent of the St. Paul sample, with an average of some four years of work experience, said they would *not* select this same career if they were to begin again. Thus, and not surprisingly, the dissatisfied group produced atypical results; occupational status, in and of itself, may therefore sometimes be a questionable way of defining a criterion group.

W. LESLIE BARNETTE, JR.

Additional support for considering occupational satisfaction is provided by the work of Ghei (1960). His study deals with three different keys based on IBM workers: a classification key to differentiate this group from TIG, a satisfaction key to separate satisfied IBM workers from TIG, and a predictor key to distinguish high-achieving and low-achieving IBM workers. Subjects used for this research were randomly selected from 453 IBM workers in five states. The reference group consisted of 575 TIG employed in fourteen different civilian occupations. The classification key was developed using occupational membership as the sole criterion. The satisfaction key was based on the IBM group who said they would select the same career again were they "to do it over." Supervisory ratings served as the criterion for the predictor key. These three keys were then compared for test-retest reliability; Tilton's percentage overlap was used to check the degree of separation between criterion and reference groups.

The results clearly indicated that the early MVII key for IBM operator (inexplicably dropped from the published inventory which now has a key for tabulating machine operators) stood up well against Ghei's cross-validation sample and that it was also effective in differentiating IBM workers from TIG. In terms of Tilton's percentage overlap, the satisfaction key did a better job than the classification key although the reliabilities were the same. The predictor key showed satisfactory reliability and correlated reasonably well with supervisory ratings, but neither the classification nor the satisfaction key correlated with the ratings. Thus the relation between achievement and job satisfaction was obscure. Nevertheless, Ghei was able to demonstrate that by including some measure of satisfaction along with occupational membership the validity of the traditional classification keys might be improved.

Christiansen (1960) tackled the old problem of the relation between measured and claimed interests. Graduating seniors ($N = 175$) in a large midwestern metropolitan vocational high school were given the MVII and twenty scales were then ranked from high to low. One week later, an alphabetical listing of these same twenty occupations was presented to the group for ranking from high to low. *Rhos* between the inventoried and claimed interest rankings for the twenty occupations ranged from −.69 to .84 with a median of .35. (Oddly enough the published report does not give the scale titles for reader inspection.) Christiansen feels that inventoried interests provide additional and different information and thus are more useful than claimed interests for counseling purposes.

103

Norman (1960) obtained completed MVII's from almost seven thousand persons representing ninety-eight occupational and seventeen reference groups. Subjects came from universities, civilian trades, navy occupations, and technical schools. Using dispersion analysis, he analyzed the interest patterns of the 115 groups with reference to the nine homogeneous or area scales developed by Gee (1955). A cluster analysis was performed and the space occupied by each cluster was geometrically projected. The smallest inter-group distance was between civilian machinists and sheet metal workers, while the largest D value occurred between liberal arts women and refrigerator repairmen. A masculine-feminine factor emerged in that the female groups and the male trade and factory occupations fell at the ends of a continuum. The groups that clustered together showed nearly congruent profiles across the area keys. Thus groups with obvious divergent interests could easily be separated.

Scott (1960) concerned himself with how the MVII was interpreted in counseling and how certain MVII scores were related to SVIB scoring keys. Three groups of subjects were employed. One was a group of 244 patients from the Minneapolis VA Hospital who had completed both the MVII and SVIB; a second group consisted of 266 former VA patients who had completed only the MVII; the third was composed of 271 senior boys from three Minneapolis high schools who had completed the SVIB. He reported that the food service manager key on the MVII was a more meaningful measure of "food" interests than the baker key which seemed to show a subject's rejection of mechanical interests. The construction keys (carpenter, painter, plasterer), which appear to be related to artistic pursuits, were not nearly as effective in indicating interests as were the electrical keys (electrician and radio/TV repairman) which were closely related to Strong's group II. High clerical scores (IBM operator and stock clerk) tended to cluster with mechanical rejection patterns and these, in turn, were associated with low MF. Conversely, high MF (high masculine) subjects usually had mechanical and electrical profile peaks.

In 1961 Clark published *The Vocational Interests of Nonprofessional Men*, a volume which carefully reported all the details involved in the construction and validation of the inventory. (Callis, in his 1962 review of this book, called it a major contribution, a fascinating landmark, and, to my surprise, a difficult book.) Clark described the scoring keys for his inventory and discussed several studies concerning the psychometric qualities of keys developed by different methods. He indicated how his scoring keys could classify individuals into occupational groups and how his interest measures could aid in predicting achievement and choice of specialty. Chapter six, for example, gives data from navy samples which indicate that the MVII, along with information from aptitude test data, was clearly helpful in predicting success and achievement in navy technical schools. An especially intriguing finding regarded ability — for the very capable and for the below average pupil, high interest in the program did not materially affect school grades. However, "when learning ability was just adequate" — i.e., for the average student — the motivational aspects of interests did play a significant part in academic achievement. The concluding section of the book suggests several ways to improve interest measures so that not only will there be better counseling of individuals but also greater understanding of the processes by which occupational choices are made.

Campbell (1960) compared the validity of two methods of scoring the MVII. One employed Clark's technique of specific scoring keys whose items differentiated between a criterion group and a reference group of TIG. The other involved a configural scoring technique based upon the six possible patterns of responses within any triad (like A and dislike B, like B and dislike C, etc.) that discriminated between the two groups. The data employed were completed inventories of some nine hundred skilled trade persons, part of Clark's original sample, divided approximately equally into electricians, painters, and printers. Clark's original TIG group was also included. The first method merely examines each choice separately and makes no attempt to look at combinations of responses; configural scoring, on the other hand, looks at the frequency of each response pattern within each triad. Tilton's percentage overlap was the validity statistic used. The results, in general, showed that the configural scoring keys were either equal to or slightly less effective than the empirically derived keys but that they accomplished this by using far fewer test items. This raises the problem of the reliability of these configural keys which Campbell examined in his study published in 1963.

Campbell's 1963 study is an extension of his 1960 work in which, as we have seen, he was concerned with the validity and reliability of pattern scoring. This second report utilized three occupational groups: painters, electricians, and IBM operators, which were further split into validation and cross-validation groups. These criterion groups were compared with Clark's TIG reference group. Again each of the six possible rank orderings of the triad was used. A tremendous amount of data was generated here since a series of scales was developed for each occupation based upon difference percentages of 25 down to 6. Thus the first scale would contain only those patterns which showed a 25 percent or more difference between criterion and TIG groups. In the end, pattern scoring was shown not to be as valid as Clark's empirical item scoring. It was also demonstrated that this configural scoring suffered from marked cross-validation shrinkage, although the reliabilities were about the same as those obtained from item scoring. This type of pattern scoring is therefore inferior and offers no advantage over the method originally used by Clark.

The MVII has proved to be essentially free of any response bias caused by the location of an item within a triad. Campbell and Sorenson (1963) suggested that if a subject chooses strictly on the basis of item content, thereby ignoring the arrangement of the items within the triad, and if the statements within triads have been randomly arranged, then each pattern should occur approximately one-sixth of the time. Should this not be the case, a response bias would be present. The appropriate tabulations for both persons and occupational groups were made, with the result that little or no response bias was indicated.

Campbell and Trockman (1963) concerned themselves with spotting individuals who respond carelessly or dishonestly to the inventory. They developed a verification scale similar to the MMPI validity scales. They first identified those MVII items endorsed infrequently by Clark's original TIG group. The rationale behind this procedure was that anyone who selects a substantial number of these unpopular items (those only endorsed by 5–9 percent) is either being careless, or does not understand the directions, or is deliberately trying to fake. An 8 percent key, consisting of fifty-eight items, was found to be superior. To establish the validity of this new scale, a new group of twenty-seven people was given the MVII answer sheet (but not the inventory booklet) and asked to respond blindly. The validation scale correctly identified them. For a further test, thirty answer sheets were completed using a table of random numbers; the mean for this group was extremely close to the mean of the blindly responding group (eighteen for the former and nineteen for the latter).

McCall (1965) reported on another characteristic of this verification scale. Special precautions were taken in administering the inventory to a vocational high school sample so McCall felt it unlikely that students had misunderstood instructions or that they were faking. It was noted that many of the boys with high scores were enrolled in the foods curriculum. Barnette observed that many of the triads showed a masculinity-femininity dimension as did many of the triads forming Campbell's verification scale. McCall also noted that several of these scale items come from the scoring keys for baker, stock clerk, and hospital attendant, but none from the more masculine groups such as carpenter, plumber, and electrician. Thus, when the MVII is carefully and honestly completed, Campbell's verification scale actually represents an MF scale, similar in nature to the MF scale on the SVIB.

To test this, McCall first administered the MVII, with the usual or normal instructions, to male and female students enrolled in both high school and college summer courses. A week later, one group of the same students was asked to assume a masculine set while a second group was to adopt a feminine ("sissy") one. With the normal set, males scored higher on the verification scale than skilled tradesmen, below the mean for chance derived scores, and far below the females. Both males and females with a masculine set scored low. Males with a feminine set scored at the same level as females under a normal set. Results for females with the "sissy" set were unclear; here it would have probably been better to have asked the females to adopt a female rather than a feminine-boy set. In general it appears that the verification scale includes considerable M-F content.

Barnette and McCall (1964) reported results of a validation study on vocational high school boys. Usable MVII protocols were obtained from 1114 boys enrolled in grades 9 and 12 in four of Buffalo's schools. School records for each student provided data including general intelligence level, results from five DAT subtests, and average grades for academic and shop courses. Approximately 10 percent of the sample were Negroes. Comparisons were made between mean MVII scores for grade 9 versus grade 12 and for Negro versus white students.

In general, grade 9 boys and Negro students showed somewhat higher clerical and personal service interests than did either grade 12 or white students. But the differences in MVII scores were greater between the two grade levels than between the two ethnic groups. The scores on the numerical and verbal DAT subtests were higher for grade 9 boys than for grade 12 boys, which suggests that brighter students may transfer out of the vocational schools. On the other hand, the spatial and mechanical test data indicate that the more technically oriented boys remain. The Negro pupils showed lower mean scores compared with whites on all the ability measures except the abstract reasoning subtest, a test generally regarded as minimizing academic content. Profiles of average MVII scores were determined separately for each trade at both grade levels. At the grade 12 level, the food, electrical, and printing trades had the most valid profiles. Here were the hits. In other curricula, mostly mechanical and building trades, the results were poor since students would usually peak on non-criterion scales. Grade 9 results were similar, although there were fewer hits than at grade 12. Students who earned high academic and shop grades tended to have higher MVII scores on criterion scales. The relationship between interest and achievement, reported earlier by Clark, did not stand up when DAT or Lorge-Thorndike IQ scores were used as the criterion measures.

A second and final report of this longitudinal study involved data collected in the spring of 1965 in three of the four Buffalo vocational high schools originally tested (Silver and Barnette, 1970). Predictive data for the grade 9 boys, first tested in 1962, and concurrent validity data for grade 12 boys in 1965 are the concern of this study. A total of 223 senior boys, previously seen when they were pupils in the ninth grade, were again administered the MVII. Usable MVII's from 215 additional twelfth-grade boys, for whom no grade 9 data were available, were picked up at the same time. Total N was 438 vocational high school seniors distributed as follows: 102 in building trades (carpentry, plumbing, sheet metal), 202 in electrical, 17 in baking, and 114 in machine shop (drafting, shop or tool design curricula).

In 1966 after these boys had graduated, such data as Lorge-Thorndike IQ's, five DAT subtests, and school grades were made available from school folders. Here the published version of the MVII was used and all answer sheets were scored for both the occupational and homogeneous scales. A multiple group discriminant analysis was employed. Sample size restricted this analysis to three major trade groups: building trades, electrical, and machine shop. These three curricula groups were shown to be distinct at both grade 9 and grade 12 levels. Rather surprisingly, the twenty-one occupational scales did a slightly better job of separation at grade 9 than they did at grade 12, although the scales still worked well at this senior level. The number of hits, or correct curriculum classifications, was very impressive; the "poorest" was an 85 percent hit rate at grade 12 for the machine shop curriculum. A similar analysis was done utilizing the nine homogeneous scales, but here the hit rate was not nearly as impressive. The occupational scales on the MVII are clearly doing an excellent job; distinct MVII patterns emerged for each of the three curricula. The trade groups peak on the appropriate occupational and area scales. Neither IQ nor the five DAT scores showed differences among these three programs that could be considered of any practical significance. The electrical students, however, were a somewhat elite group ranking ahead of the other two groups both in IQ and on the abstract, verbal, and mechanical DAT subtests. These boys were scored against Clark's normative data for employed adults with a mean standard score of 50. Clark has reported that seven out of ten men working in a given occupation score above 45 on their own scale. No student trade group came close to this level. Typically, student means were between 37 and 42. What is probably needed here is a separate set of norms for students in these nonprofessional occupations.

Doerr and Ferguson (1968) reported another study of junior and senior vocational school boys in Missouri where both the MVII and the Dailey Vocational Test were utilized. Only five MVII scales were employed (truck mechanic, sheet metal worker, machinist, electrician, and radio/ TV repairman) as criterion scales. Again a multiple discriminant function analysis was used. Hit rates for curriculum classification ranged from a high of 86 percent for electrical programs to a low of 33 percent for welding. Measurably different aptitudes and interests were demonstrated for the various programs. Hit rates might possibly have been improved had all MVII scales been employed rather than only five. Certainly the counseling functions would have been greater, although this was not the aim of the study.

Here, then, are three studies that demonstrate the usefulness of the MVII with vocational high school samples. The relevancy of these specialized scoring keys is obvious. Other interest inventories, not developed especially for such nonprofessional occupations, simply do not work well. Motto (1959), using Kuder Preference Record, Form C, scores to predict vocational school success, found that the students tested produced essentially flat profiles and that none of the Kuder scales could be used to differentiate successful from unsuccessful pupils.

It has been shown that the MVII is effective in differentiating among community college students (Johnson and St. John, 1970). Usable MVII answer sheets were obtained from 107 such students distributed among three programs: engineering technology, business administration, and liberal arts. The mechanical, health service, and office work area scales were most effective in such differentiation. For example, when a cutoff score of 50 on the mechanical scale was used, 50 percent of the engineering technology students were identified, but only 3 percent of the liberal arts majors and none of the business students were picked up. (The Allport-Vernon-Lindzey Study of Values was also administered and most of these scales — four out of six — yielded nonsignificant differences.) For counseling purposes, the area scales seemed to be of more value than the occupational scales; the latter, however, were most helpful in counseling students who became college dropouts. These data were collected at a junior college in Worcester, Massachusetts; the authors feel that comparable data from other community colleges are needed and that each community college should also develop its own local MVII norms.

## SUPPLEMENTARY RESEARCH

A relationship between MVII occupational interest scales and measured vocational needs (determined by the Minnesota Importance Questionnaire which provides scores for such needs as activity, creativity, independence, security) has been demonstrated (Thorndike, Weiss, and Dawis, 1968). Both of these inventories were administered to some five hundred male vocational rehabilitation clients. The study was principally an investigation of the value or worth of the method of canonical correlation rather than of any particular worth of the MVII. The sample was split into two approximately equal groups so that one could be used for cross-validation purposes. The results showed a moderate relationship between interests and needs (of the magnitude of .38), suggesting that similar variables underlie both of these measures.

Hale and Beal (1969) have published a MVII profile based on twenty VA housekeeping aides. Such individuals peak on white-collar, clerical type occupational scales and on the clean hands and service area scales. The MVII has also been used to develop a scale to identify high school dropouts with high ability (Bonfield, 1968). An identification key was developed after an item analysis of the MVII responses of 125 dropouts and 125 persisters with IQ's of 110 or above. Items that separated these two groups by a 17 percent difference or more were selected. A total of 107 items were located. A percentage overlap of 42 was found. About 80 percent of the sample was correctly identified (i.e., 20 percent errors-of-classification). Students who receive high dropout scores are thus easily spotted by counselors who may then be successful in helping these students to utilize their potential.

The idea that genes may help determine one's preferred occupation may seem a bit startling at first thought. Vandenberg and Stafford (1967) administered the MVII to fifty-three fraternal and seventy-one identical pairs of twins. They thought it highly probable that aptitudes and personality traits disposing a person to some vocational preference could be influenced genetically. Significant F ratios were found more frequently for boys than for girls. With the two sexes combined, significant F ratios were discovered for nine occupational scales and four area scales. Carter (1932) had long ago demonstrated that identical twins show great similarities in occupational choices as measured by the SVIB. Results now gained from the MVII suggest that hereditary influences on vocational interests are not necessarily limited to high-level abilities such as those required for scientific and professional occupations, but that they range over the entire occupational spectrum.

There are now three empirically scored interest inventories (the SVIB, the Kuder, and the MVII) where it is possible to find overlapping keys. A scale for printer, for example, is found on all these inventories. Zytowski (1968) obtained over two hundred completed forms of these three inventories from Iowa State University undergraduates and ascertained the necessary intercorrelations. A total of sixty-eight comparisons were made between the SVIB, the Kuder, and the MVII. For the MVII, the main concern of this chapter, fourteen comparisons could be made with the Kuder and only three with the SVIB. The reliability with which an individual's score on a scale from one of these inventories could be predicted from the same-named scale on another inventory was far too low (the highest $r$ obtained was a mere .49 for carpenter for the SVIB-Kuder comparison). Twelve correlations were not significantly different from zero and even one of these (that for Kuder-MVII printer) was negative. Zytowski could only conjecture upon these low intercorrelations. Sampling errors in the selection of norm group members immediately come to mind. Differences in the norming and scoring procedures for the three inventories might be another cause, as might be item format. Perhaps we should develop occupational scales on two of the three inventories from a single occupational group (for example librarians). Any increase in correlation over that found in Zytowski's 1968 report could represent the unreliability due to sampling error.

111

Zytowski (1969) proceeded with his inquiry and developed a new librarian scale on both the SVIB and the KOIS. The low congruent validity of both of these original scales was shown clearly not to arise from sampling differences. The difference between the correlation of the original scales (.53) and the new scales (.49) was so small that one could definitely conclude that no change had occurred. And so the missing congruent validity has not been located.

Kuder (1969) has his own explanation for these findings. He notes that both the SVIB and the MVII use essentially difference scores and that single KOIS scores are *not* difference scores. Both the SVIB and the MVII have partialed out the core of common interests between occupational and reference groups. Kuder argues that if we estimate conservatively that at least half the variance of a KOIS score is accounted for by common interests that have already been subtracted by the other two inventories, then an upper limit of .71 or $\sqrt{.50}$ is immediately established for the correlations computed by Zytowski. (This $r$ would become .63 if we allowed for 60 percent of the variance for common interests.) Thus low correlations are inevitable. Kuder feels that one way to attack this problem is to find the proportion of persons correctly classified when occupational groups are studied in pairs and then to do this for all possible combinations. A summary statistic could thus be obtained for each of the three inventories which would express the percentage correctly classified for all comparisons. Regardless, for the three occupational scales common to both SVIB and MVII, the median correlation was a mere .08 (Zytowski, 1968).

Lefkowitz (1970), using a sample of six hundred male professional engineers taken from McCampbell's doctoral dissertation, compared six engineering scoring keys (keys for engineers in general, agricultural, electrical, mechanics, industrial, and civil) both on the SVIB and the KOIS. Each subject was scored twice on all these six scales, first on his own occupation and then on the other five. They were first scored by the SVIB procedure (standard scores for the six keys) and then by the KOIS system, thereby obtaining lambda scores for the six engineering keys. The SVIB scoring system yielded correct classifications (hits) for 67 percent of the cases whereas the KOIS procedure only came up with 53 percent hits. Percentage overlap (Tilton, 1937) again showed the SVIB to be superior: SVIB overlaps ranging from 42 to 96 percent and KOIS overlaps from 76 to 100 percent. These results, although limited to engineers, point to the failure of the KOIS scoring system to differentiate between and within individuals as well as the SVIB does. Lefkowitz concludes on the cautionary note that the results might be different if more than one occupation were studied and this research effort should be pursued. This report, however, does show that "these two inventories are designed for different purposes and aimed at the measurement of different aspects of the domain of interests."

Cole and Hanson (1971), adopting a more "global" approach, offer less pessimistic results obtained with a technique termed Analysis of Spatial Configuration which looks at the internal structure of the various scales for any one inventory. A planar, circular configuration with two axes at right angles, originally proposed by Roe and found by Holland to characterize his Vocational Preference Inventory, was used as the basis for comparison. The method employed was to take, say, the fifty SVIB occupational scales and then fit these into Holland's six basic categories (artistic, conventional, enterprising, intellectual, realistic, and social). This was also done with the twenty-three KOIS core scales and the nine MVII homogeneous keys. A more or less uniform circular plane arrangement was found for all of these inventories, which means that those scales of interest inventory A that fall into one of Holland's categories, as a whole, tend to correlate most highly with the inventory B scales which fall into the same category. In addition, the scales in the adjacent categories (within this circular ordering) tend to produce the next highest correlations. Thus these results suggest that correspondence of scores on two or more interest inventories may best be ascertained by looking at patterns of scales rather than at individual scales. From this stance the authors then proceed to discuss the counseling implications of their findings.

CONCLUSION

With the MVII, we thus have, in the words of Callis in his *Contemporary Psychology* review (1962), a very professional job done on a group of nonprofessional men. The MVII has clearly proved its utility in the correct classification of navy technical assignments, and it has now been extended to a large number of civilian nonprofessional groups, mostly skilled trades. Other work has shown that the inventory may be profitably used for classification and counseling of vocational high school students. In a few instances, new occupational profiles have been reported, and there should be no reason why additional norm groups might not be added to the inventory in its present form. With this new inventory, we now have a very wide band of interest measurement that stretches from high-level professional careers down to relatively modest and nontechnical ones.

## References

Barnette, W. L., Jr., and J. N. McCall. Validation of the MVII for vocational high school boys. *Journal of Applied Psychology*, 1964, 48, 378–382.

Bonfield, J. Development and validation of an identification scale for high ability dropouts. *Vocational Guidance Quarterly*, 1968, 16, 177–180.

Bradley, A. D. Estimating success in technical and skilled trades courses using a multivariate statistical analysis. Ph.D. dissertation, University of Minnesota, 1958.

Callis, R. Review of Clark's "Interests of nonprofessional men." *Contemporary Psychology*, 1962, 7, 398–399.

Campbell, D. P. Psychometric analysis of response patterns to interest inventory items. Ph.D. dissertation, University of Minnesota, 1960.

————. The use of response patterns to improve item scoring. *Journal of Applied Psychology*, 1962, 46, 194–197.

————. Another attempt at configural scoring. *Educational and Psychological Measurement*, 1963, 23, 721–727.

————. The MVII. *Personnel and Guidance Journal*, 1966, 45, 854–858.

————, and W. W. Sorenson. Response set on interest inventory triads. *Educational and Psychological Measurement*, 1963, 23, 145–152.

Campbell, D. P., and R. W. Trockman. A verification scale for the MVII. *Journal of Applied Psychology*, 1963, 47, 276–279.

Carter, H. D. Twin similarities in occupational interests. *Journal of Educational Psychology*, 1932, 23, 641–655.

Christiansen, H. D. Inventories and claimed interests. *Vocational Guidance Quarterly*, 1960, 9, 128–130.

Clark, K. E. A vocational interest test at the skilled trades level. *Journal of Applied Psychology*, 1949, 33, 291–303.

————. Problems of method in interest measurement. In W. L. Layton (ed.), *The Strong Vocational Interest Blank: Research and uses*. Minnesota Studies in Student Personnel Work, No. 10. Minneapolis: University of Minnesota Press, 1960, 146–162.

————. *Vocational interests of nonprofessional men*. Minneapolis: University of Minnesota Press, 1961.

————, and D. P. Campbell. *Manual for MVII*. New York: Psychological Corporation, 1965.

Clark, K. E., and H. H. Gee. Selecting items for interest inventory keys. *Journal of Applied Psychology*, 1954, 38, 12–17.

Cole, N. S., and G. R. Hanson. An analysis of the structure of vocational interests. *ACT Research Report*, No. 40. Iowa City, Iowa: American College Testing Program, January 1971.

Doerr, J. J., and J. L. Ferguson. The selection of vocational-technical students. *Vocational Guidance Quarterly*, 1968, 16, 27–32.

Gee, H. H. A comparison of empirical and homogeneous keys in interest measurement. Ph.D. dissertation, University of Minnesota, 1955.

Ghei, S. Vocational interests, achievement and satisfaction. *Journal of Counseling Psychology*, 1960, 7, 132–136.

Hale, P. P., and L. E. Beal. MVII occupational interest profile for hospital house-keeping aides. *Vocational Guidance Quarterly*, 1969, 17, 218–220.

Johnson, R. W., and D. E. St. John. Use of the MVII in educational planning with community college "career" students. *Vocational Guidance Quarterly*, 1970, 19, 90–96.

Kuder, F. A note on the comparability of occupational scores from different interest inventories. *Measurement and Evaluation in Guidance*, 1959, 2, 94–100.

Lefkowitz, D. M. Comparison of the Strong Vocational Interest Blank and the Kuder Occupational Interest Survey scoring procedures. *Journal of Counseling Psychology*, 1970, 17, 357–363.

McCall, J. N. "Masculine striving" as a clue to skilled trade interests. *Journal of Applied Psychology*, 1965, 49, 106–109.

McCampbell, M. K. Differentiation of engineers' interests. Ph.D. dissertation, University of Kansas, 1966.

Motto, J. J. Interest scores in predicting success in vocational school programs. *Personnel and Guidance Journal*, 1959, 37, 674–676.

Norman, W. T. A spatial analysis of an interest domain. *Educational and Psychological Measurement*, 1960, 20, 347–361.

Olson, D. W., and R. W. Johnson. Reliability of measured interests of hospitalized psychiatric patients. *Measurement and Evaluation in Guidance*, 1968, 1, 115–121.

Perry, D. Problems of item form and criterion group definition. In W. L. Layton (ed.), *The Strong Vocational Interest Blank: Research and uses*. Minnesota Studies in Student Personnel Work, No. 10, Minneapolis: University of Minnesota Press, 1960, 163–177.

Scott, T. B. Counseling interpretations for the MVII based on comparisons with the SVIB. Ph.D. dissertation, University of Minnesota, 1960.

Silver, H. A., and W. L. Barnette, Jr. Predictive and concurrent validity of the Minnesota Vocational Interest Inventory for vocational high school boys. *Journal of Applied Psychology*, 1970, 34, 436–440.

Thorndike, R. M., D. J. Weiss, and R. V. Dawis. Multivariate relationships between a measure of vocational interests and a measure of vocational needs. *Journal of Applied Psychology*, 1968, 52, 491–496.

Tilton, J. W. The measurement of overlapping. *Journal of Educational Psychology*, 1937, 28, 656–662.

Vandenberg, S. G., and R. E. Stafford. Hereditary influences on vocational preferences as shown by scores of twins on the MVII. *Journal of Applied Psychology*, 1967, 51, 17–19.

Zytowski, D. G. Relationships of equivalent scales on three interest inventories. *Personnel and Guidance Journal*, 1968, 47, 44–49.

———. A test of criterion group sampling error in two comparable interest inventories. *Measurement and Evaluation in Guidance*, 1969, 2, 37–40.

# 5

# The Kuder
# Occupational Interest
# Survey

## Donald G. Zytowski

THERE ARE PROBABLY FEW PERSONS in a group of counselors and counselors-to-be who haven't at least heard of the Kuder Preference Record. Even among adults who are not counselors, many can recognize that "test you take with a pin." The present edition of the Preference Record, Form E, consists of a number of items arranged into ten homogeneous scales, from which, with norm tables, one can discover what classes of things or activities attract him most or least.

Form D of the Kuder inventory was a departure from this design. It was scored not on homogeneous scales but on normative scales that indicated what occupational groups an individual was most similar to. From this, the Form DD, or the Kuder Occupational Interest Survey (KOIS), evolved.

The KOIS has certain features in common with the Kuder Preference Record. Each has one hundred items listing three kinds of activities, not necessarily occupational in content. A person selects the alternative he likes most and the one he likes least, leaving the other blank. At this point resemblance to the Preference Record ends. The person's responses are compared with those of men in a number of different occupations, and an index of similarity with each is derived and reported on a profile. To understand the KOIS better — to see what it is like and how it differs from

116

other normative interest inventories — this process should be examined in some detail.

### LIST I

1. Cook a gourmet dinner Ⓜ L
   Play bridge M L
   Go fishing M Ⓛ

2. Collect stamps Ⓜ L
   Bowl in a tournament M Ⓛ
   Repair a car M L

3. Invest in the stock market M L
   Start a social service agency M Ⓛ
   Discover a new miracle drug Ⓜ L

In List I are three items which are similar to those on the KOIS. The instructions tell the person to identify in each item the alternative he likes *most*, and the one he likes *least*, even though he may like or dislike all three. In this sense, the KOIS has a forced-choice rather than a free-response format. Further, let it be assumed that the choices made in each item triad of List I are those of a single person, who wishes to discover his similarity with some occupational groups by taking this brief inventory. In order to establish this similarity, it is necessary to know how persons in different occupational groups respond to these same items. That means we will have had to collect their responses before scoring this person on the inventory.

The items are shown again, in List II, this time with the hypothetical proportions of two occupational groups that responded to each alternative. The categories liked least and most by the hypothetical inventory

### LIST II

| | Accountants | | Architects | |
|---|---|---|---|---|
| | M | L | M | L |
| 1. Cook a gourmet dinner | 35* | 20 | 48* | 26 |
| Play bridge | 40 | 20 | 31 | 22 |
| Go fishing | 25 | 60* | 21 | 52* |
| 2. Collect stamps | 33* | 33 | 04* | 23 |
| Bowl in a tournament | 33 | 33* | 30 | 44* |
| Repair a car | 33 | 33 | 66 | 33 |
| 3. Invest in the stock market | 72 | 25 | 70 | 20 |
| Start a social service agency | 13 | 27* | 23 | 68* |
| Discover a new drug | 15* | 38 | 07* | 12 |

117

taker are indicated by the asterisks corresponding to the percentage of accountants and architects who responded "likes most" and "likes least" to these items. Each column totals 100 percent, but each row may total any figure up to 100 percent, depending on how each group distributes its likes and dislikes. Also, it should be apparent that items vary in their descriptiveness of occupational groups. In this example, item 3 for architects shows responses allotted chiefly to two alternatives. Item 2 for accountants does not differentiate them particularly because they have distributed their responses equally among all the alternatives. *That items differ in the proportions of criterion groups which each alternative attracts is the reason why interest measurement works.* If an occupational group were not homogeneous in its likes and dislikes and heterogeneous with respect to other occupations, normative interest inventorying would not be possible.

To express how similar a person is to people in different occupational groups, the KOIS in effect awards him the proportion of the occupational group that has made the same choice as he. So our hypothetical person's score on accountant is 203, and his score on architect is 223. It should be pointed out that there is no contrast group of people-in-general, such as the SVIB uses to award points only on the basis of the criterion group's differences from men-in-general. This is an important difference between the KOIS and the SVIB, which will become more meaningful as this chapter develops.

It should be apparent that the raw score an individual receives is dependent upon how extreme the differences in proportions are on each item. That is, the highest total score a person can attain on any occupational scale will be different for each scale. It is reasonable then to express the person's score as a ratio between the score he did attain, and the highest score he could attain on that scale. The highest possible score for accountants is 276 and for architects 348. The hypothetical inventory taker has scored .64 on architect and .75 on accountant. Despite his higher raw score on architect, he is more similar to accountants.

Kuder obtains this same end by means of the lambda score. It is a more sensitive measure of the similarity derived from correlational procedures, but it is nothing more than a ratio between the highest correlation a person could receive on each occupational scale and the correlation he actually did get between his responses and the responses of the occupational group. The lambda is not a standard score like a T score, but it does have some constant characteristics which the counselor should know.

The lambda score's upper limit, being a ratio, is 1.00. Kuder reports in his interpretative leaflet that 80 percent of those who are in a given occupation (and are satisfied with it) score .45 or higher on the scale for their occupation or college major. The highest scores generally seen run to about .65, with an occasional .69 or .70. For an undifferentiated group of adults, that is, one composed of men or women in a variety of the occupations or college majors scored on the KOIS, the average score is between .40 and .45, with standard deviations between 10 and 12. Negative scores are possible and are seen for some persons; they are usually the consequence of omitted responses. A score of .45, though, can be regarded as the demarcation line between the average score of undifferentiated persons and the highest 80 percent of those people in a given occupation or major.

But Kuder cautions that the lambda score should not be taken in absolute (ratio scale) terms because a person's score on any one occupation has two components: the degree to which he is similar to people-in-general and the degree to which he is similar to the people in the occupation for which he received the score. *So, if the person's lambda score is more than the upper limit of random response, it should be understood only as it stands relative to his other lambda scores.* For this reason, a ranking procedure is used in interpreting scores. This same feature precludes meaningful comparison of two different persons' scores on the same scale.

It is important to know when two scores are truly different. From his knowledge of the psychometric characteristics of the lambda score, Kuder recommends that *all scores within .06 of each other be considered the same score.* Thus, scores of .60 and .55 would not be different, but a score of .50 would be considered lower than a score of .60.

## THE PROFILE

The KOIS profile sheet is given in Figure 5.1. It yields a number of different scores. Most obvious are the occupational scores, which show how similar the inventory taker is to persons in each occupation listed. The occupational and college major scales are listed separately for women and for men. Men are scored on only men's scales. Women are scored on women's scales and on some of the men's scales. This use of the men's scales for women was decided upon empirically: the men's scales women are scored on represent those occupations for which the characteristics of women could not be distinguished from those of men (Hornaday and Ku-

119

der, 1961). Men are scored on seventy-seven occupations and twenty-nine college majors; women are scored on thirty-seven women's occupational scales and twenty men's, and on nineteen women's college majors and eight men's.

About the coverage of the KOIS scales: there is probably no certain way to determine the degree to which a set of occupational scales is representative of the variety of occupations that exist. But Roe's classification of fields and levels of occupations makes it possible to determine more systematically what the coverage of the occupational scales of the

## Report of Scores — Kuder Occupational Interest Survey (Form DD)

NAME MAXINE   LOCATION PERSONNEL SERVICES   DATE OF SURVEY 9-14-70

### OCCUPATIONAL SCALES WOMEN

| Title | Score | Title | Score |
|---|---|---|---|
| Accountant | .49 | Nurse | .56 |
| Bank Clerk | .49 | Nutritionist | .52 |
| Beautician | .44 | Occupational Therapist | .44 |
| Bookkeeper | .49 | Office Clerk | .46 |
| Bookstore Manager | .42 | Physical Therapist | .55 |
| Computer Programmer | .45 | Primary School Teacher | .50 |
| Counselor, High School | .51 | Psychologist | .47 |
| Dean of Women | .48 | Psychologist, Clinical | .46 |
| Dental Assistant | .55 | Religious Education Director | .47 |
| Department Store Saleswoman | .42 | Science Teacher, High School | .48 |
| Dietitian, Administrative | .57 | Secretary | .49 |
| Dietitian, Public School | .55 | Social Caseworker | .49 |
| Florist | .46 | Social Worker, Group | .48 |
| Home Demonstration Agent | .48 | Social Worker, Medical | .49 |
| Home Ec Teacher, College | .54 | Social Worker, Psychiatric | .49 |
| Interior Decorator | .31 | Social Worker, School | .49 |
| Lawyer | .44 | Stenographer | .48 |
| Librarian | .41 | X-Ray Technician | .53 |
| Math Teacher, High School | .48 | | |

### COLLEGE MAJOR SCALES, WOMEN

| Title | Score |
|---|---|
| Art & Art Education | .32 |
| Biological Sciences | .58 |
| Business Ed & Commerce | .54 |
| Drama | .42 |
| Elementary Education | .60 |
| English | .45 |
| Foreign Languages | .51 |
| General Social Sciences | .57 |
| Health Professions | .64 |
| History | .48 |
| Home Economics Education | .60 |
| Mathematics | .55 |
| Music & Music Education | .48 |
| Nursing | .65 |
| Physical Education | .44 |
| Political Science | .44 |
| Psychology | .53 |
| Sociology | .54 |
| Teaching Sister, Catholic | .55 |

### OCCUPATIONAL SCALES MEN

| Title | Score | Title | Score | Title | Score | Title | Score |
|---|---|---|---|---|---|---|---|
| Acc't, Certified Public | | Engineer, Electrical | | Optometrist | .46 | Psychology Professor | .35 |
| Architect | .29 | Engineer, Heating/Air Cond. | | Osteopath | | Radio Station Manager | |
| Automobile Mechanic | | Engineer, Industrial | | Painter, House | | Real Estate Agent | .34 |
| Automobile Salesman | | Engineer, Mechanical | | Pediatrician | .46 | Sales Eng, Heating/Air Cond. | |
| Banker | | Engineer, Mining & Metal | | Personnel Manager | .36 | Science Teacher, High School | |
| Bookkeeper | | Farmer | | Pharmaceutical Salesman | | School Superintendent | |
| Bookstore Manager | | Florist | | Pharmacist | .40 | Social Caseworker | |
| Bricklayer | | Forester | | Photographer | .32 | Social Worker, Group | |
| Building Contractor | | Insurance Agent | .32 | Physical Therapist | | Social Worker, Psychiatric | |
| Buyer | .33 | Interior Decorator | | Physician | .44 | Statistician | .37 |
| Carpenter | | Journalist | .22 | Plumber | | Supv/Foreman, Industrial | |
| Chemist | .34 | Lawyer | | Plumbing Contractor | | Travel Agent | .37 |
| Clothier, Retail | | Librarian | | Podiatrist | | Truck Driver | |
| Computer Programmer | | Machinist | | Policeman | | Television Repairman | |
| Counselor, High School | | Mathematician | .33 | Postal Clerk | | University Pastor | |
| County Agricultural Agent | | Math Teacher, High School | | Printer | | Veterinarian | .37 |
| Dentist | .42 | Meteorologist | | Psychiatrist | .44 | Welder | |
| Electrician | | Minister | | Psychologist, Clinical | | X-Ray Technician | |
| Engineer, Civil | .30 | Nurseryman | | Psychologist, Counseling | | YMCA Secretary | |
| | | | | Psychologist, Industrial | | | |

### COLLEGE MAJOR SCALES MEN

| Title | Score | Title | Score |
|---|---|---|---|
| Agriculture | .35 | Foreign Languages | |
| Animal Husbandry | | Forestry | |
| Architecture | .26 | History | |
| Art & Art Education | | Law (Grad School) | |
| Biological Sciences | | Mathematics | |
| Business Acc't & Finance | | Music & Music Ed | |
| Business & Marketing | | Physical Education | |
| Business Management | | Physical Sciences | .38 |
| Economics | .36 | Political Science & Gov't | |
| Elementary Education | | Premed, Pharm & Dentistry | |
| Engineering, Chemical | .35 | Psychology | |
| Engineering, Civil | .33 | Sociology | |
| Engineering, Electrical | .33 | U.S. Air Force Cadet | |
| Engineering, Mechanical | .30 | U.S. Military Cadet | |
| English | | | |

### Summary

| OCCUPATIONAL SCALES WOMEN | | COLLEGE MAJOR SCALES WOMEN | | OCCUPATIONAL SCALES MEN | | COLLEGE MAJOR SCALES MEN | |
|---|---|---|---|---|---|---|---|
| Title | Score | Title | Score | Title | Score | Title | Score |
| DIETITIAN, ADMIN | .57 | NURSING | .65 | OPTOMETRIST | .46 | PHYSICAL SCIENCE | .38 |
| NURSE | .56 | HEALTH PROFES | .64 | PEDIATRICIAN | .46 | ECONOMICS | .36 |
| DENTAL ASSISTANT | .55 | ELEMENTARY EDUC | .60 | PHYSICIAN | .44 | AGRICULTURE | .35 |
| DIETITIAN, PUB SCH | .55 | HOME ECON EDUC | .60 | PSYCHIATRIST | .44 | ENGINEERING, CHEM | .35 |
| PHYS THERAPIST | .55 | BIOLOGICAL SCI | .58 | DENTIST | .42 | ENGINEERING, CIVIL | .33 |
| HOME EC TCHR, COL | .54 | | | PHARMACIST | .40 | ENGINEERING, ELEC | .33 |
| X-RAY TECHNICIAN | .53 | | | | | ENGINEERING, MECH | .30 |
| NUTRITIONIST | .52 | | | STATISTICIAN | .37 | ARCHITECTURE | .26 |
| COUNSELOR, HI SCH | .51 | | | TRAVEL AGENT | .37 | | |
| PRIMARY SCH TCHR | .50 | | | VETERINARIAN | .37 | | |
| | | | | PERSONNEL MANAGR | .36 | | |

V _____

Figure 5.1. Profile sheet for the KOIS. (From *Kuder Occupational Interest Survey — Form DD* by G. Frederic Kuder. Copyright © 1965, 1968, 1970, Science Research Associates, Inc. Reproduced by permission of the publisher.)

KOIS is (Roe, 1956). Table 1.2 shows that at the highest occupational levels the KOIS has scales for only services and science. This may be a function of the distribution of the occupations rather than of the scales selected by Kuder. At the next level, all fields are represented except business contact, although outdoor and arts and entertainment fields have only one occupation each. The KOIS has more scales in each field at level III than most other inventories of the same kind, except for the technology field (actually building trades) where the coverage begins to fall off. It is generally accepted that the SVIB concentrates on white-collar occupations and the MVII on blue-collar ones: perhaps one strength of the KOIS is that it samples both these composite levels. It (like others) is weakest in providing scales in the arts and entertainment and outdoor occupational fields.

The KOIS duplicates some scales on other inventories that provide normative occupational scores. There are thirty to thirty-five scales for the same occupations on both the male SVIB and the KOIS (depending on such things as whether buyer and purchasing agent are the same). Fourteen are identical to scales on the MVII. About thirty women's KOIS scales are also represented on the SVIB, but none on the MVII, since the latter is intended exclusively for men. Each inventory is scored for occupations that are unique to it; if the counselor is attempting to provide information to a client on his similarity to one or several of these occupations, he should select the inventory with that coverage. It should be noted here that experience has shown that some individuals score at vastly different levels on the equivalent scales of the KOIS and another inventory. There are a number of possible reasons for this, which are explored in the introductory chapter to this book. Suffice it here to say, a counselor who gives two inventories to his client and then finds scores with distinctly different interpretations on the scales of the same name is in an awkward position. About all he can say is that the client is high on one and low on the other, and that there might be some question whether he should consider that occupation as seriously as those on which he scores high on both inventories.

At the bottom of the profile the computer prints out the ten occupational and college major scales with the highest scores. If the range of scores is more than six, it underlines the last one which does not differ more than .06 from the top one. This is consistent with Kuder's instruction to take the scores in terms of their relative standing, and the information is placed here on the profile to facilitate the ranking procedure. It is not necessarily complete on the profile.

At the lower right of the profile sheet, the V score is given, which is precisely the same here as it was on the pinprick (Form C and now E) version. It consists of extremely unpopular responses. If "clean out a stopped-up sewer" were an item on the KOIS, it would probably be included on the V scale. Points are given for *avoiding* these alternatives, so that omitting responses does not increase the V score. Kuder has studied the V scores of persons instructed to take the KOIS insincerely and of randomly answered inventories, and concluded that a 45 is the lowest possible score which would not cast doubt on the validity of the entire profile of scores. If the score is lower than 45, it is possible that the inventory taker was careless, and with appropriate motivation he could take it again and produce a valid profile. It is also possible that he or she misunderstood the instructions or is a poor reader and answered positively to some items that most people avoid. Or it is possible that the person does like a lot of things that most people do not. What the counselor does in the last situation is a test of his clinical ability.

On the original, but not on the carbon copy, eight more scores are printed out under the V score. Kuder (1966) points out that these are experimental scales, and that although they clearly differentiate between groups, their meaning has not been adequately enough established to be communicated to the client. It is my opinion that, if they are cautiously used, they may add a dimension to understanding the client which may be explored and validated with him. Their interpretation and potential utility will be discussed here, however, rather than in the part of this presentation that deals with scores which are communicated or interpreted to the client.

M and W stand for men-in-general and women-in-general. M scores for men, and W scores for women co-vary closely with the overall elevation of scores on the occupations and majors. They represent, to some degree, the component of the person's score mentioned before which is in common with people-in-general, rather than that which is in common with the differentiating interests of an occupational group. The M and W scores vary through a wide range, and this variation *may* be taken to represent something like the breadth of a person's interests.

MBI and WBI denote "best impression." These scales are based on the responses of the same men and women who formed the M and W scales when they were instructed to make the best impression possible. Scores for the appropriate sex on the MBI or the WBI scale should be compared with the corresponding M or W score, and the differences should be taken as an index of the social desirability response set of the person. M typically runs 30 or 40 points higher than MBI, but when the two begin to approach the same magnitude, or MBI is greater than M, the counselor has to judge the meaningfulness of the occupational and major scale scores.

Comparison of the M and W scores yields what may be called a scale of masculinity-femininity of interests. It is inappropriate to use this contrast diagnostically, but a lack of difference in this score may reflect some lack of a clear role identification or some confusion that the client might be aided in solving within the stream of his vocational development. A skillful counselor would take the problem up with the client not in terms of his masculinity or her femininity, but in terms of his comfort in occupations that have a high population of women, or of her feelings about having to compete with men in her career.

The S and F scales were derived from the responses of a group of 250 high school boys (S) and their fathers (F). The D and Mo scales were likewise developed from 330 high school girls and their mothers. Again, these scores afford comparisons that may yield useful information. The S-D comparison may be more relevant than the M-W one, depending upon how young the inventory taker is. More directly, since differences in interests between children and their parents may be more a function of their ages than of their environments, it is possible that differences between these scores may reflect the child's level of maturity. Just what is to be concluded or what action is to be taken toward an "immature" client depends upon the skill of the counselor, and would well be approached cautiously and sensitively.

INTERPRETATION OF THE KOIS PROFILE

There is an almost regular sequence of steps that may be taken in interpreting the KOIS profile to a client. One begins this procedure by deciding whether the client's profile is usable.

Step 1 is to inspect the V score. If it is over 45, go to Step 2. If it is not above 45, there are a number of options. The counselor may conclude that the inventory must be repeated for one of the several reasons given previously when the V score was discussed. If it is only a few points below the cutting score, the counselor may decide from what he knows or might find out from his client that the latter has truly unusual interest patterns which for him are valid even though untypical for the ordinary run of people. Bobby Fischer, who even as a teen-ager was a chess prodigy, might have had a suspect V score because of the obsessive quality of his interests at that time.

For Step 2, inspect the general level of the lambda scores on the profile. If some are higher than .40, the profile is interpretable and the counselor can proceed to Step 3. If the lambda scores are between .32 and .39, the counselor may still go to Step 3, with the understanding that the interpretations are tentative and perhaps incorrect. If all scores are less than .31, the profile is uninterpretable, and all attempts to derive conclusions from it should be terminated. This is a rare event; I have seen only three such profiles in approximately one thousand cases in a college counseling service. It appears more frequently among younger persons, but it is still an uncommon occurrence.

The cause of such low scores can be an indifferently answered inventory, which would be accompanied by a suspect V score. They may also be the result of immature, yet sincere, interests. That is, the person's interests may not have yet developed any patterning or crystallization that allows them to be significantly like those of persons who are stable and satisfied members of occupational groups.

For Step 3, it is useful to check the eight research scale scores. From these scores one can gain some impression of the range of interests reflected by the M or W score and some insight into the possibility that the occupational scores are influenced by a social desirability set (MBI or WBI) or reflect interests that are "masculine" or "feminine" as defined by contemporary culture. This step tends to make the whole profile more understandable and offers an opportunity to check its validity against other data obtained from the client.

Step 4 returns to Kuder's recommended procedure of transferring the highest ranked scales from the bottom of the profile to the interpretative leaflet. The leaflet is received when the KOIS "test booklets" are ordered and contains information for the inventory taker about vocational interests and how to interpret the results from the profile. It is especially useful in group interpretations and will supplement individual ones. If there are more than ten scores in the range of .06 from the highest score, all of them are listed on the leaflet. Occupations are placed in one rank, and college majors in another. Kuder recommends that women's scores on their own scales and on the men's scales be ranked separately. The two, however, should be considered together. Although ranks are to be numbered, the rankings do not matter if the scores are not more than .06 apart. *They have all come in first.* If the .06 range does not place ten occupations in the ranking, those which are one point under the .06 line may be added.

The use of the .06 span to identify the top-ranking scales permits the number of occupations that will be given serious consideration to vary widely. This is partly a result of the number of similar occupations for which the inventory is scored. If a person has psychological interests, four scales relating to psychologists are likely to be included in the list within .06 of the highest scored scale; if an individual is oriented toward skilled trades, more than ten scales may be added to others which he may have similarities with. Alternatively, a person may have many scales in the top .06 range because his pattern of interests is not differentiated to a high degree. In addition, if a person's M or W score is very close to the general level of the occupational or college major scales, there may be very little distinctive occupational content in the lambda scores.

For Step 5 I again propose a departure from Kuder. There is a developing body of theory (Tyler, 1955; Gribbons and Lohnes, 1969) postulating that vocational development consists of a series of successive eliminations of alternatives. Added to this should be the understanding (Campbell, 1971) that the prediction from a person's low scores of what occupations he won't enter is more powerful than the prediction from his high scores of what he will enter. I suggest that the counselor scan the profile for the ten or so lowest scoring occupations to gain some impression of what the client has eliminated or what he should avoid consideration of.

This still leaves the counselor with (in the case of occupations for men) more than fifty scores that are pretty much ignored, unless they include one which the client specifically wants an opinion on.

Step 6 is also an addition to the procedure recommended by Kuder. This step gives the counselor an opportunity to compare the general level of lambda scores for occupations with the level of college majors. Differences between the average scores in the two series might be interpreted as a crude kind of academic orientation scale. There is no empirical basis for comparing these scores, but if a student has higher scores on certain occupations, particularly those in the building trades or in other blue-collar occupations, than he does on college majors, one is tempted to put this profile in a special folder and look at it again four years later to see whether or not he completed college.

The profile offers similarity indices on a large number of occupations, each with varying overlap with the others. For instance, psychologist and social worker must be more like each other than, say, psychologist and forester, or engineer and plumber. To comprehend the variable relationships among the scales, one would be tempted to group them into families of like occupations. This has been the approach used by the SVIB and the MVII. But one of the unusual qualities of the KOIS is that no such grouping is done, and the ranking procedure affords infinitely variable possibilities for sensitive interpretation. This is the essence of the next step.

Step 7 is to inspect the highest ranking occupations and "educe" what they have in common or conceptualize the underlying similarities in the series. This is not a difficult task; there are a number of occupational grouping systems to work from as well as the grouping of occupations from the SVIB. Its lack of rigidity also permits flexible interpretation of any of these occupational scores within the context of the other high scores. For instance, photographer at the head of a list including florist, interior decorator, and art major would have different implications than if the remainder of the list included small businessmen, such as retail clothier, radio station manager, and the like. In addition, the counselor may encounter unique combinations of occupations, not found in any classification system, which would suggest directions that would not otherwise come to attention.

The following tabulation is a ranked set of men's occupational scales from one KOIS profile. What underlying similarity intuitively comes to mind? Note sciences. Mathematician, statistician, and computer programmer. Psychology professor. But no biological sciences. The communality? The underlying dimension? Mathematics, or mathematically oriented sciences. Higher levels first; B.S. levels second.

Now the counselor is prepared to speak to the client and convey some kind of statement summarizing the essence of the whole profile to him. The interpretive formula first suggested for the SVIB is useful here: "Your interests are similar to those of (name underlying similarity), such as (name high-scoring occupations)." For the individual whose profile is presented in the tabulation below, the counselor might say, "Your interests are similar to those of mathematical scientists, such as chemists, psy-

126

| Rank | Title | Score |
|------|-------|-------|
| 1 | Mathematician | .56 |
| 2.5 | Chemist | .55 |
| 2.5 | Electrical engineer | .55 |
| 4 | Statistician | .53 |
| 5 | Computer programmer | .52 |
| 6.5 | Psychology professor | .50 |
| 6.5 | High school science teacher | .50 |
| 8.5 | Civil engineer | .49 |
| 8.5 | Mechanical engineer | .49 |
| 10 | Industrial psychologist | .47 |

chologists, engineers, mathematicians of various kinds, and high school science teachers."

Obviously there is more to interpretation than one sentence, but that is the kernel of it. That information, clearly communicated, perhaps repeated, aids the client in clarifying his self-concept, which Super (1953) maintains he needs for effective vocational development. Then attention should be given to helping the client integrate the interpretation into his self-concept; elaboration will be required to resolve any conflict between the interpretation and what he already thinks about himself. Implications must be discussed: what kinds and levels of abilities are necessary for success in the occupations named; what else is demanded of the client in order to perform well in a particular job; and what rewards the occupations have to offer if he could enter one or another of them.

SOME ILLUSTRATIVE PROFILES

The following are profiles from a number of young persons. They have been selected to show how interpretations generate from the ranks and other scores and to illustrate some features of the KOIS that will prove helpful to the counselor.

James has as straightforward a profile as one typically finds on the KOIS (see Fig. 5.2). All his occupational scores within .06 of the highest point to just one thing: public contact, selling, and at their broadest interpretation, business. The college major scores also support this conclusion. They are well over the minimum interpretable level; there is nothing that would lead the counselor to question their validity. There is evidence at the lower ranks of the ten scales of some real-thing orientation (bricklayer, mechanical and civil engineer), but there is sufficiently good proof of James's interest in selling that it need not be attended to especially. His

127

lowest scores have in common a high level of education (architect, mathematician, psychology professor, pastor), which is supported by a slightly (but significantly) lower average level of college major scale scores than of occupational scores.

James's reason for taking an interest inventory was that he had just decided not to be a mathematician, and he was anxious to explore some new alternatives. He had experience working in short-order food sales (hamburger stand), and the interest inventory clarified that this experience was something real to him, and that there were further avenues through which it might be expressed.

**Report of Scores**   *Kuder Occupational Interest Survey*   (Form DD)

NAME ___JAMES_____ 1 LOCATION _____ 000-38744 ___ DATE OF SURVEY 05-24-71

| OCCUPATIONAL SCALES WOMEN | | COLLEGE MAJOR SCALES, WOMEN | OCCUPATIONAL SCALES MEN | | | | COLLEGE MAJOR SCALES MEN | |
|---|---|---|---|---|---|---|---|---|
| Accountant | Nurse | Art & Art Education | Acc't, Certified Public .46 | Engineer, Electrical .38 | Optometrist .42 | Radio Station Manager .46 | Agriculture .39 | Foreign Languages .21 |
| Bank Clerk | Nutritionist | Biological Sciences | Architect .27 | Engineer, Heating/Air Cond. .42 | Osteopath .33 Painter, House .38 | Real Estate Agent .47 Animal Husbandry .35 | | Forestry .30 |
| Beautician | Occupational Therapist | Business Ed & Commerce | Automobile Mechanic .40 | Engineer, Industrial .43 | Pediatrician .26 | Sales Eng, Heating/Air Cond .51 Architecture .25 | | History .24 |
| Bookkeeper | Office Clerk | Drama | Automobile Salesman .57 | Engineer, Mechanical .39 | Personnel Manager .44 | Science Teacher, High School .30 Art & Art Education .14 | | Law (Grad School) .33 |
| Bookstore Manager | Physical Therapist | Elementary Education | Banker .49 | Engineer, Mining & Metal .36 | Pharmaceutical Salesman .50 | School Superintendent .34 Biological Sciences .24 | | Mathematics .32 |
| Computer Programmer | Primary School Teacher | English | Bookkeeper .42 | Farmer .35 | Pharmacist .42 | Social Caseworker .32 Business Acc't & Finance .47 | | Music & Music Ed .27 |
| Counselor, High School | Psychologist | Foreign Languages | Bookstore Manager .37 | Florist .45 | Photographer .39 | Social Worker, Group .34 Business & Marketing .48 | | Physical Education .47 |
| Dean of Women | Psychologist, Clinical | General Social Sciences | Bricklayer .46 | Forester .34 | Physical Therapist .40 | Social Worker, Psychiatric .28 Business Management .51 | | Physical Sciences .23 |
| Dental Assistant | Religious Education Director | Health Professions | Building Contractor .39 | Insurance Agent .52 | Physician .29 | Statistician .26 Economics .42 | | Political Science & Gov't .29 |
| Department Store Saleswoman | Science Teacher, High School | History | Buyer .54 | Interior Decorator .24 | Plumber .40 | Supv/Foreman, Industrial .43 Elementary Education .40 | | Premed, Pharm & Dentistry .33 |
| Dietitian, Administrative | Secretary | Home Economics Education | Carpenter .38 | Journalist .22 | Plumbing Contractor .45 | Travel Agent .44 Engineering, Chemical .36 | | Psychology .27 |
| Dietitian, Public School | Social Caseworker | Mathematics | Chemist .23 | Lawyer .29 | Podiatrist .41 | Truck Driver .43 Engineering, Civil .40 | | Sociology .32 |
| Florist | Social Worker, Group | Music & Music Education | Clothier, Retail .54 | Librarian .23 | Policeman .42 | Television Repairman .42 Engineering, Electrical .37 | | U.S. Air Force Cadet .41 |
| Home Demonstration Agent | Social Worker, Medical | Nursing | Computer Programmer .28 | Machinist .39 | Postal Clerk .43 | University Pastor .44 Engineering, Mechanical .41 | | U.S. Military Cadet .44 |
| Home Ec Teacher, College | Social Worker, Pyschiatric | Physical Education | Counselor, High School .38 | Mathematician .21 | Printer .38 | Veterinarian .31 English .11 | | |
| Interior Decorator | Social Worker, School | Political Science | County Agricultural Agent .32 | Math Teacher, High School .36 | Psychiatrist .24 | Welder .42 | | |
| Lawyer | Stenographer | Psychology | Dentist .38 | Meteorologist .31 | Psychologist, Clinical .25 | X-Ray Technician .38 | | |
| Librarian | X-Ray Technician | Sociology | Electrician .41 | Minister .23 | Psychologist, Counseling .28 | YMCA Secretary .40 | | |
| Math Teacher, High School | | Teaching Sister, Catholic | Engineer, Civil .39 | Nurseryman .38 | Psychologist, Industrial .36 | | | |

| OCCUPATIONAL SCALES WOMEN | | COLLEGE MAJOR SCALES WOMEN | | OCCUPATIONAL SCALES MEN | | COLLEGE MAJOR SCALES MEN | | | |
|---|---|---|---|---|---|---|---|---|---|
| Title | Score | Title | Score | Title | Score | Title | Score | | |
| | | | | AUTO SALESMAN | .57 | BUS MANAGEMENT | .51 | V | 49 |
| | | | | BUYER | .54 | BUS & MARKETING | .48 | | |
| | | | | CLOTHIER, RETAIL | .54 | BUS ACCT AND FIN | .47 | | |
| | | | | INSURANCE AGENT | .52 | PHYSICAL EDUC | .47 | | |
| | | | | SALES ENG,HT/AIR | .51 | | | M .43 S .50 | |
| | | | | PHARMACEUT SALES | .50 | MILITARY CADET | .44 | MBI .17 F .48 |
| | | | | BANKER | .49 | ECONOMICS | .42 | | |
| | | | | REAL ESTATE AGT | .47 | ENGINEERING,MECH | .41 | W .26 D .31 |
| | | | | AGCT,CERT PUBLIC | .46 | AIR FORCE CADET | .41 | | |
| | | | | BRICKLAYER | .46 | ELEMENTARY EDUC | .40 | WBI .19 MO .28 |
| | | | | | | ENGINEERNG,CIVIL | .40 | | |

Figure 5.2. James's KOIS profile. (From *Kuder Occupational Interest Survey — Form DD* by G. Frederic Kuder. Copyright © 1965, 1968, 1970, Science Research Associates, Inc. Reproduced by permission of the publisher.)

128

Kathleen's profile is just as clear-cut as James's, but appears to give a good deal more information because she is scored for some occupations also scored for men (see Fig. 5.3). There can be no doubt that Kathleen's interests are oriented toward health or medical occupations. That she has higher scores on occupational or physical therapist, nurse, and X-ray technician than she has on dentist, pediatrician, physician, and psychiatrist suggests too that she might be more satisfied in a four-year or shorter curriculum of study. Notice that on the men's college major scales she scores highest on architecture, physical science, and engineering, but also that their lambda coefficients are 39 or lower. These are her high scores be-

**Report of Scores** — **Kuder Occupational Interest Survey** (Form DD)

NAME KATHLEEN  LOCATION  000-38648  DATE OF SURVEY 02-01-71

**OCCUPATIONAL SCALES, WOMEN**

| Scale | λ | Scale | λ |
|---|---|---|---|
| Accountant | .34 | Nurse | .52 |
| Bank Clerk | .39 | Nutritionist | .40 |
| Beautician | .41 | Occupational Therapist | .57 |
| Bookkeeper | .40 | Office Clerk | .40 |
| Bookstore Manager | .38 | Physical Therapist | .54 |
| Computer Programmer | .49 | Primary School Teacher | .43 |
| Counselor, High School | .37 | Psychologist | .45 |
| Dean of Women | .38 | Psychologist, Clinical | .44 |
| Dental Assistant | .45 | Religious Education Director | .41 |
| Department Store Saleswoman | .34 | Science Teacher, High School | .39 |
| Dietitian, Administrative | .43 | Secretary | .41 |
| Dietitian, Public School | .41 | Social Caseworker | .43 |
| Florist | .45 | Social Worker, Group | .42 |
| Home Demonstration Agent | .44 | Social Worker, Medical | .41 |
| Home Ec Teacher, College | .39 | Social Worker, Psychiatric | .42 |
| Interior Decorator | .32 | Social Worker, School | .42 |
| Lawyer | .27 | Stenographer | .41 |
| Librarian | .37 | X-Ray Technician | .51 |
| Math Teacher, High School | .39 | | |

**COLLEGE MAJOR SCALES, WOMEN**

| Scale | λ | Scale | λ |
|---|---|---|---|
| Art & Art Education | .48 | History | .40 |
| Biological Sciences | .54 | Home Economics Education | .53 |
| Business Ed & Commerce | .41 | Mathematics | .55 |
| Drama | .37 | Music & Music Education | .46 |
| Elementary Education | .48 | Nursing | .54 |
| English | .39 | Physical Education | .56 |
| Foreign Languages | .47 | Political Science | .33 |
| General Social Sciences | .48 | Psychology | .51 |
| Health Professions | .58 | Sociology | .45 |
| | | Teaching Sister, Catholic | .50 |

**OCCUPATIONAL SCALES, MEN**

| Scale | λ | Scale | λ | Scale | λ | Scale | λ |
|---|---|---|---|---|---|---|---|
| Acc't, Certified Public | | Engineer, Electrical | | Optometrist | .39 | Psychology Professor | .36 |
| Architect | .32 | Engineer, Heating/Air Cond. | | Osteopath | | Radio Station Manager | .35 |
| Automobile Mechanic | | Engineer, Industrial | | Painter, House | | Real Estate Agent | .24 |
| Automobile Salesman | | Engineer, Mechanical | | Pediatrician | .42 | Sales Eng, Heating/Air Cond. | .39 |
| Banker | | Engineer, Mining & Metal | | Personnel Manager | .27 | Science Teacher, High School | |
| Bookkeeper | | Farmer | | Pharmaceutical Salesman | | School Superintendent | |
| Bookstore Manager | | Florist | | Pharmacist | .37 | Social Caseworker | |
| Bricklayer | | Forester | | Photographer | .36 | Social Worker, Group | |
| Building Contractor | .25 | Insurance Agent | .25 | Physical Therapist | | Social Worker, Psychiatric | |
| Buyer | | Interior Decorator | | Physician | .41 | Statistician | .30 |
| Carpenter | | Journalist | .28 | Plumber | | Supv/Foreman, Industrial | |
| Chemist | .32 | Lawyer | | Plumbing Contractor | | Travel Agent | .25 |
| Clothier, Retail | | Librarian | | Podiatrist | | Truck Driver | |
| Computer Programmer | | Machinist | | Policeman | | Television Repairman | |
| Counselor, High School | | Mathematician | .36 | Postal Clerk | | University Pastor | |
| County Agricultural Agent | | Math Teacher, High School | | Printer | | Veterinarian | .37 |
| Dentist | .44 | Meteorologist | | Psychiatrist | .40 | Welder | |
| Electrician | | Minister | | Psychologist, Clinical | | X-Ray Technician | |
| Engineer, Civil | .33 | Nurseryman | | Psychologist, Counseling | | YMCA Secretary | |
| | | | | Psychologist, Industrial | | | |

**COLLEGE MAJOR SCALES, MEN**

| Scale | λ | Scale | λ |
|---|---|---|---|
| Agriculture | | Foreign Languages | |
| Animal Husbandry | | Forestry | |
| Architecture | .39 | History | |
| Art & Art Education | | Law (Grad School) | |
| Biological Sciences | | Mathematics | |
| Business Acc't & Finance | | Music & Music Ed | |
| Business & Marketing | | Physical Education | |
| Business Management | | Physical Sciences | .38 |
| Economics | .25 | Political Science & Gov't | |
| Elementary Education | | Premed, Pharm & Dentistry | |
| Engineering, Chemical | .34 | Psychology | |
| Engineering, Civil | .39 | Sociology | |
| Engineering, Electrical | .39 | U.S. Air Force Cadet | |
| Engineering, Mechanical | .39 | U.S. Military Cadet | |
| English | | | |

**Summary of high scores**

| OCCUPATIONAL SCALES WOMEN | Score | COLLEGE MAJOR SCALES WOMEN | Score | OCCUPATIONAL SCALES MEN | Score | COLLEGE MAJOR SCALES MEN | Score |
|---|---|---|---|---|---|---|---|
| OCCUPA THERAPIST | .57 | HEALTH PROFES | .58 | DENTIST | .44 | ARCHITECTURE | .39 |
| PHYS THERAPIST | .54 | PHYSICAL EDUC | .56 | PEDIATRICIAN | .42 | ENGINEERNG,CIVIL | .39 |
| NURSE | .52 | MATHEMATICS | .55 | PHYSICIAN | .41 | ENGINEERING,ELEC | .39 |
| X-RAY TECHNICIAN | .51 | BIOLOGICAL SCI | .54 | PSYCHIATRIST | .40 | ENGINEERING,MECH | .39 |
| COMPUTR PROGRAMR | .49 | NURSING | .54 | OPTOMETRIST | .39 | PHYSICAL SCIENCE | .38 |
| DENTAL ASSISTANT | .45 | | | PHARMACIST | .37 | AGRICULTURE | .35 |
| FLORIST | .45 | | | VETERINARIAN | .37 | ENGINEERING,CHEM | .34 |
| PSYCHOLOGIST | .45 | | | MATHEMATICIAN | .36 | ECONOMICS | .25 |
| HOME DEMO AGENT | .44 | | | PHOTOGRAPHER | .36 | | |
| PSYCH, CLINICAL | .44 | | | PSYCHOLGY PROF | .36 | | |

V 58

| | | | |
|---|---|---|---|
| M | .37 | S | .42 |
| MBI | -.03 | F | .34 |
| W | .46 | D | .50 |
| WBI | .02 | MO | .43 |

Figure 5.3. Kathleen's KOIS profile. (From *Kuder Occupational Interest Survey — Form DD* by G. Frederic Kuder. Copyright © 1965, 1968, 1970, Science Research Associates, Inc. Reproduced by permission of the publisher.)

cause they are most similar to the interests that she expresses, but they are not similar enough to make her really like anyone in those fields. Since she has a clear pattern of interests elsewhere on her profile, the men's college major scores should be ignored. Her lowest scores are in business and selling occupations. Kathy has a good grasp of the import of her interests, for she wants to be a nurse or a physical therapist.

Three years before taking the KOIS, Steve flunked out of his aeronautical engineering course and went into the army to "find himself." He topped most of the routine college ability tests, and there were semesters when he earned almost all A's, but others when he received all F's. In the army he was trained to be a meteorologist, and he became friends with a young man who had a bachelor's degree in economics. On getting out of the army, he decided to return to school and major in economics. As a condition of his readmission, he was required to be tested and inventoried as to his interests.

Steve's scores are not very high on the average, showing that his occupational interests are still not well crystallized; he has few interests similar to those of people in occupations and yet distinct from those of people-in-general (see Fig. 5.4). Nevertheless, engineering is not among his high scores. The mathematical content of his previous major and perhaps his work in meteorology seem to express themselves in his similarities with computer programmers, mathematicians, and statisticians, plus some occupations in the physical sciences. The remaining ranks in the occupations and the college majors in general seem to compose a kind of Mulligan stew of interests. It is significant that economics is not among the top ten ranks. This is a dilemma to a counselor: expressed interests at variance with measured interests. Which should be given greater weight as being more valid? There is no general agreement on this question, but expressed interests should not be overlooked. Steve might be encouraged to explore his expressed interests early in his choice of courses, and possibly take courses to confirm or disconfirm his measured interests, and to be alert to shift his emphasis if he feels from his experience that one field of interest would be preferable to another. Opposition to his choice of economics as a major is not necessarily called for since there is a role in the field, econometrics, which is congruent with his measured interests, shown by the profile. One may conclude from this discussion that results from the interest profile are not necessarily more valid than expressed interests, and certainly that no final and irreversible decisions should be made from them.

Shellie came to a university counseling service because she felt she was pushing too hard for a goal, medicine, of which she wasn't sure. Her KOIS profile is marked by the variety of her occupational similarities and by her scores on the women's scales, which are at the same level as her scores on the men's scales (see Fig. 5.5). Her scores on medical and biological sciences, occupations with art content, verbal occupations (law, drama), and numerical work are all at approximately equivalent levels. Since each of these is virtually mutually exclusive, it will be necessary for her to pursue only one and drop serious pursuit of the rest. It is interesting to conjecture

# Report of Scores    *Kuder Occupational Interest Survey*    (Form DD)

NAME STEVE    LOCATION    000-38752    DATE OF SURVEY 06-03-71

**OCCUPATIONAL SCALES, WOMEN**

| (col 1) | (col 2) |
|---|---|
| Accountant | Nurse |
| Bank Clerk | Nutritionist |
| Beautician | Occupational Therapist |
| Bookkeeper | Office Clerk |
| Bookstore Manager | Physical Therapist |
| Computer Programmer | Primary School Teacher |
| Counselor, High School | Psychologist |
| Dean of Women | Psychologist, Clinical |
| Dental Assistant | Religious Education Director |
| Department Store Saleswoman | Science Teacher, High School |
| Dietitian, Administrative | Secretary |
| Dietitian, Public School | Social Caseworker |
| Florist | Social Worker, Group |
| Home Demonstration Agent | Social Worker, Medical |
| Home Ec Teacher, College | Social Worker, Psychiatric |
| Interior Decorator | Social Worker, School |
| Lawyer | Stenographer |
| Librarian | X-Ray Technician |
| Math Teacher, High School | |

**COLLEGE MAJOR SCALES, WOMEN**

Art & Art Education; Biological Sciences; Business Ed & Commerce; Drama; Elementary Education; English; Foreign Languages; General Social Sciences; Health Professions; History; Home Economics Education; Mathematics; Music & Music Education; Nursing; Physical Education; Political Science; Psychology; Sociology; Teaching Sister, Catholic

**OCCUPATIONAL SCALES, MEN**

| Occupation | Score | Occupation | Score | Occupation | Score | Occupation | Score |
|---|---|---|---|---|---|---|---|
| Acc't, Certified Public | .28 | Engineer, Electrical | .37 | Optometrist | .34 | Psychology Professor | .40 |
| Architect | .40 | Engineer, Heating/Air Cond. | .36 | Osteopath | .33 | Radio Station Manager | .33 |
| Automobile Mechanic | .24 | Engineer, Industrial | .32 | Painter, House | .26 | Real Estate Agent | .26 |
| Automobile Salesman | .18 | Engineer, Mechanical | .38 | Pediatrician | .38 | Sales Eng, Heating/Air Cond | .29 |
| Banker | .24 | Engineer, Mining & Metal | .37 | Personnel Manager | .22 | Science Teacher, High School | .37 |
| Bookkeeper | .27 | Farmer | .22 | Pharmaceutical Salesman | .22 | School Superintendent | .24 |
| Bookstore Manager | .38 | Florist | .31 | Pharmacist | .31 | Social Caseworker | .24 |
| Bricklayer | .24 | Forester | .36 | Photographer | .38 | Social Worker, Group | .21 |
| Building Contractor | .29 | Insurance Agent | .23 | Physical Therapist | .31 | Social Worker, Psychiatric | .27 |
| Buyer | .27 | Interior Decorator | .31 | Physician | .31 | Statistician | .41 |
| Carpenter | .22 | Journalist | .38 | Plumber | .26 | Supv/Foreman, Industrial | .24 |
| Chemist | .42 | Lawyer | .29 | Plumbing Contractor | .27 | Travel Agent | .26 |
| Clothier, Retail | .24 | Librarian | .36 | Podiatrist | .26 | Truck Driver | .21 |
| Computer Programmer | .47 | Machinist | .25 | Policeman | .23 | Television Repairman | .33 |
| Counselor, High School | .28 | Mathematician | .43 | Postal Clerk | .27 | University Pastor | .24 |
| County Agricultural Agent | .29 | Math Teacher, High School | .34 | Printer | .40 | Veterinarian | .30 |
| Dentist | .35 | Meteorologist | .36 | Psychiatrist | .36 | Welder | .25 |
| Electrician | .27 | Minister | .24 | Psychologist, Clinical | .38 | X-Ray Technician | .33 |
| Engineer, Civil | .36 | Nurseryman | .36 | Psychologist, Counseling | .34 | YMCA Secretary | .18 |
| | | | | Psychologist, Industrial | .33 | | |

**COLLEGE MAJOR SCALES, MEN**

| Major | Score | Major | Score |
|---|---|---|---|
| Agriculture | .33 | Foreign Languages | .39 |
| Animal Husbandry | .35 | Forestry | .40 |
| Architecture | .42 | History | .28 |
| Art & Art Education | .46 | Law (Grad School) | .30 |
| Biological Sciences | .42 | Mathematics | .42 |
| Business Acc't & Finance | .30 | Music & Music Ed | .38 |
| Business & Marketing | .29 | Physical Education | .27 |
| Business Management | .28 | Physical Sciences | .47 |
| Economics | .30 | Political Science & Gov't | .27 |
| Elementary Education | .35 | Premed, Pharm & Dentistry | .36 |
| Engineering, Chemical | .37 | Psychology | .41 |
| Engineering, Civil | .34 | Sociology | .34 |
| Engineering, Electrical | .42 | U.S. Air Force Cadet | .35 |
| Engineering, Mechanical | .37 | U.S. Military Cadet | .28 |
| English | .41 | | |

**Summary**

| OCCUPATIONAL SCALES WOMEN | | COLLEGE MAJOR SCALES WOMEN | | OCCUPATIONAL SCALES MEN | | COLLEGE MAJOR SCALES MEN | |
|---|---|---|---|---|---|---|---|
| Title | Score | Title | Score | Title | Score | Title | Score |
| | | | | COMPUTR PROGRAMR | .47 | PHYSICAL SCIENCE | .47 |
| | | | | MATHEMATICIAN | .43 | ART AND ART EDUC | .46 |
| | | | | CHEMIST | .42 | ARCHITECTURE | .42 |
| | | | | STATISTICIAN | .41 | BIOLOGICAL SCI | .42 |
| | | | | | | ENGINEERING,ELEC | .42 |
| | | | | ARCHITECT | .40 | MATHEMATICS | .42 |
| | | | | PRINTER | .40 | ENGLISH | .41 |
| | | | | PSYCHOLOGY PROF | .40 | PSYCHOLOGY | .41 |
| | | | | BOOKSTOR MANAGER | .38 | | |
| | | | | ENGINEER, MECH | .38 | FORESTRY | .40 |
| | | | | JOURNALIST | .38 | FOREIGN LANGUAGE | .39 |

V 51

| | | | |
|---|---|---|---|
| M | .34 | S | .33 |
| MBI | .09 | F | .29 |
| W | .33 | D | .24 |
| WBI | .11 | MO | .27 |

Figure 5.4. Steve's KOIS profile. (From *Kuder Occupational Interest Survey — Form DD* by G. Frederic Kuder. Copyright © 1965, 1968, 1970, Science Research Associates, Inc. Reproduced by permission of the publisher.)

131

about some of Shellie's experimental scale scores relative to her profile. Her WBI and W scores are very close, suggesting that she reveals a strong need to convey the best possible image of herself. There are other bits of evidence from her contact with the counselor that this is so. She also seemed to identify more strongly than is usual with her father, which might account for the closeness of her scores on the M and W or S and D scales. All in all, Shellie's complex profile reveals a complex person, probably one who is trying rather hard at this time to establish a comfortable concept of herself.

The evidence from her profile convinced Shellie that it was all right to

## Report of Scores — Kuder Occupational Interest Survey (Form DD)

NAME SHELLIE LOCATION 000-38654 DATE OF SURVEY 02-08-71

### Occupational Scales, Women

| Title | Score | Title | Score |
|---|---|---|---|
| Accountant | .32 | Nurse | .36 |
| Bank Clerk | .26 | Nutritionist | .38 |
| Beautician | .33 | Occupational Therapist | .42 |
| Bookkeeper | .25 | Office Clerk | .27 |
| Bookstore Manager | .40 | Physical Therapist | .49 |
| Computer Programmer | .49 | Primary School Teacher | .33 |
| Counselor, High School | .31 | Psychologist | .43 |
| Dean of Women | .36 | Psychologist, Clinical | .44 |
| Dental Assistant | .37 | Religious Education Director | .32 |
| Department Store Saleswoman | .24 | Science Teacher, High School | .36 |
| Dietitian, Administrative | .38 | Secretary | .35 |
| Dietitian, Public School | .34 | Social Caseworker | .40 |
| Florist | .39 | Social Worker, Group | .38 |
| Home Demonstration Agent | .30 | Social Worker, Medical | .41 |
| Home Ec Teacher, College | .33 | Social Worker, Psychiatric | .44 |
| Interior Decorator | .46 | Social Worker, School | .38 |
| Lawyer | .44 | Stenographer | .31 |
| Librarian | .33 | X-Ray Technician | .38 |
| Math Teacher, High School | .24 | | |

### College Major Scales, Women

| Title | Score |
|---|---|
| Art & Art Education | .53 |
| Biological Sciences | .55 |
| Business Ed & Commerce | .41 |
| Drama | .54 |
| Elementary Education | .48 |
| English | .49 |
| Foreign Languages | .55 |
| General Social Sciences | .52 |
| Health Professions | .49 |
| History | .55 |
| Home Economics Education | .46 |
| Mathematics | .47 |
| Music & Music Education | .49 |
| Nursing | .43 |
| Physical Education | .48 |
| Political Science | .55 |
| Psychology | .54 |
| Sociology | .45 |
| Teaching Sister, Catholic | .33 |

### Occupational Scales, Men

| Title | Score | Title | Score |
|---|---|---|---|
| Acc't, Certified Public | .44 | Optometrist | .44 |
| Architect | .44 | Osteopath | |
| Automobile Mechanic | | Painter, House | |
| Automobile Salesman | .54 | Pediatrician | .45 |
| Banker | | Personnel Manager | .33 |
| Bookkeeper | | Pharmaceutical Salesman | |
| Bookstore Manager | | Pharmacist | .35 |
| Bricklayer | | Photographer | .47 |
| Building Contractor | | Physical Therapist | |
| Buyer | .28 | Physician | .37 |
| Carpenter | | Plumber | |
| Chemist | .38 | Plumbing Contractor | |
| Clothier, Retail | | Podiatrist | |
| Computer Programmer | | Policeman | |
| Counselor, High School | | Postal Clerk | |
| County Agricultural Agent | | Printer | |
| Dentist | .42 | Psychiatrist | .45 |
| Electrician | | Psychologist, Clinical | |
| Engineer, Civil | .32 | Psychologist, Counseling | |
| Engineer, Electrical | | Psychologist, Industrial | |
| Engineer, Heating/Air Cond. | | Psychology Professor | .34 |
| Engineer, Industrial | | Radio Station Manager | |
| Engineer, Mechanical | | Real Estate Agent | .30 |
| Engineer, Mining & Metal | | Sales Eng, Heating/Air Cond. | |
| Farmer | | Science Teacher, High School | |
| Florist | | School Superintendent | |
| Forester | | Social Caseworker | |
| Insurance Agent | .24 | Social Worker, Group | |
| Interior Decorator | | Social Worker, Psychiatric | |
| Journalist | .31 | Statistician | .38 |
| Lawyer | | Supv/Foreman, Industrial | |
| Librarian | | Travel Agent | .38 |
| Machinist | | Truck Driver | |
| Mathematician | .37 | Television Repairman | |
| Math Teacher, High School | | University Pastor | |
| Meteorologist | | Veterinarian | .35 |
| Minister | | Welder | |
| Nurseryman | | X-Ray Technician | |
| | | YMCA Secretary | |

### College Major Scales, Men

| Title | Score | Title | Score |
|---|---|---|---|
| Agriculture | .32 | Foreign Languages | |
| Animal Husbandry | | Forestry | |
| Architecture | .50 | History | |
| Art & Art Education | | Law (Grad School) | |
| Biological Sciences | | Mathematics | |
| Business Acc't & Finance | | Music & Music Ed | |
| Business & Marketing | | Physical Education | |
| Business Management | | Physical Sciences | .46 |
| Economics | .41 | Political Science & Gov't | .41 |
| Elementary Education | | Premed, Pharm & Dentistry | |
| Engineering, Chemical | .40 | Psychology | |
| Engineering, Civil | .37 | Sociology | |
| Engineering, Electrical | .37 | U.S. Air Force Cadet | |
| Engineering, Mechanical | .37 | U.S. Military Cadet | |
| English | | | |

### Ranked Summaries

**Occupational Scales, Women**

| Title | Score |
|---|---|
| COMPUTR PROGRAMR | .49 |
| PHYS THERAPIST | .49 |
| INTERIOR DECORAT | .46 |
| LAWYER | .44 |
| PSYCH, CLINICAL | .44 |
| SOC WRKER,PSYCH | .44 |
| PSYCHOLOGIST | .43 |
| OCCUPA THERAPIST | .42 |
| SOC WORKER,MEDIC | .41 |
| BOOKSTOR MANAGER | .40 |

**College Major Scales, Women**

| Title | Score |
|---|---|
| BIOLOGICAL SCI | .55 |
| FOREIGN LANGUAGE | .55 |
| HISTORY | .55 |
| POLITICAL SCIENC | .55 |
| DRAMA | .54 |

**Occupational Scales, Men**

| Title | Score |
|---|---|
| PHOTOGRAPHER | .47 |
| PEDIATRICIAN | .45 |
| PSYCHIATRIST | .45 |
| ARCHITECT | .44 |
| OPTOMETRIST | .44 |
| DENTIST | .42 |
| CHEMIST | .38 |
| STATISTICIAN | .38 |
| TRAVEL AGENT | .38 |
| MATHEMATICIAN | .37 |

**College Major Scales, Men**

| Title | Score |
|---|---|
| ARCHITECTURE | .50 |
| PHYSICAL SCIENCE | .46 |
| ECONOMICS | .41 |
| ENGINEERING,CHEM | .40 |
| ENGINEERNG,CIVIL | .37 |
| ENGINEERING,ELEC | .37 |
| ENGINEERING,MECH | .37 |
| AGRICULTURE | .32 |

V 48

| | | | |
|---|---|---|---|
| M | .30 | S | .38 |
| MBI | .30 | F | .31 |
| W | .38 | D | .44 |
| WBI | .32 | MO | .36 |

Figure 5.5. Shellie's KOIS profile. (From *Kuder Occupational Interest Survey — Form DD* by G. Frederic Kuder. Copyright © 1965, 1968, 1970, Science Research Associates, Inc. Reproduced by permission of the publisher.)

explore occupational possibilities other than medicine, and she began to seek information on other fields of medical service as well as on some of the additional areas reflected by her KOIS scores.

Although Don's profile is relatively simple to interpret, it illustrates a problem that some young people have to face (see Fig. 5.6). The highest scores appear quite clearly to contain an engineering and outdoor orientation. But the range of .06 from Don's highest score contains no fewer than twenty-five occupational scales, and almost half of the college major scales, which is more than most individuals can consider easily. Some young persons whose profiles turn out this way express considerable dis-

## Report of Scores — Kuder Occupational Interest Survey (Form DD)

NAME. DON — LOCATION — 000-38722 — DATE OF SURVEY 04-27-71

| OCCUPATIONAL SCALES WOMEN | | COLLEGE MAJOR SCALES, WOMEN |
|---|---|---|
| Accountant | Nurse | Art & Art Education |
| Bank Clerk | Nutritionist | Biological Sciences |
| Beautician | Occupational Therapist | Business Ed & Commerce |
| Bookkeeper | Office Clerk | Drama |
| Bookstore Manager | Physical Therapist | Elementary Education |
| Computer Programmer | Primary School Teacher | English |
| Counselor, High School | Psychologist | Foreign Languages |
| Dean of Women | Psychologist, Clinical | General Social Sciences |
| Dental Assistant | Religious Education Director | Health Professions |
| Department Store Saleswoman | Science Teacher, High School | History |
| Dietitian, Administrative | Secretary | Home Economics Education |
| Dietitian, Public School | Social Caseworker | Mathematics |
| Florist | Social Worker, Group | Music & Music Education |
| Home Demonstration Agent | Social Worker, Medical | Nursing |
| Home Ec Teacher, College | Social Worker, Psychiatric | Physical Education |
| Interior Decorator | Social Worker, School | Political Science |
| Lawyer | Stenographer | Psychology |
| Librarian | X-Ray Technician | Sociology |
| Math Teacher, High School | | Teaching Sister, Catholic |

| OCCUPATIONAL SCALES MEN | | | | Optometrist .53 | Psychology Professor .43 | COLLEGE MAJOR SCALES MEN | |
|---|---|---|---|---|---|---|---|
| Acc't, Certified Public .44 | Engineer, Electrical .54 | Osteopath .53 | Radio Station Manager .45 | Agriculture .50 | Foreign Languages .30 |
| Architect .45 | Engineer, Heating/Air Cond. .55 | Painter, House .47 | Real Estate Agent .46 | Animal Husbandry .50 | Forestry .55 |
| Automobile Mechanic .45 | Engineer, Industrial .53 | Pediatrician .48 | Sales Eng, Heating/Air Cond. .52 | Architecture .40 | History .31 |
| Automobile Salesman .43 | Engineer, Mechanical .55 | Personnel Manager .49 | Science Teacher, High School .50 | Art & Art Education .29 | Law (Grad School) .38 |
| Banker .46 | Engineer, Mining & Metal .54 | Pharmaceutical Salesman .51 | School Superintendent .48 | Biological Sciences .46 | Mathematics .45 |
| Bookkeeper .43 | Farmer .46 | Pharmacist .50 | Social Caseworker .41 | Business Acc't & Finance .40 | Music & Music Ed .39 |
| Bookstore Manager .43 | Florist .49 | Photographer .47 | Social Worker, Group .39 | Business & Marketing .40 | Physical Education .54 |
| Bricklayer .51 | Forester .54 | Physical Therapist .55 | Social Worker, Psychiatric .39 | Business Management .46 | Physical Sciences .47 |
| Building Contractor .53 | Insurance Agent .50 | Physician .50 | Statistician .40 | Economics .42 | Political Science & Gov't .32 |
| Buyer .49 | Interior Decorator .31 | Plumber .48 | Supv/Foreman, Industrial .49 | Elementary Education .49 | Premed, Pharm & Dentistry .47 |
| Carpenter .45 | Journalist .33 | Plumbing Contractor .53 | Travel Agent .46 | Engineering, Chemical .46 | Psychology .39 |
| Chemist | Lawyer .39 | Podiatrist .48 | Truck Driver .40 | Engineering, Civil .54 | Sociology .38 |
| Clothier, Retail .45 | Librarian .33 | Policeman .49 | Television Repairman .51 | Engineering, Electrical .54 | U.S. Air Force Cadet .50 |
| Computer Programmer .48 | Machinist .46 | Postal Clerk .45 | University Pastor .36 | Engineering, Mechanical .52 | U.S. Military Cadet .49 |
| Counselor, High School .48 | Mathematician .42 | Printer .43 | Veterinarian .53 | English .23 | |
| County Agricultural Agent .47 | Math Teacher, High School .49 | Psychiatrist .44 | Welder .47 | | |
| Dentist .54 | Meteorologist .51 | Psychologist, Clinical .41 | X-Ray Technician .54 | | |
| Electrician .48 | Minister .36 | Psychologist, Counseling .42 | YMCA Secretary .46 | | |
| Engineer, Civil .56 | Nurseryman .50 | Psychologist, Industrial .45 | | | |

| OCCUPATIONAL SCALES WOMEN | | COLLEGE MAJOR SCALES WOMEN | | OCCUPATIONAL SCALES MEN | | COLLEGE MAJOR SCALES MEN | |
|---|---|---|---|---|---|---|---|
| Title | Score | Title | Score | Title | Score | Title | Score |
| | | | | ENGINEER, CIVIL | .56 | FORESTRY | .55 |
| | | | | ENG, HEAT/AIR CON | .55 | ENGINEERNG, CIVIL | .54 |
| | | | | ENGINEER, MECH | .55 | ENGINEERING, ELEC | .54 |
| | | | | PHYS THERAPIST | .55 | PHYSICAL EDUC | .54 |
| | | | | DENTIST | .54 | ENGINEERING, MECH | .52 |
| | | | | ENGINEER, ELEC | .54 | AGRICULTURE | .50 |
| | | | | ENG, MINING/METAL | .54 | ANIMAL HUSBANDRY | .50 |
| | | | | FORESTER | .54 | ENGINEERING, CHEM | .50 |
| | | | | X-RAY TECHNICIAN | .54 | AIR FORCE CADET | .50 |
| | | | | BLDG CONTRACTOR | .53 | ELEMENTARY EDUC | .49 |

V __55

| | | | |
|---|---|---|---|
| M | .52 | S | .47 |
| MBI | .13 | F | .51 |
| W | .28 | D | .22 |
| WBI | .11 | MO | .23 |

Figure 5.6. Don's KOIS profile. (From *Kuder Occupational Interest Survey — Form DD* by G. Frederic Kuder. Copyright © 1965, 1968, 1970, Science Research Associates, Inc. Reproduced by permission of the publisher.)

133

appointment, even hostility toward the inventory. A response such as this suggests that the person was depending too exclusively on inventory data and too little on his own rational processes to make decisions regarding his future occupational life. Counseling with Don should emphasize the latter approach without downgrading the information gained from the KOIS.

The most obvious import of all Michael's KOIS scores is his similarity with those in occupations not requiring college training and his very low scores on the college major scales (see Fig. 5.7). He could be described as having a "masculine" profile; his interests center on mostly physical or

## Report of Scores — Kuder Occupational Interest Survey (Form DD)

NAME __MICHAEL__ LOCATION _____ 000-38718 DATE OF SURVEY 04-22-71

### OCCUPATIONAL SCALES, MEN

| Title | Score | Title | Score | Title | Score | Title | Score |
|---|---|---|---|---|---|---|---|
| Acc't, Certified Public | .20 | Engineer, Electrical | .35 | Optometrist | .21 | Psychology Professor | .15 |
| Architect | .18 | Engineer, Heating/Air Cond. | .33 | Osteopath | .21 | Radio Station Manager | .16 |
| Automobile Mechanic | .48 | Engineer, Industrial | .25 | Painter, House | .41 | Real Estate Agent | .25 |
| Automobile Salesman | .16 | Engineer, Mechanical | .32 | Pediatrician | .16 | Sales Eng, Heating/Air Cond | .25 |
| Banker | .38 | Engineer, Mining & Metal | .33 | Personnel Manager | .09 | Science Teacher, High School | .27 |
| Bookkeeper | .45 | Farmer | .42 | Pharmaceutical Salesman | .06 | School Superintendent | .22 |
| Bookstore Manager | .33 | Florist | .33 | Pharmacist | .29 | Social Caseworker | .02 |
| Bricklayer | .40 | Forester | .38 | Photographer | .18 | Social Worker, Group | -.02 |
| Building Contractor | .41 | Insurance Agent | .27 | Physical Therapist | .18 | Social Worker, Psychiatric | .00 |
| Buyer | .33 | Interior Decorator | .08 | Physician | .22 | Statistician | .22 |
| Carpenter | .45 | Journalist | .18 | Plumber | .48 | Supv/Foreman, Industrial | .40 |
| Chemist | .26 | Lawyer | .16 | Plumbing Contractor | .40 | Travel Agent | .17 |
| Clothier, Retail | .23 | Librarian | .17 | Podiatrist | .06 | Truck Driver | .38 |
| Computer Programmer | .31 | Machinist | .45 | Policeman | .33 | Television Repairman | .38 |
| Counselor, High School | .11 | Mathematician | .33 | Postal Clerk | .47 | University Pastor | -.08 |
| County Agricultural Agent | .32 | Math Teacher, High School | .40 | Printer | .37 | Veterinarian | .33 |
| Dentist | .28 | Meteorologist | .35 | Psychiatrist | .07 | Welder | .43 |
| Electrician | .46 | Minister | -.01 | Psychologist, Clinical | .04 | X-Ray Technician | .28 |
| Engineer, Civil | .36 | Nurseryman | .32 | Psychologist, Counseling | .04 | YMCA Secretary | .05 |
| | | | | Psychologist, Industrial | .07 | | |

### COLLEGE MAJOR SCALES, MEN

| Title | Score | Title | Score |
|---|---|---|---|
| Agriculture | .37 | Foreign Languages | .05 |
| Animal Husbandry | .35 | Forestry | .32 |
| Architecture | .11 | History | .01 |
| Art & Art Education | .05 | Law (Grad School) | .03 |
| Biological Sciences | .11 | Mathematics | .30 |
| Business Acc't & Finance | .28 | Music & Music Ed | .06 |
| Business & Marketing | .14 | Physical Education | .16 |
| Business Management | .16 | Physical Sciences | .23 |
| Economics | .13 | Political Science & Gov't | .04 |
| Elementary Education | .10 | Premed, Pharm & Dentistry | .09 |
| Engineering, Chemical | .24 | Psychology | .01 |
| Engineering, Civil | .34 | Sociology | .03 |
| Engineering, Electrical | .32 | U.S. Air Force Cadet | .14 |
| Engineering, Mechanical | .31 | U.S. Military Cadet | .12 |
| English | -.02 | | |

(Women occupational and college major scales shown but unscored.)

### OCCUPATIONAL SCALES, MEN (ranked)

| Title | Score |
|---|---|
| AUTO MECHANIC | .48 |
| PLUMBER | .48 |
| POSTAL CLERK | .47 |
| ELECTRICIAN | .46 |
| BOOKKEEPER | .45 |
| CARPENTER | .45 |
| MACHINIST | .45 |
| WELDER | .43 |
| FARMER | .42 |
| BLDG CONTRACTOR | .41 |

### COLLEGE MAJOR SCALES, MEN (ranked)

| Title | Score |
|---|---|
| AGRICULTURE | .37 |
| ANIMAL HUSBANDRY | .35 |
| ENGINEERNG,CIVIL | .34 |
| ENGINEERING,ELEC | .32 |
| FORESTRY | .32 |
| ENGINEERING,MECH | .31 |
| MATHEMATICS | .30 |
| BUS ACCT AND FIN | .28 |
| ENGINEERING,CHEM | .24 |
| PHYSICAL SCIENCE | .23 |

V 55

| M | .38 | S | .34 |
|---|---|---|---|
| MBI | -.34 | F | .32 |
| W | .19 | D | .01 |
| WBI | .33 | MO | .15 |

Figure 5.7. Michael's KOIS profile. (From *Kuder Occupational Interest Survey — Form DD* by G. Frederic Kuder. Copyright © 1965, 1968, 1970, Science Research Associates, Inc. Reproduced by permission of the publisher.)

134

mechanical work, out of doors, and when abstract or numerical, at a level performed by persons with no college training. It is interesting to note how low his score on the best impression scale is relative to his M score: no window dressing here, just his real self, take it or leave it. Michael's profile also shows a few negative scores. This is possible even with his high V score, reflecting almost nothing in common with persons in social welfare occupations. Clearly, the sooner Michael can get out of school and into the world working, the better he will like it.

It should be evident from both the discussion of the inventory and of the illustrative profiles that the use of the KOIS ought to be cautious or reserved. Such statements as "You ought to be a . . ." or "You'll regret it if you don't . . ." are too strong for what interest inventories yield. The KOIS is no exception.

Further, its unique solutions to some of the problems of interest measurement, such as the elicitation of preferences rather than of absolute likes and dislikes, the scoring of a broad range of occupations, and the use of the lambda coefficient and its attendant ranking procedure, require the user to be meticulous in its application and interpretation.

Still, for purposes of supplying alternatives to explore, of strengthening tentative choices, or of confirming plans already actualized, the KOIS is an excellent source.

## References

Campbell, D. P. *Handbook for the Strong Vocational Interest Blank*, Stanford: Stanford University Press, 1971.

Gribbons, W. D., and P. R. Lohnes. Career development from age 13 to age 25. Final Report of Project No. 6-2151, U.S. Department of Health, Education, and Welfare, Grant No. OEG-1-7-062151-0471, Office of Education, Bureau of Research, 1969.

Hornaday, J. A., and G. F. Kuder. A study of male occupational interest scales applied to women. *Educational and Psychological Measurement*, 1961, 19, 413–420.

Kuder, G. F. *Manual, Kuder (DD) Occupational Interest Survey*. Chicago: Science Research Associates, 1966.

———. A note on the comparability of occupational scores from different interest inventories. *Measurement and Evaluation in Guidance*, 1969, 2, 94–100.

Roe, A. *The psychology of occupations*. New York: Wiley, 1956.

Super, D. E. A theory of vocational development. *American Psychologist*, 1953, 8, 185–190.

Tyler, L. The development of "vocational interests": The organization of likes and dislikes in ten year old children. *Journal of Genetic Psychology*, 1955, 86, 33–44.

Wilson, R. N., and H. E. Kaiser. A comparison of similar scales on the SVIB and the Kuder, Form DD. *Journal of Counseling Psychology*, 1968, 15, 468–470.

Zytowski, D. G. Relationships of equivalent scales on three interest inventories. *Personnel and Guidance Journal*, 1968, 47, 44–49.

135

# 6

# The Minnesota
# Importance Questionnaire

David J. Weiss

THE MINNESOTA IMPORTANCE QUESTIONNAIRE (MIQ) was developed within the framework of the Theory of Work Adjustment (Dawis, England, and Lofquist, 1964; Dawis, Lofquist, and Weiss, 1968; Lofquist and Dawis, 1969) which is the major focus of research of the Work Adjustment Project at the University of Minnesota. The Work Adjustment Project derives from Viteles's early research in vocational psychology, which led to the development of the job psychograph, and from the later work of Paterson and his colleagues at the Minnesota Employment Stabilization Research Institute in the early 1930s. In more recent years, Work Adjustment Project research has been influenced primarily by the work of the British psychologists Alec Roger and Alistair Heron on job satisfaction and satisfactoriness, as well as by recent American research and theory relating to job satisfaction.

The Work Adjustment Project has been supported for over ten years by the Social and Rehabilitation Service (formerly the Vocational Rehabilitation Administration) of the United States Department of Health, Education, and Welfare. Its mission is to develop a psychology of work for the disabled individual, but its research also has implications for the vocational problems of persons who are not disabled. Since the MIQ derives directly from the Theory of Work Adjustment, comprehensive understanding of its development and use requires some explanation of this theory.

## THE THEORY OF WORK ADJUSTMENT

*Basic concepts.* The two major components of the Theory of Work Adjustment are the individual and the work environment. It is an interactionist theory in the sense that the individual and the environment can influence each other; the individual can change the environment and the environment can change the individual. It is both a stable and a dynamic theory. Using the theory and its instruments, a vocational counselor can predict an individual's probable work adjustment at some point in time. The theory can also help the counselor make predictions concerning how an individual might progress through a series of work environments, and how both he and the environment might change as a function of that sequence of events. The Theory of Work Adjustment deals with the style and the structure of the work personality. This includes the development and stability of the work personality and the effects on the work personality of changes in person, such as might occur when he becomes disabled. The theory also involves the effects on the work personality of alterations in the environment, such as those resulting from unemployment, job transfers, and changes in job duties.

Figure 6.1 is a schematic representation of the major components of

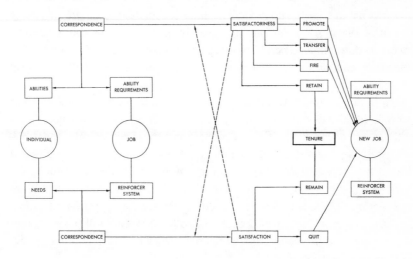

Figure 6.1. The Theory of Work Adjustment. (Reprinted from A theory of work adjustment (a revision), *Minnesota Studies in Vocational Rehabilitation*, 1968, 23, 12, copyright © 1968, University of Minnesota, by permission of the publisher and author.)

the Theory of Work Adjustment. The theory is an individual-environment matching model. Characteristics of the individual are matched with characteristics of occupational environments to predict adjustment in a given occupation.

The individual's work personality is defined by his abilities and his "needs." The MIQ is a measure of vocational needs. Needs are not the same as interests, but there is some relation between the two concepts (Thorndike, Weiss, and Dawis, 1968a, 1968b).

*Prediction of satisfactoriness.* An occupation can be described by its two major components: ability requirements and the reinforcer system. For the last thirty years, vocational psychologists have been concerned primarily with the prediction of satisfactoriness. To predict how an individual will perform in an occupation — what the Theory of Work Adjustment calls satisfactoriness — the counselor determines the correspondence between the individual's abilities and the ability requirements of the occupation. For example, the job of watchmaker demands that an individual have very fine finger dexterity. If an individual does not have this quality, he will probably not be satisfactory on that job. In contrast, the job of a high school mathematics teacher requires a certain level of mathematical ability. If the individual does not have that level of ability, he will not be satisfactory in that occupation. The man-job matching model originally operationalized by Viteles is used in matching abilities with ability requirements to determine some index of correspondence. From that match the counselor can predict satisfactoriness — how an individual will perform on a given job.

On the basis of satisfactoriness the counselor can also predict whether an individual will be promoted on that job. The individual who is very satisfactory — whose abilities are higher than those required by the job — will probably (everything else being equal) be promoted. The individual who is less satisfactory, but satisfactory enough to perform at minimally acceptable levels, will be retained on that job. The individual who is not satisfactory will be transferred or fired. In three cases (promotion, transfer, firing) the individual proceeds to another job that will have another set of ability requirements from which the theory assists in making predictions of satisfactoriness.

The prediction of satisfactoriness has been continually researched by vocational-industrial psychologists for over thirty years. An important contribution of the Work Adjustment Project is in the prediction of job

138

satisfaction, the other major indicator of work adjustment. The Theory of Work Adjustment applies the man-job matching model and specifies the variables that are relevant to the prediction of satisfaction in both the individual and his environment.

*Prediction of satisfaction.* Individuals can be differentiated by their "vocational needs," which are preferences for certain kinds of reinforcers, satisfiers, or rewards in occupations. For example, one individual might prefer a job in which he has the opportunity to be busy and to experience a feeling of achievement. Another person might prefer a job in which the primary rewards are suitable working conditions, security, and a good supervisor. These two individuals would differ, then, in their preferences for certain kinds of satisfiers, rewards, or reinforcers in the work environment and would be likely to be satisfied in different kinds of occupations.

Occupations can be described in terms of differential reinforcer systems. That is, some occupations provide opportunities for advancement; others do not. In some occupations an individual can be busy all the time; in others he is not. By matching the individual's needs with the reinforcer characteristics of an occupation — matching what the individual prefers with what the job offers — one can determine some measure of correspondence. It is from this measure of correspondence, according to the Theory of Work Adjustment, that an individual's satisfaction in an occupation can be predicted.

The Theory of Work Adjustment holds that occupational satisfaction is independent of satisfactoriness. Although both satisfaction and satisfactoriness are predictive of job tenure, only satisfaction can forecast whether an individual will voluntarily quit or remain on a job, other things being equal. If the individual quits, he will move to an occupation which has a different reinforcer system which can then be matched with his needs to predict his satisfaction and tenure in that occupation.

*Research on the Theory of Work Adjustment.* The research relevant to the Theory of Work Adjustment supports several of these hypotheses. First, satisfaction and satisfactoriness are linearly independent of each other (Weiss, Dawis, England, and Lofquist, 1966). An individual can be satisfied on a job and not be satisfactory; he can be satisfactory and not satisfied; or any number of possible combinations. Other recent data indicate that job satisfaction will predict tenure outcomes in terms of job turnover (Taylor and Weiss, 1969a, 1969b). Individuals who are satisfied are more likely to remain on the job; those who are not satisfied are more likely to leave the job. In addition, data show that correspondence between the individual's needs and the reinforcer systems of jobs will predict job satisfaction (Betz, 1968). Job satisfaction in turn predicts tenure. These data support two major propositions of the Theory of Work Adjustment.

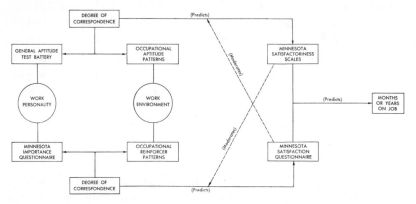

Figure 6.2. The Theory of Work Adjustment in operational terms. (Reprinted from A theory of work adjustment (a revision), *Minnesota Studies in Vocational Rehabilitation*, 1968, 23, 14, copyright © 1968, University of Minnesota, by permission of the publisher and author.)

Figure 6.2 specifies the instruments used to operationalize the Theory of Work Adjustment. To predict satisfactoriness the Work Adjustment Project has been using the General Aptitude Test Battery (GATB) and the Occupational Aptitude Patterns (OAPs) of the United States Employment Service. The correspondence between GATB scores and OAPs predicts scores on the Minnesota Satisfactoriness Scales (MSS), which measures several kinds of satisfactoriness — performance, conformance, dependability, and personal adjustment (Gibson, Weiss, Dawis, and Lofquist, 1970). The other side of the diagram illustrates that the MIQ is used to measure an individual's vocational needs. Occupational Reinforcer Patterns (ORPs) have been developed to measure the reinforcer characteristics of the job or work environment (Borgen, Weiss, Tinsley, Dawis, and Lofquist, 1968a, 1968b). The correspondence between the MIQ and the ORPs predicts scores on the Minnesota Satisfaction Questionnaire (Weiss, Dawis, Lofquist, and England, 1967), a measure of job satisfaction.

140

OCCUPATIONAL REINFORCER PATTERNS

As the Theory of Work Adjustment indicates, utilization of the MIQ in vocational counseling requires that there be information available on the reinforcer characteristics of work environments with which to match an individual's preferences. If a person prefers an occupation in which he can have a lot of activity, can the counselor find him a job in which he is likely to be busy all the time? If another person happens to want a job in which he can gain a feeling of achievement in his work, can the counselor help him to find a job which will meet his needs so that he can be satisfied in his job? The Occupational Reinforcer Patterns were designed to make this information readily available to vocational counselors (Borgen et al., 1968a, b).

*The Minnesota Job Description Questionnaire.* The following twenty-one statements constitute the Minnesota Job Description Questionnaire (MJDQ).[1] The first twenty of these scales parallel the scales included on the Minnesota Importance Questionnaire. This set of twenty variables originated from research on job satisfaction conducted by the Work Adjustment Project. It was reasoned that since it was possible to measure individual differences in job satisfaction in relation to such aspects of job environments as achievement, activity, advancement, and authority, it should be possible to (1) differentiate occupations on these variables, and (2) measure an individual's preferences for these variables. Then, by matching the individual's preferences with characteristics of the environment, it would be possible to predict job satisfaction. In this way, Work Adjustment Project research made its way back from job satisfaction through reinforcer patterns to vocational needs.

The MJDQ is administered to supervisors of occupations to determine how much of each of the twenty-one reinforcers that occupation provides. In essence, the supervisors are asked to do a "job analysis," but in a very structured fashion. The MJDQ is a multiple rank orders variation of a pair comparison instrument (Borgen et al., 1968b); the MIQ is also a pair comparison instrument. The same methodology is used to measure needs and reinforcer patterns in order to obtain comparable results for the scaling characteristics of the instruments.

*Scaling of Occupational Reinforcer Patterns.* In the MJDQ the twenty-

1. Minnesota Job Description Questionnaire, copyright © 1968, Vocational Psychology Research, University of Minnesota.

| Scale | Item |
|-------|------|
| 1. Ability utilization . . . . . . . . . . . . . | make use of their individual abilities |
| 2. Achievement . . . . . . . . . . . . . . | get a feeling of accomplishment |
| 3. Activity . . . . . . . . . . . . . . . . . . . | are busy all the time |
| 4. Advancement . . . . . . . . . . . . . . | have opportunities for advancement |
| 5. Authority . . . . . . . . . . . . . . . . . | tell other workers what to do |
| 6. Company policies and practices . . | have a company which administers its policies fairly |
| 7. Compensation . . . . . . . . . . . . . | are paid well in comparison with other workers |
| 8. Co-workers . . . . . . . . . . . . . . . | have co-workers who are easy to make friends with |
| 9. Creativity . . . . . . . . . . . . . . . . | try out their own ideas |
| 10. Independence . . . . . . . . . . . . . | do their work alone |
| 11. Moral values . . . . . . . . . . . . . . | do work without feeling that it is morally wrong |
| 12. Recognition . . . . . . . . . . . . . . | receive recognition for the work they do |
| 13. Responsibility . . . . . . . . . . . . . | make decisions on their own |
| 14. Security . . . . . . . . . . . . . . . . . | have steady employment |
| 15. Social service . . . . . . . . . . . . . | have work where they do things for other people |
| 16. Social status . . . . . . . . . . . . . | have the position of "somebody" in the community |
| 17. Supervision-human relations . . . . | have bosses who back up their men (with top management) |
| 18. Supervision-technical . . . . . . . . | have bosses who train their men well |
| 19. Variety . . . . . . . . . . . . . . . . . | have something different to do every day |
| 20. Working conditions . . . . . . . . . | have good working conditions |
| 21. Autonomy . . . . . . . . . . . . . . . | plan their work with little supervision |

one statements are organized into subsets of all the possible combinations of five statements. The supervisor is instructed to rank each block of five statements according to which characteristics are most and least descriptive of the job he supervises. The supervisor ranks each block of five separately; there are twenty-one such blocks of five statements. By means of a complete pair comparison scaling, the composite scale values indicate the relative distances between the twenty-one stimuli as distributed around an arbitrary zero point. To permit inter-job comparisons of reinforcer patterns and to interpret scale values in terms of an "absolute" or psychologically meaningful zero point, Gulliksen and Tucker's (1961) method was applied to the MJDQ. On the last page of the MJDQ, the supervisor is asked to indicate categorically whether or not each of the characteristics being scaled is descriptive of the job he is rating. These data then are scaled in the usual pair comparison model to yield a neutral or zero point. The last column in Table 6.1 shows the results of pair comparison scaling without the neutral point. Half of the unadjusted scale values are positive and half are negative; this is characteristic of pair comparison scaling. When the scale values are adjusted for the zero point, only six of the twenty-one scale values are below zero, as shown in the first column of Table 6.1. Scale values below the zero point are preceded by a minus sign; those above the zero point are positive.

Table 6.1. Occupational Reinforcer Pattern for Fire Fighter

| Scale | Adjusted Value | −1 SE | +1 SE | P | Q | Unadjusted Value |
|---|---|---|---|---|---|---|
| 1. Ability utilization ...... | .38 | .31 | .45 | .31 | 1.03 | −.04 |
| 2. Achievement .......... | 1.05 | .98 | 1.13 | .02 | 3.00 | .63 |
| 3. Activity .............. | −.55 | −.62 | −.48 | .94 | 1.53 | −.97 |
| 4. Advancement ......... | .83 | .76 | .90 | .02 | 2.26 | .41 |
| 5. Authority ............ | −.49 | −.56 | −.43 | .82 | 1.41 | −.91 |
| 6. Company policies ...... | .79 | .73 | .85 | .04 | 2.40 | .37 |
| 7. Compensation ......... | −.01 | −.10 | .09 | .67 | .01 | −.43 |
| 8. Co-workers ........... | .84 | .78 | .90 | .02 | 2.59 | .42 |
| 9. Creativity ............ | −.06 | −.11 | −.00 | .47 | .18 | −.48 |
| 10. Independence ......... | −.73 | −.81 | −.66 | .94 | 2.05 | −1.15 |
| 11. Moral values .......... | .76 | .65 | .86 | .04 | 1.59 | .34 |
| 12. Recognition .......... | .49 | .42 | .56 | .24 | 1.30 | .07 |
| 13. Responsibility ........ | .12 | .04 | .19 | .55 | .30 | −.30 |
| 14. Security .............. | 1.74 | 1.65 | 1.85 | 0.00 | 5.42 | 1.32 |
| 15. Social service ......... | 1.23 | 1.14 | 1.31 | 0.00 | 3.37 | .81 |
| 16. Social status ........... | .13 | .05 | .21 | .43 | .31 | −.29 |
| 17. Supervision-hum.-rel. ... | .80 | .75 | .85 | 0.00 | 2.67 | .38 |
| 18. Supervision-technical ... | .93 | .88 | .99 | .02 | 2.97 | .51 |
| 19. Variety .............. | .37 | .28 | .46 | .41 | .84 | −.05 |
| 20. Working conditions ..... | .69 | .59 | .79 | .20 | 1.50 | .27 |
| 21. Autonomy ............ | −.11 | −.19 | −.03 | .78 | .27 | −.53 |
| Adjusted neutral point ..... | 0.000 | −.038 | .038 | | | |
| Unadjusted neutral point ... | −.420 | −.459 | −.383 | | | |

For the occupation represented in Table 6.1 the most descriptive characteristic, as rated by a group of forty-nine supervisors, is security. Security is 1.74 standard deviations above the perceived zero point for that occupation. The next most descriptive characteristic is social service, which is 1.23 standard deviations above the rated zero point. Third highest is achievement. The occupation for which the adjusted scale value is shown in Table 6.1 is, therefore, characterized by security, social service, and achievement as defined by the twenty-one statements used in the MJDQ. The occupation is not characterized by independence, which is

## (N = 49 Supervisors)

O.A.P. = 10                                        1965 D.O.T. = 373.884

### Descriptive Characteristics

**Have steady employment**
**Do not do their work alone**
**Are not busy all the time**
Have work where they do things for other people
Get a feeling of accomplishment
Do not tell other workers what to do
Do not plan their work with little supervision
Are not paid well in comparison with other workers

### Occupations with Similar ORPs

None

Figure 6.3. Descriptive statements for fire fighter. (Reprinted from *Occupational Reinforcer Patterns*, rev. ed., vol. 1, p. 85, copyright © 1972, Vocational Psychology Research, University of Minnesota, by permission of the publisher and author.)

almost three-fourths of a standard deviation below the zero point; it is also not distinguished by activity or by authority.

To make it easier for counselors to use this type of occupational information the statistical statements given in Table 6.1 are converted into descriptive statements, as shown in Figure 6.3. This figure interprets the Occupational Reinforcer Pattern (ORP) for the job of fire fighter as rated by forty-nine supervisors in this occupation. What is *not* descriptive of this occupation? Activity — fire fighters are usually not busy all the time; authority — a fire fighter is someone who does not have much authority over other workers; independence — a fire fighter hardly ever works alone; and autonomy — he does not plan his work by himself. Thus the occupation of fire fighter can be described by reinforcers that can be used by counselors. Fire fighters have steady employment, they do not work alone, they are not busy all the time, they do work which helps other people, they can get a feeling of accomplishment out of their work, and so on. The bold-face statements in Figure 6.3 are highly descriptive characteristics; all the rest are moderately descriptive characteristics. A graphic presentation of the ORP for fire fighters is shown in Figure 6.4.

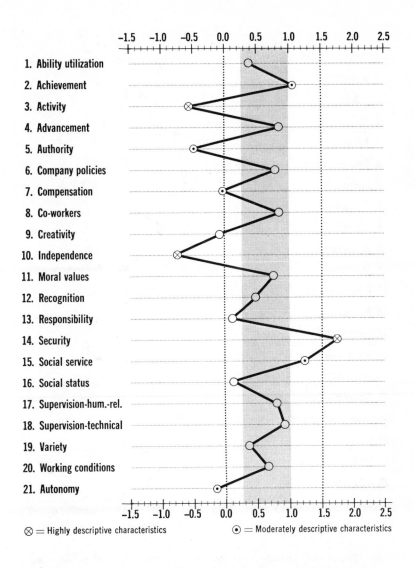

Figure 6.4. Occupational Reinforcer Pattern for fire fighter. (Reprinted from *Occupational Reinforcer Patterns*, rev. ed., vol. 1, p. 84, copyright © 1972, Vocational Psychology Research, University of Minnesota, by permission of the publisher and author.)

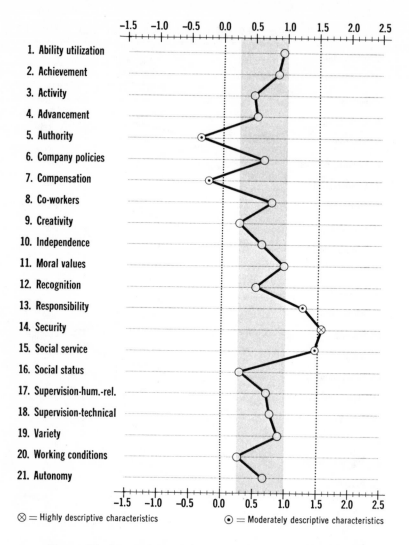

|  | -1.5 | -1.0 | -0.5 | 0.0 | 0.5 | 1.0 | 1.5 | 2.0 | 2.5 |
|---|---|---|---|---|---|---|---|---|---|

1. Ability utilization
2. Achievement
3. Activity
4. Advancement
5. Authority
6. Company policies
7. Compensation
8. Co-workers
9. Creativity
10. Independence
11. Moral values
12. Recognition
13. Responsibility
14. Security
15. Social service
16. Social status
17. Supervision-hum.-rel.
18. Supervision-technical
19. Variety
20. Working conditions
21. Autonomy

⊗ = Highly descriptive characteristics          ⊙ = Moderately descriptive characteristics

Figure 6.5. Occupational Reinforcer Pattern for policeman. (Reprinted from *Occupational Reinforcer Patterns*, rev. ed., vol. 1, p. 128, copyright © 1972, Vocational Psychology Research, University of Minnesota, by permission of the publisher and author.)

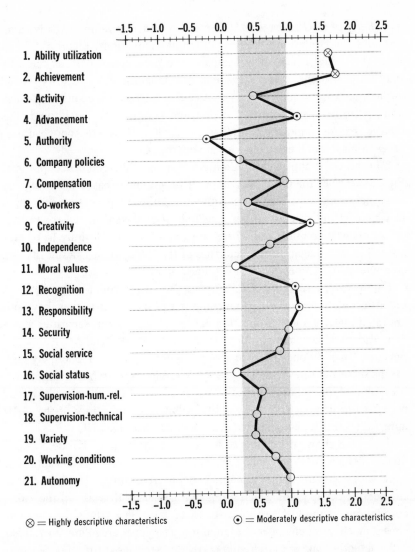

Figure 6.6. Occupational Reinforcer Pattern for computer programmer. (Reprinted from *Occupational Reinforcer Patterns*, rev. ed., vol. 1, p. 132, copyright © 1972, Vocational Psychology Research, University of Minnesota, by permission of the publisher and author.)

*Validity of ORPs.* If the MJDQ method of determining ORPs is valid, it should yield different ORPs for different occupations. Figure 6.5 illustrates the ORP profile for policeman. The policeman ORP, as rated by sixty-six police chiefs and sergeants, is characterized by security, social service, and responsibility. The negative characteristics are authority (they don't tell other *workers* what to do) and compensation. Although this ORP has some similarity to that of fire fighter, there are enough differences to show that the occupations are not the same.

Can the ORP approach differentiate among white-collar occupations? Figure 6.6 gives the ORP for computer programmer based on ratings by forty-eight supervisors of that occupation. Computer programmer is a job in which an individual can get a feeling of achievement, where he can utilize his best abilities, and where he can have an opportunity to be creative. The only negative characteristic of this occupation is authority — a computer programmer doesn't tell other workers what to do.

Figure 6.7 presents the ORP for another white-collar occupation. A securities salesman is similar to a computer programmer in that they both are rated high on ability utilization and achievement, but securities salesmen also consider compensation, social status, and social service of importance. In addition, variety and working conditions are moderately high for the securities salesman. These sample ORPs suggest that the approach is capable of differentiating specific occupations. But further analysis was necessary to demonstrate the validity, reliability, and utility of the ORP approach before it could be used in conjunction with the MIQ.

Figure 6.8 shows the results of a cluster analysis of eighty-one occupations for which ORPs are available. The analysis yielded nine clusters plus a group of occupations that remained unclustered. Cluster 1 includes three engineering occupations which grouped together on the basis of the intercorrelations of the ORP profiles for these jobs. The ORPs for civil engineer, mechanical engineer, and time study engineer are highly correlated with each other and are not highly correlated with those for other occupations. Cluster 2 comprises cost accountant, computer programmer, statistician, technical writer, and several other occupations. Although these clusters in some cases are not similar to what would be expected on the basis of other occupational taxonomies, there is little reason to expect that analogous clusters would result from grouping reinforcer patterns and other job characteristics.

A contrast of the two most different clusters is shown in Figure 6.9.

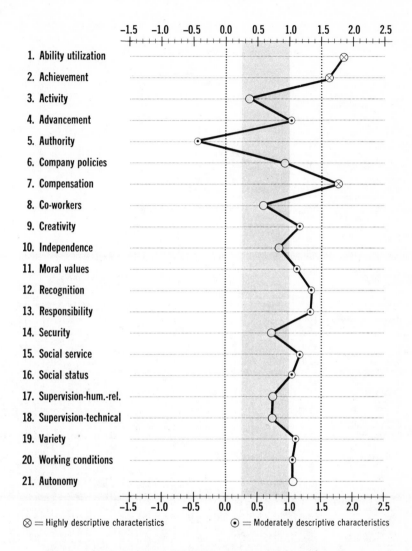

1. Ability utilization
2. Achievement
3. Activity
4. Advancement
5. Authority
6. Company policies
7. Compensation
8. Co-workers
9. Creativity
10. Independence
11. Moral values
12. Recognition
13. Responsibility
14. Security
15. Social service
16. Social status
17. Supervision-hum.-rel.
18. Supervision-technical
19. Variety
20. Working conditions
21. Autonomy

⊗ = Highly descriptive characteristics          ⊙ = Moderately descriptive characteristics

Figure 6.7. Occupational Reinforcer Pattern for securities salesman. (Reprinted from *Occupational Reinforcer Patterns*, rev. ed., vol. 1, p. 146, copyright © 1972, Vocational Psychology Research, University of Minnesota, by permission of the publisher and author.)

(Occupations are listed alphabetically within each cluster)

| | | | 1 | 2 | 3 | 4 | 5 | 6 | 7 | 8 | 9 | 10 | 11 | 12 | 13 | 14 | 15 | 16 | 17 | 18 | 19 | 20 | 21 | 22 | 23 | 24 | 25 | 26 | 27 | 28 | 29 | 30 | 31 | 32 | 33 | 34 | 35 | |
|---|---|---|---|---|---|---|---|---|---|---|---|---|---|---|---|---|---|---|---|---|---|---|---|---|---|---|---|---|---|---|---|---|---|---|---|---|---|---|
| C. 1 | Engineer, Civil | 1 | | | | | | | | | | | | | | | | | | | | | | | | | | | | | | | | | | | | |
| | Engineer, Mechanical | 2 | 89 | | | | | | | | | | | | | | | | | | | | | | | | | | | | | | | | | | | |
| | Engineer, Time Study | 3 | 81 | 84 | | | | | | | | | | | | | | | | | | | | | | | | | | | | | | | | | | |
| C. 2 | Accountant, Cost | 4 | 85 | 78 | 79 | | | | | | | | | | | | | | | | | | | | | | | | | | | | | | | | | |
| | Programmer (Business, Eng,&Sci) | 5 | 68 | 77 | 78 | 84 | | | | | | | | | | | | | | | | | | | | | | | | | | | | | | | | |
| | Statistician | 6 | 85 | 87 | 82 | 89 | 91 | | | | | | | | | | | | | | | | | | | | | | | | | | | | | | | |
| | Writer, Technical Publications | 7 | 82 | 82 | 80 | 92 | 91 | 92 | | | | | | | | | | | | | | | | | | | | | | | | | | | | | | |
| C. 3 | Beauty Operator | 8 | 50 | 55 | 68 | 60 | 77 | 81 | 74 | | | | | | | | | | | | | | | | | | | | | | | | | | | | | |
| | Salesman, Real Estate | 9 | 45 | 50 | 58 | 53 | 73 | 70 | 68 | 83 | | | | | | | | | | | | | | | | | | | | | | | | | | | | |
| | Salesman, Securities | 10 | 33 | 47 | 49 | 46 | 75 | 63 | 62 | 70 | 89 | | | | | | | | | | | | | | | | | | | | | | | | | | | |
| Cluster 4 | Caseworker | 11 | 62 | 50 | 59 | 66 | 65 | 74 | 72 | 81 | 77 | 60 | | | | | | | | | | | | | | | | | | | | | | | | | | |
| | Counselor, School | 12 | 59 | 49 | 48 | 49 | 55 | 69 | 56 | 75 | 72 | 51 | 80 | | | | | | | | | | | | | | | | | | | | | | | | | |
| | Counselor, Vocational Rehab. | 13 | 76 | 71 | 74 | 70 | 78 | 84 | 75 | 79 | 80 | 64 | 83 | 87 | | | | | | | | | | | | | | | | | | | | | | | | |
| | Instructor, Vocational School | 14 | 70 | 70 | 64 | 64 | 79 | 86 | 78 | 84 | 72 | 65 | 79 | 84 | 84 | | | | | | | | | | | | | | | | | | | | | | | |
| | Librarian | 15 | 70 | 56 | 52 | 69 | 59 | 78 | 72 | 74 | 63 | 42 | 84 | 85 | 76 | 79 | | | | | | | | | | | | | | | | | | | | | | |
| | Occupational Therapist | 16 | 77 | 77 | 64 | 64 | 66 | 86 | 74 | 76 | 66 | 49 | 78 | 86 | 84 | 89 | 88 | | | | | | | | | | | | | | | | | | | | | |
| | Physical Therapist | 17 | 67 | 61 | 54 | 67 | 65 | 82 | 71 | 76 | 57 | 40 | 75 | 81 | 72 | 86 | 94 | 90 | | | | | | | | | | | | | | | | | | | | |
| | Teacher, Elementary School | 18 | 69 | 62 | 61 | 59 | 66 | 79 | 71 | 83 | 71 | 53 | 88 | 93 | 87 | 93 | 84 | 91 | 84 | | | | | | | | | | | | | | | | | | | |
| | Teacher, Secondary School | 19 | 63 | 54 | 63 | 54 | 63 | 73 | 65 | 85 | 75 | 57 | 85 | 93 | 87 | 89 | 81 | 83 | 80 | 95 | | | | | | | | | | | | | | | | | | |
| Clus. 5 | Accounting Clerk, Civil Serv | 20 | 51 | 31 | 37 | 70 | 52 | 55 | 70 | 46 | 43 | 29 | 60 | 39 | 44 | 42 | 64 | 40 | 57 | 44 | 47 | | | | | | | | | | | | | | | | | |
| | Auto Service Station Attendant | 21 | 46 | 25 | 39 | 52 | 33 | 52 | 51 | 61 | 45 | 22 | 80 | 59 | 51 | 53 | 79 | 59 | 72 | 64 | 68 | 74 | | | | | | | | | | | | | | | | |
| | Clerk, General Office, C. S. | 22 | 26 | 01 | 18 | 43 | 19 | 29 | 40 | 40 | 22 | 01 | 59 | 34 | 25 | 27 | 59 | 28 | 50 | 40 | 44 | 84 | 87 | | | | | | | | | | | | | | | |
| | Stenographer, Technical, C. S. | 23 | 34 | 16 | 33 | 54 | 41 | 48 | 58 | 62 | 50 | 31 | 68 | 50 | 42 | 46 | 70 | 43 | 63 | 53 | 60 | 88 | 88 | 89 | | | | | | | | | | | | | | |
| | Typist, Civil Service | 24 | 27 | 06 | 24 | 48 | 31 | 38 | 45 | 51 | 43 | 22 | 68 | 49 | 41 | 36 | 70 | 39 | 60 | 47 | 54 | 80 | 89 | 87 | 93 | | | | | | | | | | | | | |
| Cluster 6 | Embalmer | 25 | 43 | 34 | 40 | 40 | 49 | 61 | 56 | 82 | 68 | 47 | 78 | 79 | 67 | 75 | 83 | 75 | 83 | 79 | 86 | 60 | 80 | 62 | 74 | 67 | | | | | | | | | | | | |
| | Medical Technologist | 26 | 44 | 25 | 32 | 48 | 41 | 51 | 58 | 59 | 50 | 30 | 66 | 53 | 46 | 51 | 73 | 54 | 67 | 56 | 63 | 84 | 81 | 84 | 84 | 76 | 83 | | | | | | | | | | | |
| | Nurse Aid | 27 | 11 | -06 | 01 | 26 | 19 | 27 | 35 | 50 | 37 | 19 | 59 | 40 | 21 | 39 | 65 | 38 | 61 | 45 | 46 | 68 | 79 | 82 | 80 | 79 | 75 | 80 | | | | | | | | | | |
| | Nurse, Licensed Practical | 28 | 33 | 18 | 12 | 35 | 31 | 46 | 46 | 58 | 47 | 29 | 71 | 60 | 40 | 61 | 80 | 64 | 79 | 65 | 62 | 63 | 80 | 71 | 70 | 69 | 84 | 81 | 92 | | | | | | | | | |
| | Orderly | 29 | 07 | -12 | 02 | 14 | 05 | 20 | 21 | 49 | 39 | 10 | 59 | 47 | 25 | 31 | 65 | 40 | 57 | 45 | 50 | 57 | 82 | 78 | 78 | 82 | 77 | 77 | 92 | 85 | | | | | | | | |
| | Radiologic Technologist | 30 | 46 | 30 | 32 | 46 | 41 | 57 | 55 | 70 | 50 | 26 | 71 | 72 | 55 | 66 | 87 | 70 | 86 | 72 | 75 | 70 | 83 | 76 | 79 | 73 | 93 | 89 | 84 | 90 | 83 | | | | | | | |
| | Waiter-Waitress | 31 | 25 | 11 | 23 | 41 | 32 | 42 | 50 | 57 | 56 | 37 | 61 | 40 | 31 | 38 | 68 | 44 | 59 | 41 | 46 | 77 | 79 | 77 | 86 | 81 | 73 | 85 | 87 | 79 | 87 | 78 | | | | | | |
| Clus. 7 | Carpenter | 32 | 35 | 42 | 35 | 55 | 52 | 48 | 64 | 44 | 52 | 53 | 53 | 20 | 32 | 43 | 41 | 36 | 37 | 38 | 28 | 53 | 39 | 36 | 47 | 36 | 29 | 36 | 48 | 43 | 29 | 31 | 54 | | | | | |
| | Heavy Equipment Operator | 33 | 38 | 48 | 46 | 64 | 62 | 57 | 69 | 49 | 69 | 64 | 54 | 25 | 42 | 40 | 44 | 41 | 39 | 35 | 28 | 53 | 34 | 28 | 44 | 38 | 29 | 36 | 38 | 36 | 27 | 28 | 59 | 89 | | | | |
| | Painter/Paperhanger | 34 | 26 | 24 | 26 | 52 | 43 | 41 | 56 | 45 | 56 | 48 | 61 | 28 | 33 | 36 | 50 | 34 | 42 | 38 | 34 | 68 | 59 | 58 | 67 | 64 | 42 | 52 | 67 | 57 | 55 | 45 | 72 | 92 | 86 | | | |
| | Pipefitter | 35 | 34 | 40 | 31 | 53 | 54 | 51 | 65 | 45 | 61 | 63 | 55 | 20 | 35 | 40 | 42 | 38 | 36 | 33 | 28 | 61 | 44 | 38 | 53 | 43 | 37 | 50 | 49 | 48 | 34 | 34 | 64 | 91 | 88 | 89 | | |
| | Plumber | 36 | 39 | 42 | 39 | 57 | 65 | 60 | 69 | 61 | 81 | 73 | 64 | 41 | 57 | 48 | 55 | 48 | 46 | 45 | 43 | 60 | 42 | 33 | 53 | 45 | 51 | 53 | 48 | 48 | 39 | 45 | 67 | 79 | 88 | 81 | 88 | |
| Cluster 8 | Accounting Clerk, Manufacturing | 37 | 38 | 20 | 40 | 58 | 38 | 40 | 60 | 46 | 41 | 26 | 59 | 22 | 30 | 29 | 52 | 27 | 42 | 33 | 39 | 88 | 77 | 86 | 87 | 80 | 53 | 78 | 71 | 55 | 64 | 61 | 82 | 63 | 59 | 76 | 65 | 59 |
| | Assembler (Electrical Equipment) | 38 | 02 | -08 | 03 | 27 | 14 | 08 | 35 | 18 | 19 | 16 | 27 | -11 | -06 | 03 | 15 | -07 | 06 | 03 | 05 | 70 | 45 | 66 | 67 | 52 | 23 | 53 | 60 | 37 | 44 | 31 | 65 | 70 | 55 | 75 | 70 | 53 |
| | Assembler-Small Parts | 39 | 33 | 24 | 28 | 51 | 35 | 36 | 58 | 35 | 33 | 26 | 44 | 08 | 17 | 27 | 37 | 20 | 32 | 25 | 24 | 80 | 59 | 68 | 73 | 58 | 37 | 61 | 63 | 48 | 48 | 45 | 71 | 79 | 65 | 82 | 79 | 61 |
| | Baker | 40 | 33 | 17 | 20 | 47 | 26 | 29 | 52 | 26 | 18 | 10 | 44 | 07 | 10 | 22 | 38 | 17 | 31 | 25 | 22 | 82 | 62 | 80 | 73 | 59 | 37 | 70 | 66 | 54 | 49 | 50 | 66 | 66 | 49 | 70 | 67 | 46 |
| | Marker | 41 | 34 | 15 | 25 | 53 | 34 | 33 | 55 | 31 | 34 | 19 | 53 | 13 | 23 | 24 | 40 | 20 | 32 | 27 | 25 | 84 | 64 | 75 | 73 | 67 | 36 | 62 | 66 | 52 | 54 | 46 | 72 | 73 | 65 | 82 | 73 | 62 |
| | Meat Cutter | 42 | 09 | -06 | -01 | 29 | 16 | 14 | 39 | 18 | 20 | 16 | 32 | -08 | -04 | 06 | 25 | 03 | 14 | 06 | 05 | 74 | 50 | 68 | 67 | 55 | 29 | 62 | 66 | 49 | 51 | 37 | 72 | 62 | 50 | 69 | 72 | 54 |
| | Production Helper (Food) | 43 | 43 | 30 | 36 | 59 | 35 | 46 | 61 | 41 | 37 | 21 | 56 | 20 | 26 | 29 | 55 | 36 | 48 | 32 | 33 | 86 | 78 | 81 | 82 | 73 | 52 | 77 | 72 | 63 | 64 | 61 | 84 | 68 | 64 | 79 | 75 | 62 |
| | Punch-Press Operator | 44 | 17 | 10 | 15 | 35 | 25 | 27 | 46 | 40 | 41 | 27 | 48 | 18 | 18 | 23 | 40 | 20 | 30 | 30 | 30 | 74 | 63 | 71 | 78 | 65 | 47 | 61 | 71 | 55 | 62 | 50 | 75 | 75 | 61 | 84 | 76 | 64 |
| | Sewing-Machine Opr., Automatic | 45 | 01 | -06 | 08 | 31 | 23 | 14 | 40 | 30 | 37 | 31 | 37 | 00 | 01 | 11 | 24 | 02 | 15 | 13 | 11 | 63 | 41 | 60 | 62 | 50 | 28 | 49 | 66 | 45 | 50 | 35 | 70 | 76 | 70 | 82 | 69 | 63 |
| Cluster 9 | Automobile-Body Repairman | 46 | 54 | 46 | 47 | 60 | 66 | 69 | 72 | 71 | 72 | 51 | 82 | 63 | 69 | 69 | 69 | 66 | 66 | 74 | 70 | 70 | 69 | 58 | 70 | 61 | 71 | 68 | 59 | 68 | 56 | 65 | 64 | 60 | 59 | 64 | 67 | 71 |
| | Automobile Mechanic | 47 | 48 | 33 | 41 | 57 | 55 | 64 | 65 | 73 | 71 | 49 | 85 | 69 | 65 | 68 | 74 | 63 | 70 | 76 | 75 | 74 | 81 | 70 | 80 | 72 | 79 | 73 | 71 | 76 | 69 | 75 | 74 | 59 | 57 | 70 | 62 | 68 |
| | Draftsman, Architectural | 48 | 57 | 57 | 64 | 71 | 67 | 67 | 81 | 70 | 51 | 45 | 66 | 39 | 53 | 62 | 58 | 52 | 57 | 60 | 59 | 70 | 61 | 61 | 68 | 52 | 57 | 63 | 53 | 49 | 37 | 59 | 56 | 76 | 62 | 70 | 68 | 61 |
| | Electrical Technician | 49 | 65 | 62 | 65 | 79 | 78 | 83 | 88 | 83 | 72 | 59 | 81 | 64 | 72 | 77 | 76 | 71 | 77 | 76 | 74 | 81 | 74 | 65 | 80 | 67 | 75 | 74 | 61 | 64 | 51 | 73 | 70 | 70 | 67 | 72 | 71 | 72 |
| | Electrician | 50 | 57 | 56 | 55 | 67 | 75 | 70 | 81 | 66 | 66 | 70 | 69 | 41 | 59 | 69 | 54 | 53 | 53 | 56 | 57 | 68 | 54 | 44 | 60 | 47 | 55 | 58 | 47 | 50 | 29 | 48 | 55 | 78 | 68 | 73 | 83 | 75 |
| | Electronics Mechanic | 51 | 59 | 49 | 56 | 71 | 61 | 66 | 76 | 65 | 54 | 40 | 72 | 47 | 58 | 59 | 63 | 50 | 61 | 61 | 61 | 82 | 74 | 72 | 80 | 64 | 63 | 68 | 58 | 55 | 48 | 64 | 64 | 71 | 60 | 72 | 67 | 64 |
| | Machinist | 52 | 58 | 52 | 61 | 77 | 68 | 66 | 82 | 59 | 52 | 42 | 60 | 29 | 51 | 47 | 50 | 39 | 47 | 45 | 46 | 84 | 60 | 63 | 74 | 57 | 49 | 63 | 46 | 40 | 33 | 49 | 60 | 70 | 66 | 69 | 72 | 69 |
| | Maintenance Man, Factory or Mill | 53 | 60 | 61 | 59 | 70 | 76 | 78 | 76 | 75 | 71 | 57 | 77 | 60 | 76 | 73 | 64 | 68 | 68 | 70 | 68 | 63 | 62 | 44 | 60 | 54 | 64 | 52 | 45 | 53 | 39 | 56 | 52 | 63 | 62 | 65 | 68 | 71 |
| | Office-Machine Serviceman | 54 | 60 | 50 | 56 | 69 | 67 | 70 | 77 | 67 | 60 | 45 | 75 | 53 | 65 | 62 | 66 | 57 | 64 | 63 | 67 | 84 | 75 | 70 | 80 | 66 | 72 | 77 | 54 | 58 | 48 | 67 | 64 | 53 | 51 | 58 | 63 | 64 |
| | Photoengraver (Stripper) | 55 | 55 | 61 | 60 | 69 | 76 | 75 | 82 | 72 | 74 | 59 | 64 | 47 | 65 | 60 | 58 | 58 | 58 | 57 | 56 | 70 | 51 | 44 | 64 | 48 | 60 | 58 | 42 | 45 | 36 | 53 | 61 | 68 | 74 | 65 | 74 | 82 |
| | Screw-Machine Opr., Production | 56 | 53 | 55 | 60 | 71 | 68 | 59 | 78 | 49 | 46 | 44 | 51 | 13 | 41 | 43 | 34 | 30 | 35 | 36 | 34 | 71 | 44 | 49 | 55 | 39 | 33 | 47 | 36 | 30 | 17 | 32 | 45 | 78 | 70 | 70 | 75 | 65 |
| | Sheet Metal Worker | 57 | 63 | 63 | 61 | 79 | 75 | 75 | 88 | 66 | 64 | 56 | 73 | 40 | 59 | 63 | 64 | 58 | 63 | 58 | 54 | 78 | 64 | 57 | 69 | 57 | 57 | 63 | 55 | 56 | 39 | 56 | 65 | 85 | 80 | 81 | 86 | 81 |
| | Television Service & Repairman | 58 | 59 | 48 | 58 | 64 | 68 | 73 | 78 | 84 | 79 | 58 | 88 | 72 | 75 | 79 | 79 | 71 | 76 | 81 | 83 | 73 | 77 | 65 | 79 | 66 | 84 | 77 | 68 | 73 | 64 | 80 | 74 | 65 | 61 | 69 | 65 | 75 |
| | Welder, Combination | 59 | 59 | 63 | 56 | 73 | 76 | 71 | 85 | 58 | 68 | 64 | 63 | 42 | 59 | 63 | 53 | 55 | 53 | 56 | 51 | 73 | 46 | 42 | 60 | 45 | 46 | 54 | 40 | 43 | 25 | 43 | 55 | 82 | 82 | 77 | 85 | 79 |
| Nonclustered Occupations | Airline Stewardess | 60 | 18 | 03 | 08 | 27 | 23 | 32 | 32 | 43 | 48 | 39 | 57 | 47 | 33 | 40 | 63 | 47 | 55 | 39 | 45 | 54 | 64 | 55 | 60 | 68 | 65 | 71 | 71 | 73 | 72 | 67 | 78 | 27 | 35 | 48 | 42 | 48 |
| | Bartender | 61 | 20 | 03 | 18 | 27 | 18 | 31 | 35 | 47 | 41 | 12 | 44 | 35 | 25 | 26 | 50 | 34 | 46 | 33 | 39 | 64 | 65 | 68 | 72 | 59 | 66 | 74 | 68 | 61 | 74 | 70 | 83 | 31 | 38 | 45 | 39 | 50 |
| | Bus Driver | 62 | -10 | -28 | 03 | 12 | 13 | 06 | 20 | 35 | 40 | 26 | 36 | 10 | 08 | 05 | 27 | -02 | 18 | 07 | 22 | 59 | 53 | 65 | 67 | 62 | 50 | 65 | 68 | 48 | 68 | 50 | 79 | 32 | 38 | 51 | 42 | 53 |
| | Cashier | 63 | -05 | -27 | -13 | 21 | 02 | 04 | 23 | 18 | 21 | 07 | 34 | 05 | -05 | -01 | 36 | 01 | 22 | 05 | 08 | 72 | 59 | 78 | 76 | 74 | 38 | 66 | 79 | 58 | 73 | 51 | 84 | 47 | 45 | 67 | 54 | 50 |
| | Claim Adjuster | 64 | 64 | 56 | 74 | 71 | 73 | 74 | 75 | 77 | 79 | 63 | 81 | 66 | 84 | 66 | 65 | 60 | 59 | 69 | 76 | 64 | 65 | 48 | 66 | 58 | 67 | 58 | 34 | 38 | 37 | 55 | 53 | 50 | 56 | 54 | 54 | 70 |
| | Claim Examiner | 65 | 77 | 59 | 70 | 72 | 48 | 63 | 68 | 47 | 42 | 19 | 59 | 44 | 60 | 44 | 63 | 54 | 55 | 48 | 51 | 66 | 63 | 54 | 58 | 49 | 49 | 61 | 30 | 33 | 34 | 55 | 52 | 40 | 44 | 40 | 40 | 50 |
| | Commercial Artist, Illustrating | 66 | 57 | 75 | 74 | 71 | 89 | 82 | 82 | 79 | 75 | 74 | 64 | 56 | 75 | 76 | 51 | 64 | 58 | 68 | 65 | 41 | 34 | 15 | 42 | 29 | 48 | 28 | 15 | 24 | 07 | 34 | 28 | 61 | 65 | 51 | 59 | 64 |
| | Cook (Hotel-Restaurant) | 67 | 66 | 57 | 62 | 71 | 62 | 69 | 77 | 58 | 41 | 33 | 61 | 31 | 46 | 61 | 59 | 54 | 65 | 51 | 52 | 75 | 68 | 62 | 66 | 52 | 58 | 69 | 57 | 59 | 42 | 63 | 63 | 65 | 54 | 61 | 64 | 54 |
| | Dietitian | 68 | 78 | 67 | 55 | 60 | 52 | 75 | 63 | 49 | 36 | 17 | 51 | 58 | 62 | 63 | 75 | 80 | 77 | 59 | 56 | 42 | 49 | 25 | 35 | 30 | 59 | 54 | 26 | 51 | 29 | 62 | 38 | 10 | 19 | 07 | 20 | 33 |
| | Engineer, Stationary | 69 | 39 | 32 | 45 | 49 | 57 | 55 | 63 | 67 | 68 | 48 | 61 | 46 | 58 | 53 | 47 | 42 | 46 | 53 | 58 | 68 | 55 | 52 | 68 | 50 | 64 | 62 | 48 | 44 | 46 | 56 | 63 | 54 | 54 | 56 | 59 | 72 |
| | Fire Fighter | 70 | 15 | 07 | 17 | 19 | 20 | 25 | 29 | 42 | 21 | 20 | 45 | 18 | 15 | 36 | 41 | 29 | 45 | 28 | 40 | 50 | 68 | 62 | 57 | 54 | 64 | 70 | 71 | 68 | 62 | 64 | 62 | 33 | 17 | 43 | 42 | 29 |
| | Landscape Gardener | 71 | 30 | 26 | 25 | 41 | 23 | 34 | 36 | 38 | 47 | 32 | 64 | 45 | 39 | 35 | 62 | 46 | 53 | 47 | 43 | 42 | 64 | 48 | 50 | 61 | 46 | 41 | 59 | 60 | 59 | 50 | 57 | 64 | 63 | 78 | 55 | 55 |
| | Nurse, Professional | 72 | 50 | 33 | 23 | 42 | 30 | 52 | 44 | 47 | 24 | 07 | 62 | 61 | 44 | 61 | 84 | 70 | 85 | 65 | 60 | 51 | 74 | 60 | 55 | 58 | 75 | 70 | 70 | 87 | 66 | 85 | 55 | 19 | 12 | 28 | 21 | 23 |
| | Pharmacist | 73 | 08 | -12 | -05 | 16 | 20 | 20 | 32 | 33 | 29 | 24 | 32 | 26 | 15 | 25 | 42 | 19 | 33 | 22 | 31 | 63 | 45 | 57 | 65 | 53 | 57 | 75 | 61 | 55 | 54 | 59 | 67 | 12 | 11 | 24 | 32 | 37 |
| | Policeman | 74 | 41 | 20 | 34 | 34 | 31 | 45 | 35 | 57 | 46 | 24 | 74 | 66 | 61 | 53 | 66 | 53 | 63 | 63 | 72 | 53 | 80 | 66 | 61 | 62 | 80 | 73 | 56 | 66 | 64 | 76 | 52 | 09 | 07 | 25 | 19 | 32 |
| | Receptionist, Civil Service | 75 | 45 | 30 | 41 | 57 | 47 | 59 | 52 | 66 | 54 | 32 | 74 | 75 | 68 | 59 | 83 | 64 | 77 | 68 | 74 | 63 | 82 | 63 | 79 | 87 | 75 | 62 | 59 | 62 | 66 | 74 | 61 | 20 | 26 | 43 | 26 | 40 |
| | Salesman, Automobile | 76 | 36 | 43 | 55 | 54 | 65 | 56 | 70 | 61 | 71 | 74 | 54 | 20 | 39 | 48 | 35 | 37 | 34 | 36 | 40 | 55 | 41 | 31 | 52 | 37 | 43 | 47 | 41 | 37 | 28 | 32 | 63 | 78 | 82 | 74 | 84 | 78 |
| | Salesman-Driver | 77 | 48 | 38 | 57 | 61 | 66 | 61 | 74 | 69 | 72 | 55 | 69 | 47 | 61 | 52 | 51 | 43 | 43 | 56 | 59 | 75 | 56 | 59 | 72 | 55 | 58 | 68 | 45 | 42 | 43 | 52 | 65 | 57 | 63 | 60 | 63 | 73 |
| | Salesperson, General (Dept Store) | 78 | 56 | 42 | 49 | 70 | 49 | 58 | 71 | 57 | 48 | 29 | 76 | 44 | 50 | 52 | 71 | 54 | 63 | 58 | 52 | 78 | 79 | 76 | 78 | 75 | 56 | 66 | 71 | 66 | 63 | 66 | 73 | 78 | 68 | 84 | 70 | 64 |
| | Salesperson, Shoe | 79 | 43 | 36 | 54 | 58 | 55 | 54 | 69 | 63 | 48 | 43 | 59 | 24 | 38 | 50 | 47 | 36 | 47 | 41 | 49 | 74 | 66 | 67 | 74 | 57 | 59 | 69 | 62 | 51 | 48 | 59 | 70 | 68 | 56 | 68 | 68 | 60 |
| | Teller (Banking) | 80 | 07 | -13 | 12 | 28 | 20 | 19 | 31 | 39 | 33 | 22 | 39 | 20 | 14 | 20 | 40 | 10 | 36 | 18 | 35 | 76 | 68 | 79 | 83 | 75 | 60 | 77 | 75 | 56 | 70 | 65 | 82 | 32 | 31 | 52 | 41 | 43 |
| | Truck Driver | 81 | -07 | -16 | -05 | 13 | 14 | 09 | 28 | 27 | 38 | 30 | 31 | 03 | 02 | 06 | 22 | 01 | 13 | 07 | 14 | 66 | 49 | 60 | 71 | 60 | 41 | 62 | 64 | 47 | 60 | 39 | 78 | 51 | 49 | 64 | 68 | 60 |

Figure 6.8. Cluster analysis for eighty-one occupations.

Cluster 4, composed of service occupations (social-educational), is primarily characterized by intrinsic reinforcers; cluster 8, formed principally of extrinsic reinforcers, is almost a mirror image of cluster 4. In general, the results of the cluster analysis supported the validity of the method.

*Reliability of ORPs.* The reliability of the ratings was studied by taking a group of supervisors, splitting them randomly into two groups, and computing ORPs separately for each. Figure 6.10 shows the split-group ORPs for two random groups of high school teachers. The correlation between the two ORPs was .96. The same procedure was followed for each of the other eighty-one occupations, splitting every group randomly and computing the within-group correlation of the two ORP profiles. Figure 6.11 presents the distributions of within occupation reliability correlations in contrast to the between occupation correlations. The reliabilities for the within occupations varied from .78 to .98 with a median of .91, while the between occupation correlations ranged from −.08 to .98 with a median

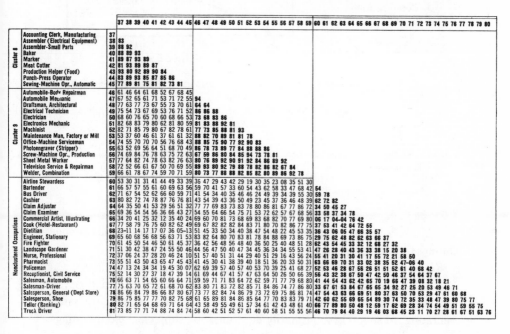

Figure 6.8 — continued. (Reprinted from *Occupational Reinforcer Patterns,* vol. 1, pp. 201–203, in *Minnesota Studies in Vocational Rehabilitation,* 1968, 24, copyright © 1968, University of Minnesota, by permission of the publisher and author.)

151

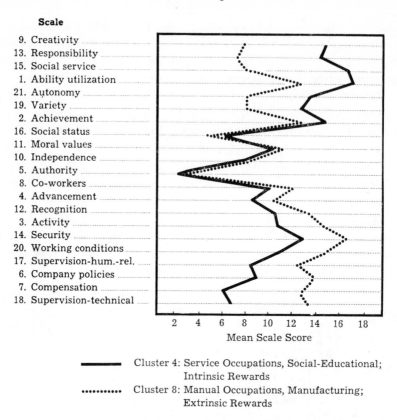

**Scale**

9. Creativity
13. Responsibility
15. Social service
1. Ability utilization
21. Autonomy
19. Variety
2. Achievement
16. Social status
11. Moral values
10. Independence
5. Authority
8. Co-workers
4. Advancement
12. Recognition
3. Activity
14. Security
20. Working conditions
17. Supervision-hum.-rel.
6. Company policies
7. Compensation
18. Supervision-technical

2  4  6  8  10  12  14  16  18

Mean Scale Score

────────  Cluster 4: Service Occupations, Social-Educational;
Intrinsic Rewards

··········  Cluster 8: Manual Occupations, Manufacturing;
Extrinsic Rewards

Figure 6.9. Contrast of two occupational clusters. (Reprinted from
The measurement of occupational reinforcer patterns, *Minnesota Studies in Vocational Rehabilitation*, 1968, 25, 54, copyright © 1968, University of Minnesota, by permission of the publisher and author.)

of .55. These data indicate that the MJDQ rating method yields similar
ratings from different supervisors of the same occupation.

*Generalizability of ORPs.* Occupational Reinforcer Patterns have been
published for eighty-one occupations, and data for another sixty-seven
are now being prepared for publication. ORPs available thus far are based
on ratings of supervisors primarily in Minnesota, supplemented by ratings
for some occupations from supervisors in Iowa, Wisconsin, Nebraska, and
Illinois. To determine whether there are regional differences in ORPs,
data for one occupation were obtained from a location in New York State.
Supervisors of social workers in New York and in Minnesota independ-

152

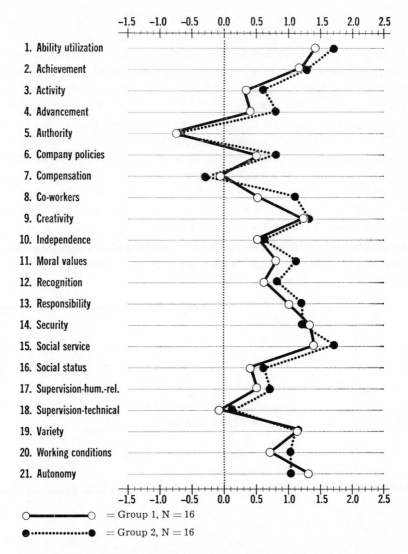

Figure 6.10. Reliability of Occupational Reinforcer Pattern ratings (split-group ORPs for high school teachers, r = .96). (Reprinted from The measurement of occupational reinforcer patterns, *Minnesota Studies in Vocational Rehabilitation*, 1968, 25, 37, copyright © 1968, University of Minnesota, by permission of the publisher and author.)

153

ently rated the job of social worker on the MJDQ. The correlation between the two ORP profiles was .71, which is within the reliability range. An analysis of the characteristics of supervisors as they are related to their ratings — their age, sex, number of employees, and number of years as a supervisor — found that there were almost no differences in the ratings as a function of these four characteristics. However, there was a tendency for the occupational level of the supervisors to be related to their ratings.

To discover whether supervisors and employees in the same occupation yielded similar ORPs, MJDQ ratings were obtained from supervisors and employees in three occupations — telephone operator, vocational rehabilitation counselor, and telephone service representative. The correlations between the supervisors' ORP profiles and those of employees were in the 80's. There was a level difference that seemed to be primarily the result of dissatisfied employees who saw their jobs differently than did satisfied employees. But in general, the employees and supervisors appeared to be rating the same job in a highly similar fashion.

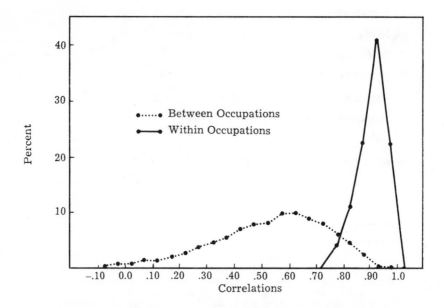

Figure 6.11. Reliability of Reinforcer Patterns for within occupations as contrasted with between occupations. (Reprinted from The measurement of occupational reinforcer patterns, *Minnesota Studies in Vocational Rehabilitation*, 1968, 25, 39, copyright © 1968, University of Minnesota, by permission of the publisher and author.)

## THE MEASUREMENT OF VOCATIONAL NEEDS

*Development of the Minnesota Importance Questionnaire.* Earlier forms of the MIQ (Weiss, Dawis, England, and Lofquist, 1964) used a Likert-type format, consisting of one hundred items; five items for each of the twenty scales. After several years of research with the Likert format, the one item that correlated most highly with each of the twenty scale scores was identified and put into a pair comparisons format with a neutral point. The following twenty statements make up the questionnaire; these statements also appear as items 191 through 210 in the MIQ *Booklet.* Each statement is paired once and only once with each other statement in random order. The order of presentation is counterbalanced with the only restriction being that no statement appear following itself in another pair. The MIQ is, therefore, a complete pair comparison of twenty state-

| Scale | Item |
|---|---|
| 1. Ability utilization | I could do something that makes use of my abilities. |
| 2. Achievement | The job could give me a feeling of accomplishment. |
| 3. Activity | I could be busy all the time. |
| 4. Advancement | The job would provide an opportunity for advancement. |
| 5. Authority | I could tell people what to do. |
| 6. Company policies and practices | The company would administer its policies fairly. |
| 7. Compensation | My pay would compare well with that of others workers. |
| 8. Co-workers | My co-workers would be easy to make friends with. |
| 9. Creativity | I could try out some of my own ideas. |
| 10. Independence | I could work alone on the job. |
| 11. Moral values | I could do the work without feeling it is morally wrong. |
| 12. Recognition | I could get recognition for the work I do. |
| 13. Responsibility | I could make decisions on my own. |
| 14. Security | The job would provide for steady employment. |
| 15. Social service | I could do things for other people. |
| 16. Social status | I could be "somebody" in the community. |
| 17. Supervision-human relations | My boss would back up his men (with top management). |
| 18. Supervision-technical | My boss would train his men well. |
| 19. Variety | I could do something different every day. |
| 20. Working conditions | The job would have good working conditions. |

ments, which are representative of the larger domain of needs that was defined by job satisfaction literature. The twenty MIQ statements also parallel the first twenty statements in the MJDQ.

The individual completing the MIQ is asked to "draw a verbal picture" of his ideal job. By pair comparison scaling this "verbal picture" is translated into a psychometric picture. The respondent is asked to choose between each pair of statements and to indicate his preference for each of the 190 pairs that constitute the complete pair comparison. On the last page he is asked to define his psychological zero point utilizing the same procedure used in the MJDQ.

If the zero point scaling were not included in the MIQ, two different people could rank their preferences in the same order, but the absolute level of these preferences could still be quite different. One individual might place his neutral point to show that, say, seven characteristics would be important to him in his ideal job. Another person could indicate that only one of the twenty variables is really important to him. To eliminate this problem, the MIQ uses a comparative judgment procedure in the first 190 items, followed by the absolute judgment procedure of Gulliksen to define the zero point.

*Scoring the MIQ.* Three steps are involved in this procedure. First, it is necessary to determine the frequency with which the individual has chosen one characteristic over all others. If he has chosen ability utilization over advancement when that pair is presented, he receives one point for the former. If he has chosen activity over ability utilization, he gets a "zero" for ability utilization and a "one" for activity. The raw scale score is the total number of times the individual has chosen a statement over all other statements.

For the absolute judgment items (191–210) a "one" is scored for those scales for which the individual indicates, by answering "yes," that a vocational need dimension is important to him on his ideal job. A "zero" is scored if the individual responds negatively, which means that the vocational need dimension is *not* important on his ideal job. The raw score for the zero-point scale is obtained by counting the number of "no" responses to the absolute judgment items.

Raw scale scores, therefore, range from 0 to 20 for each of the vocational need dimensions and for the zero-point scale. A raw score of 20 means that an individual has chosen the statement for that scale over all the other nineteen statements and has answered "yes" to the statement in the absolute judgment section (items 191–210). A raw score of 0 indicates that the individual has chosen all other statements over a given statement, and that he has answered "no" to the statement in the absolute judgment section. Other raw scale score values are defined similarly.

Since the MIQ represents a complete pair comparisons scaling, with a psychological zero point, values are determined for each scale by following the usual scaling procedures for pair comparisons (e.g. Guilford, 1954). For each raw scale score the scale values are determined by converting raw scores to z scores based on the normal curve. Each of the twenty-one raw scores for an individual is converted to a proportion of possible raw scores, which in turn is converted to the appropriate z value of the cumulative normal distribution. No reference is made to scores of other individuals in determining this z score. Z scores (scale values) for an individual are based only on his raw scale scores, and the characteristics of the cumulative normal distribution. Therefore, because of the pair comparison scaling technique, the z scores determine how far a given scale value deviates from the *individual's* own mean scale value (which is arbitrarily defined as 0.0). The z-score scale values represent purely ipsative or intraindividual scores, i.e., the individual is the base of comparison rather than some normative group.

The procedure above, because of its mathematics, always yields a set of scale values that are equally distributed around zero, with half the scale values positive and half negative. That is, the zero point is arbitrarily defined by the mathematics used to form the scale values. Scale values (z scores) are half positive and half negative for all individuals, although individuals may have different scale values for the various scales. Such scale values reflect only the *relative* levels of the measured vocational needs and allow only very limited comparisons among different individuals.

No matter what transformations are made on the raw scores or unadjusted scale values, they are initially derived by a scaling method that ranks them intraindividually. Therefore interperson comparisons of *un*adjusted MIQ scale values cannot give an estimate of the absolute elevation of the measured needs within a single individual. Scaling the zero point scale in conjunction with the values for the twenty scales provides a measure of the *absolute* levels of the twenty vocational needs, thereby permitting more meaningful comparison among individuals. The following discussion summarizes the method used to equate MIQ scale values across persons.

As indicated above, an individual's zero-point raw score is derived from items 191–210 of the MIQ. The z score (unadjusted scale value) of the zero point is determined in the same way as the z scores for the twenty vocational need scales. Once the unadjusted scale value for the zero point is fixed, scale values for the other twenty scales are adjusted to the zero point by subtracting the zero-point scale value from the scale values of each of the twenty vocational need scales, and from itself. This procedure yields a set of twenty-one *adjusted* scale values with the perceived zero point adjusted to zero and the vocational need scales adjusted to the individual's zero point.

Because of this adjustment procedure, the sign of each vocational need scale indicates whether the need is above or below the individual's zero point. Adjusted scale values with positive signs represent "important" dimensions of the individual's ideal job and therefore a "significant" need. The magnitude of the adjusted scale value indicates *how* important a particular variable is. Adjusted scale values with negative signs point to characteristics which are *not* important to the individual, and which, therefore, may not be relevant occupational needs *for the individual in question.* All scale values reported for the 1967 revision of the MIQ are adjusted with respect to each individual's scaled zero point.

In summary, the three steps in scoring the MIQ involve the computation of raw scores, unadjusted scale values, and adjusted scale values. The adjusted scale values are expressed in the same measurement terms as the adjusted scale values used for the ORPs. The zero point is defined in the same way, and the ORPs are essentially a complete pair comparison. Zero points are scaled in both the MIQ and the ORPs to permit a direct match between an individual's preferences as described by his pair comparison scaling and the characteristics of the occupation as described by the supervisor. The matching procedure is done by computer.

*Circular triads.* There is one other score in the MIQ that derives from pair comparisons scaling. That score can be used as a "validity" scale. In using the MIQ in counseling it is important to identify individuals who do not or cannot fully cooperate in completing the questionnaire. For these people, the counselor should not waste his time in occupational planning on the basis of the client's responses if they have been shown to be invalid. Furthermore, scores from such individuals should not be used in research studies since they will only add error to the results.

It is important, therefore, to identify (1) individuals who do not understand the questionnaire because the items are written at too high a level for them, (2) those who cannot choose between the alternatives because they have not had enough exposure to occupations to make meaningful choices, (3) respondents who are careless in marking the answer sheet, and (4) persons who are not motivated to complete the questionnaire meaningfully. The MIQ utilizes the Total Circular Triads score (TCT) to identify these people. TCT scores can be developed from any kind of experiment or instrument using pair comparisons (Kendall, 1955).

The TCT score has a known theoretical distribution which has been verified empirically by generating large numbers of random response records. By using the TCT score the counselor, without reference to norms, can indentify those individuals whose responses to the MIQ appear to be random.

The TCT score indicates the logical consistency with which an individual has responded to the MIQ items. A circular triad occurs when an individual responds to a group of three items in the following manner: (1) he chooses statement A over statement B; (2) he chooses statement B over statement C; (3) he chooses statement C over statement A. This sequence of choices can be described as illogical or inconsistent. A circular triad represents illogical or inconsistent choices among any three stimuli.

At a more operational level, a circular triad can be illustrated by the following example. Suppose you are asked which you prefer — chocolate ice cream or vanilla? You say that you prefer chocolate over vanilla. Then you are asked which do you prefer — vanilla or strawberry? You say you prefer vanilla. Finally you are asked to choose between chocolate or strawberry. If you like chocolate better than vanilla, and vanilla better than strawberry, but, when asked to choose between chocolate and strawberry, you indicate a preference for strawberry, then you are being inconsistent. If your preferences were completely consistent you would have chosen chocolate over vanilla, vanilla over strawberry, and chocolate over strawberry.

Circular and noncircular triads are presented in Figure 6.12, where the direction of the arrow indicates the direction of preference. The diagram in Figure 6.12a shows this person preferred chocolate over vanilla, vanilla over strawberry, but strawberry over chocolate. The reasoning is circular (note that the arrows go in a circle), reflecting an illogical set of choices among three stimuli. A noncircular triad is given in Figure 6.12b. In the MIQ there are 1330 possible combinations of three different statements

159

(including the zero point). Each person's responses are examined to determine the number of these triads that are circular. The Total Circular Triad score (for twenty-one stimuli) has a random response mean of 335 and a standard deviation of about 16. To ensure identification of virtually all random response records, the cutoff score used in the MIQ is 255, which is five standard deviations below the random response mean. If a person exhibits 255 or more circularities in his responses, it implies that he wasn't paying attention to the MIQ items, didn't care to respond meaningfully, or for several reasons could not respond meaningfully. His MIQ profile can therefore be considered invalid.

For those individuals whose MIQ responses are valid, the circular triads data appear to be more significant. On the computer it iş possible to determine how many times any given stimulus appears in a circular triad. It is also possible to identify those triads which are circular and to "reverse" the circularity (DeWitt and Weiss, 1968). After this reversal, it is possible to recompute raw scores (and scale values) for the stimuli in the circular triads. If this process is repeated across all circular triads, each stimulus obtains a "maximum" and "minimum" score reflecting the number of circularities associated with that stimulus.

This information can be used to compute "error bands" on each stimulus which indicate the degree of uncertainty related to that stimulus. If a person is very uncertain about his choice for achievement, it will frequently appear in circular triads. That person's reasoning regarding achievement will be circular because he is not really sure how he feels about it. For any given stimulus it can be determined where it appears in circular triads; the circularity is then reversed, and his raw scale scores are decreased or increased by the number of circularities in each direction. Scale

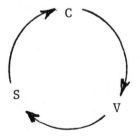 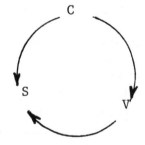

Figure 6.12. Circular and noncircular triads
Left, circular triad
Right, noncircular triad

160

values based on these pluses or minuses give an "error band" that demonstrates the degree of uncertainty relative to that score. Thus, when an MIQ is not invalid because of a high number of circular triads, an analysis of the circular triads information permits the development of "error bands" which help to interpret the amount of uncertainty associated with each stimulus.

## SOME ILLUSTRATIVE PROFILES

A sample MIQ report, for the hypothetical John, is shown in Figure 6.13.[2] John's highest preference is for security, which received a scale value of 2.8, meaning that his preference for security was 2.8 standard deviations above his own zero point. It should be kept in mind that John's set of MIQ scores is completely nonnormative; it is without reference to anyone else. The scale values simply point to deviations from his *own* zero point.

John's next highest preference was recognition which received a scale value of 2.0. The dash lines indicate that there is some indecision in his choice of recognition, and that his scale value of 2.0 on recognition could have been as high as 2.3, if all the circularities associated with recognition were eliminated. John's third preference was advancement. His adjusted scale value for advancement is somewhere between 1.6 and 2.3 standard deviations above his zero point. The next highest preference in John's MIQ profile is company policies and practices (a company that is fair to its employees), which obtained a scale value of 1.6, with a range from 1.4 to 2.0.

The reinforcers not important to John are social status and authority, which both have a scale value of −.7. The "true" scale value for authority is probably lower because the error band extends to the left of the plotted scale value. Other reinforcers not essential to John are independence, with a scale value of −.2, and moral values, with a scale value of 0.0 plus or minus a few decimal points in either direction.

On the co-workers scale John obtained a value of .6 and on supervision — human relations a value of .7, but he is much more decided about su-

2. This profile is actually only representative of the profile which is produced for the present MIQ. As new research results suggest modifications, they are immediately incorporated into the profile. At the time this book went to press, the number of occupations for which $D^2$ figures are given was increased to 148, and the likelihood of satisfaction associated with each is printed on the profile.

REPORT ON THE MINNESOTA IMPORTANCE QUESTIONNAIRE
(MIQ)
1967 REVISION

CIRCULAR TRIAD SCORE= 45
INVALID RESPONSE RANGE
BEGINS AT 255.
MIQ IS VALID.

| MIQ SCALE | SCALE VALUE |
|---|---|
| ABILITY UTILIZATION ......... | 1.2 |
| ACHIEVEMENT ................. | 1.2 |
| ACTIVITY .................... | .6 |
| ADVANCEMENT ................. | 1.8 |
| AUTHORITY ................... | -.7 |
| COMPANY POLICIES AND PRACTICES | 1.6 |
| COMPENSATION ................ | 1.4 |
| COWORKERS ................... | .6 |
| CREATIVITY .................. | 1.4 |
| INDEPENDENCE ................ | -.2 |
| MORAL VALUES ................ | 0.0 |
| RECOGNITION ................. | 2.0 |
| RESPONSIBILITY .............. | .9 |
| SECURITY .................... | 2.8 |
| SOCIAL SERVICE .............. | .2 |
| SOCIAL STATUS ............... | -.7 |
| SUPERVISION—HUMAN RELATIONS . | .7 |
| SUPERVISION—TECHNICAL ....... | .6 |
| VARIETY ..................... | .3 |
| WORKING CONDITIONS .......... | 1.4 |
| MIQ SCALE | SCALE VALUE |

SCALE VALUE

-4.0  -3.0  -2.0     VERY LOW -1.0     .LO. 0.0     .MOD. +1.0     HIGH +2.0     +3.0     +4.0

162

CORRESPONDENCE BETWEEN OCCUPATIONAL REINFORCER PATTERNS AND MIQ SCALE VALUES FOR SAMPLE REPORT NO. 1

81 OCCUPATIONS LISTED IN DECREASING ORDER OF CORRESPONDENCE, USING D-SQUARED INDEX.
OCCUPATIONS AT THE TOP OF THIS LIST ARE THOSE IN WHICH THIS INDIVIDUAL IS MOST LIKELY TO BE SATISFIED.
OCCUPATIONS AT THE BOTTOM OF THE LIST ARE THOSE IN WHICH HE(SHE) IS LEAST LIKELY TO BE SATISFIED.

| OCCUPATION | CLUSTER | D-SQUARED |
|---|---|---|
| SCREW-MACHINE OPERATOR, PRODUCTION | 9 | 6.15 |
| SALESPERSON, SHOE | 1 | 7.13 |
| ELECTRICIAN | 9 | 7.19 |
| WRITER, TECHNICAL PUBLICATIONS | 2 | 7.38 |
| COOK(HOTEL-RESTAURANT) | 1 | 7.54 |
| SALESMAN, AUTOMOBILE | 1 | 7.90 |
| MACHINIST | 9 | 7.90 |
| ASSEMBLER, SMALL PARTS | 8 | 7.97 |
| SHEET METAL WORKER | 9 | 8.09 |
| ELECTRONICS MECHANIC | 9 | 8.50 |
| DRAFTSMAN, ARCHITECTURAL | 9 | 8.55 |
| OFFICE-MACHINE SERVICEMAN | 9 | 8.58 |
| ELECTRICAL TECHNICIAN | 9 | 8.59 |
| SALESMAN-DRIVER | 1 | 8.64 |
| MARKER | 8 | 8.83 |
| WELDER, COMBINATION | 9 | 8.84 |
| SALESPERSON, GENERAL (DEPARTMENT STORE) | 1 | 9.00 |
| PHOTOENGRAVER(STRIPPER) | 9 | 9.06 |
| BARTENDER | 1 | 15.07 |
| FIRE FIGHTER | 8 | 15.08 |
| SEWING-MACHINE OPERATOR, AUTOMATIC | 8 | 15.21 |
| WAITER-WAITRESS | 6 | 15.22 |
| TEACHER, SECONDARY SCHOOL | 4 | 15.31 |
| BUS DRIVER | 1 | 15.55 |
| RADIOLOGIC TECHNOLOGIST | 6 | 16.21 |
| NURSE, PROFESSIONAL | 1 | 16.26 |
| AIRPLANE STEWARDESS | 1 | 16.61 |
| RECEPTIONIST, CIVIL SERVICE | 1 | 16.73 |
| POLICEMAN | 6 | 16.75 |
| NURSE, LICENSED PRACTICAL | 6 | 18.22 |
| NURSE AID | 4 | 19.32 |
| COUNSELOR, SCHOOL | 1 | 20.69 |
| LANDSCAPE GARDENER | 6 | 24.89 |
| ORDERLY | | |

9 OCCUPATIONAL FAMILIES LISTED IN DECREASING ORDER OF CORRESPONDENCE, USING D-SQUARED INDEX

| | | |
|---|---|---|
| CLUSTER 9 | -- MANUAL OCCUPATIONS, SERVICE-MAINTENANCE | 8.20 |
| CLUSTER 2 | -- TECHNICAL OCCUPATIONS, SEMI-PROFESSIONAL | 9.26 |
| CLUSTER 8 | -- MANUAL OCCUPATIONS, MANUFACTURING | 10.04 |
| CLUSTER 1 | -- TECHNICAL OCCUPATIONS, PROFESSIONAL | 10.41 |
| CLUSTER 7 | -- MANUAL OCCUPATIONS, BUILDING TRADES | 11.32 |
| CLUSTER 3 | -- SALES OCCUPATIONS, SERVICE | 12.56 |
| CLUSTER 5 | -- SERVICE OCCUPATIONS, BUSINESS DETAIL | 12.87 |
| CLUSTER 4 | -- SERVICE OCCUPATIONS, SOCIAL-EDUCATIONAL | 13.77 |
| CLUSTER 6 | -- SERVICE OCCUPATIONS, PERSONAL | 15.51 |

Figure 6.13. John's MIQ profile.
(Arrow indicates that items
have been dropped for
reasons of space.)

163

pervision than he is about co-workers since there is a smaller error band associated with supervision — human relations.

After an individual's MIQ profile is drawn, it can be matched up with the eighty-one ORPs to predict job satisfaction (Betz, 1968). There are many ways of matching one profile with another. For the purposes of vocational counselors, MIQ reports use total D-squared ($D^2$) to match the individual's MIQ profile with each job's ORP. To compute $D^2$, take the individual's MIQ profile and the ORP profile for one occupation and compute the "distance" (or the difference) between the similar points of the profile. These differences are then squared and summed across the twenty common scales on the MIQ and ORP profiles. For example, on ability utilization John obtained an adjusted scale value of 1.2. In the ORP for cost accountant the scale value for ability utilization is 1.46 (Borgen et al., 1968b); the difference is .26. The value that is summed is the square of the difference, which in this case is .07. The differences in scale values are then obtained between John's scale value for achievement and the ORP scale value on the achievement scale, the difference is squared, and added to $D^2$ for ability utilization. This process is repeated for each of the twenty common points of the MIQ and ORP profiles, the result being the total squared distance ($D^2$) between the two profiles.

This procedure is repeated for each individual on all eighty-one ORPs, yielding eighty-one $D^2$ values. To facilitate use of the $D^2$ information by vocational counselors, the computer ranks the occupations on the second page by *decreasing* similarity (or increasing $D^2$). When there is no difference between two profiles, $D^2$ will be zero. As the ORP profile for an occupation becomes different from an individual's MIQ profile in shape and/or level, $D^2$ increases. Occupations at the top of the computer-ranked list are those in which the individual is *most* likely to be satisfied. Occupations at the bottom are those in which he is *least* likely to be satisfied.

According to the $D^2$ values, John's profile is closest to the ORP profile for screw-machine operator. John has high preferences for security, recognition, and advancement, and low preferences for authority, social status, and independence. The ORP for screw-machine operator (Borgen et al., 1968b) shows that three of the "moderately" descriptive characteristics for that occupation are security, recognition, and advancement. Other "moderately" descriptive characteristics are ability utilization and achievement which have scale values not very different from John's preferences for these two variables on the MIQ. The reinforcers judged "not

164

descriptive" of the occupation of screw-machine operator include authority, social status, and social service, all of which obtained negative scale values. Although John's MIQ profile and the ORP for screw-machine operator do not match on all points of the total profile, there is considerable similarity between the two profiles, and the match is the best among the eighty-one occupations for which ORPs are available.

The next occupation listed in the ORP ranking for John is shoe salesperson. According to the ORP for the occupation (Borgen et al., 1968b), the moderately descriptive characteristics are security, recognition, and ability utilization. Both security and recognition are "highly important" to John. The occupation of shoe salesperson was also judged to be characterized by good working conditions, which was not indicated to be of high importance to John. The "not descriptive" characteristics of the salesperson job are similar to John's preferences only in "low" security. It is evident that, while the occupation of shoe salesperson has some similarity to John's MIQ pattern, it is not as good a match as the ORP for screw-machine operator.

At the bottom of John's list of occupations is the job of orderly. A comparison of the characteristics of this job with John's preferences on the MIQ shows that they are quite dissimilar. The highest ORP scale values for orderly are social service and security. Although John's preference for security is high, there is a considerable difference in the scale values for social service. In addition, the occupation of orderly is unlikely to satisfy John's needs for recognition, advancement, good company policies, authority, ability utilization, and achievement, among others. It would therefore be expected that John would not be satisfied in this job.

The MIQ report also assists the counselor in relating specific occupations to the clusters to which they belong. The cluster numbers are printed alongside the occupational titles to help counselors go from the individual occupations to the clusters. In the column for "cluster" a dash means that it was an unclustered occupation. At the end of the third page of the MIQ report, the individual's MIQ profile is compared to the composite ORP for each of the nine clusters of occupations. In John's case, his preferences are most similar to the ORP for manual occupations and service-maintenance, and least similar to the ORP for personal service occupations.

Figure 6.14 is the MIQ profile of another individual, William. William's preferences as measured by the MIQ are quite different from John's. His profile is characterized by high scale values for social service,

165

REPORT ON THE MINNESOTA IMPORTANCE QUESTIONNAIRE
(MIQ)
1967 REVISION

CIRCULAR TRIAD SCORE= 36
INVALID RESPONSE RANGE
BEGINS AT 255.
MIQ IS VALID.

| MIQ SCALE | SCALE VALUE |
|---|---|
| ABILITY UTILIZATION | 1.5 |
| ACHIEVEMENT | 2.0 |
| ACTIVITY | .5 |
| ADVANCEMENT | .6 |
| AUTHORITY | -1.0 |
| COMPANY POLICIES AND PRACTICES | 0.0 |
| COMPENSATION | 1.0 |
| COWORKERS | -.3 |
| CREATIVITY | -.5 |
| INDEPENDENCE | .5 |
| MORAL VALUES | .7 |
| RECOGNITION | 1.3 |
| RESPONSIBILITY | .5 |
| SECURITY | .6 |
| SOCIAL SERVICE | 2.5 |
| SOCIAL STATUS | -1.0 |
| SUPERVISION—HUMAN RELATIONS | -.7 |
| SUPERVISION—TECHNICAL | .1 |
| VARIETY | 1.5 |
| WORKING CONDITIONS | .9 |

166

CORRESPONDENCE BETWEEN OCCUPATIONAL REINFORCER PATTERNS AND MIQ SCALE VALUES FOR SAMPLE REPORT NO. 2

81 OCCUPATIONS LISTED IN DECREASING ORDER OF CORRESPONDENCE, USING D-SQUARED INDEX.
OCCUPATIONS AT THE TOP OF THIS LIST ARE THOSE IN WHICH THIS INDIVIDUAL IS MOST LIKELY TO BE SATISFIED.
OCCUPATIONS AT THE BOTTOM OF THE LIST ARE THOSE IN WHICH HE(SHE) IS LEAST LIKELY TO BE SATISFIED.

| OCCUPATION | CLUSTER | D-SQUARED |
| --- | --- | --- |
| RECEPTIONIST, CIVIL SERVICE | 1 | 7.51 |
| TYPIST, CIVIL SERVICE | 5 | 9.45 |
| STENOGRAPHER, TECHNICAL, CIVIL SERVICE | 5 | 10.73 |
| NURSE, LICENSED PRACTICAL | 6 | 10.90 |
| WAITER-WAITRESS | 6 | 11.15 |
| EMBALMER | 5 | 11.16 |
| AUTOMOBILE SERVICE STATION ATTENDANT | 9 | 11.18 |
| AUTOMOBILE MECHANIC | 4 | 11.29 |
| PHYSICAL THERAPIST | 6 | 11.30 |
| RADIOLOGIC TECHNOLOGIST | 1 | 11.43 |
| LANDSCAPE GARDENER | 7 | 11.55 |
| PAINTER/PAPERHANGER | 3 | 11.69 |
| SALESMAN, REAL ESTATE | 4 | 11.82 |
| LIBRARIAN | 6 | 11.83 |
| NURSE AID | 9 | 11.92 |
| MAINTENANCE MAN, FACTORY OR MILL | 9 | 12.09 |
| PHOTOENGRAVER(STRIPPER) | 9 | 12.25 |
| AUTOMOBILE-BODY REPAIRMAN | | 12.27 |
| MARKER | 8 | 16.17 |
| SALESMAN-DRIVER | 4 | 16.23 |
| INSTRUCTOR, VOCATIONAL SCHOOL | 1 | 16.25 |
| BARTENDER | 1 | 16.36 |
| ENGINEER, STATIONARY | | 16.40 |
| BUS DRIVER | 9 | 16.64 |
| SCREW-MACHINE OPERATOR, PRODUCTION | 1 | 16.69 |
| ENGINEER, CIVIL | 8 | 16.72 |
| BAKER | 8 | 16.99 |
| FIRE FIGHTER | 1 | 17.48 |
| SEWING-MACHINE OPERATOR, AUTOMATIC | 8 | 17.55 |
| ENGINEER, TIME STUDY | 8 | 17.64 |
| MEAT CUTTER | 1 | 17.83 |
| CLAIM EXAMINER | 8 | 17.86 |
| PHARMACIST | | 17.91 |
| ASSEMBLER(ELECTRICAL EQUIPMENT) | | 19.47 |

9 OCCUPATIONAL FAMILIES LISTED IN DECREASING ORDER OF CORRESPONDENCE, USING D-SQUARED INDEX

| | | |
| --- | --- | --- |
| CLUSTER 6 | -- SERVICE OCCUPATIONS, PERSONAL | 10.93 |
| CLUSTER 5 | -- SERVICE OCCUPATIONS, BUSINESS DETAIL | 12.05 |
| CLUSTER 2 | -- TECHNICAL OCCUPATIONS, SEMI-PROFESSIONAL | 12.31 |
| CLUSTER 3 | -- SALES OCCUPATIONS, SERVICE | 12.64 |
| CLUSTER 7 | -- MANUAL OCCUPATIONS, BUILDING TRADES | 12.64 |
| CLUSTER 9 | -- MANUAL OCCUPATIONS, SERVICE-MAINTENANCE | 12.67 |
| CLUSTER 4 | -- SERVICE OCCUPATIONS, SOCIAL-EDUCATIONAL | 12.68 |
| CLUSTER 8 | -- MANUAL OCCUPATIONS, MANUFACTURING | 15.67 |
| CLUSTER 1 | -- TECHNICAL OCCUPATIONS, PROFESSIONAL | 16.42 |

Figure 6.14. William's MIQ profile.
(Arrow indicates that items
have been dropped for
reasons of space.)

167

variety, and achievement. In comparing his profile to the eighty-one ORPs the computer indicates that his preferences are most similar to the ORPs for receptionist, stenographer, typist, licensed practical nurse, waiter-waitress, and embalmer. In terms of clusters, his preferences are most similar to the ORPs for service occupations, business detail, and personal service occupations. This different MIQ profile has, of course, different implications for William's vocational counseling.

Research with the $D^2$ correspondence index (Gay, Weiss, Hendel, Dawis, and Lofquist, 1971) suggest the following guidelines for interpretation of the $D^2$ values reflecting MIQ-ORP correspondence: (1) a $D^2$ value of less than 9.00 suggests that the individual *would be satisfied* in the occupation; (2) a $D^2$ of greater than 9.00 but less than 20.00 suggests that the individual is *likely to be satisfied* in the occupation; and (3) a $D^2$ of greater than 20.00 suggests that the individual is *not likely to be satisfied* in the occupation.

These guidelines were based on the analysis of MIQ-ORP $D^2$ values with one occupation ORP for employed workers. The cutting scores were developed on five occupational groups, and were set to predict about 25 percent of each group as "satisfied," 50 percent as "likely satisfied," and 25 percent as "not likely satisfied." Appropriate interpretative statements accompany the $D^2$ values on the MIQ computer report to assist the counselor in using the MIQ-ORP information in vocational counseling.

## IMPLEMENTATION OF THE THEORY OF WORK ADJUSTMENT

According to the Theory of Work Adjustment, the vocational counselor should be interested in predicting both job satisfaction and job satisfactoriness. These two indicators of work adjustment are independent of each other. An individual can be highly satisfied and highly satisfactory; he can have low satisfaction and high satisfactoriness; or there can be either of the other combinations of the two variables. To predict work adjustment maximally the counselor should assist the counselee in finding those occupations in which he is likely to be both satisfied and satisfactory. The MIQ will help to differentiate occupations into predicted high satisfaction or low satisfaction, currently on a relative basis and soon on a categorical "satisfied"/"not satisfied" basis. Within the "predicted satisfied" occupations, the counselor will be able to use information on the client's vocational abilities in conjunction with ability requirements information on occupations to determine which of the "predicted satisfied" occupations are also "predicted satisfactory" for that individual.

Eventually, the Work Adjustment Project intends to develop a new multifactor ability measure and corresponding occupational information to assist in the prediction of satisfactoriness. This information, combined with MIQ-ORP data, would be put into a computer which could yield such statements as the following: "These are the occupations that are relevant possibilities for this individual based on the best predictions of satisfaction and satisfactoriness"; or "These are the occupations he should avoid because he is not qualified for them nor is he likely to be satisfied in them." This information, based on a synthesis of the individual's work personality information and the characteristics of hundreds or thousands of occupations, can then be considered in relation to the client's interests, personal situation, and other characteristics and can help him to develop realistic vocational plans designed to maximize his career adjustment.

## References

Betz, E. Need-reinforcer correspondence as a predictor of job satisfaction. *Personnel and Guidance Journal*, 1968, 47, 878–883.

Borgen, F. H., D. J. Weiss, H. E. A. Tinsley, R. V. Dawis, and L. H. Lofquist. Occupational reinforcer patterns. *Minnesota Studies in Vocational Rehabilitation*, 1968, 24 (a).

———. The measurement of occupational reinforcer patterns. *Minnesota Studies in Vocational Rehabilitation*, 1968, 25 (b).

Dawis, R. V., G. W. England, and L. H. Lofquist. A theory of work adjustment. *Minnesota Studies in Vocational Rehabilitation*, 1964, 15.

Dawis, R. V., L. H. Lofquist, and D. J. Weiss. A theory of work adjustment (a revision). *Minnesota Studies in Vocational Rehabilitation*, 1968, 23.

DeWitt, L. J., and D. J. Weiss. Applications of circular triad data in individual measurement. *Proceedings, 77th Annual Convention of the American Psychological Association*, 1969, 147–148.

Gay, E. G., D. J. Weiss, D. D. Hendel, R. V. Dawis, and L. H. Lofquist. Manual for the Minnesota Importance Questionnaire. *Minnesota Studies in Vocational Rehabilitation*, 1971, 28.

Gibson, D. L., D. J. Weiss, R. V. Dawis, and L. H. Lofquist. Manual for the Minnesota satisfactoriness scales. *Minnesota Studies in Vocational Rehabilitation*, 1970, 27.

Guilford, J. P. *Psychometric methods*. New York: McGraw-Hill, 1954.

Gulliksen, H., and L. R. Tucker. A general procedure for obtaining paired comparisons from multiple rank orders. *Psychometrika*, 1961, 26, 173–183.

Kendall, M. G. *Rank correlation methods*. New York: Hafner, 1955.

Lofquist, L. H., and R. V. Dawis. *Adjustment to work: A psychological view of man's problems in a work-oriented society*. New York: Appleton-Century-Crofts, 1969.

Taylor, K. E., and D. J. Weiss. Prediction of individual job turnover from measured job satisfaction. *Proceedings, 77th Annual Convention of the American Psychological Association*, 1969, 587–588 (a).

————. Prediction of individual job termination from measured job satisfaction and biographical data. *Experimental Publication System*, 1969, No. 3, Ms. 102a (b).

Thorndike, R. M., D. J. Weiss, and R. V. Dawis. The canonical correlation of vocational interests and vocational needs. *Journal of Counseling Psychology*, 1968, 15, 101–106 (a).

————. Multivariate relationships between a measure of vocational interests and a measure of vocational needs. *Journal of Applied Psychology*, 1968, 52, 491–496 (b).

Weiss, D. J., R. V. Dawis, G. W. England, and L. H. Lofquist. The measurement of vocational needs. *Minnesota Studies in Vocational Rehabilitation*, 1964, 16.

————. Manual for the Minnesota satisfaction questionnaire. *Minnesota Studies in Vocational Rehabilitation*, 1967, 22.

Weiss, D. J., R. V. Dawis, L. H. Lofquist, and G. W. England. Instrumentation for the Theory of Work adjustment. *Minnesota Studies in Vocational Rehabilitation*, 1966, 21.

# 7

# The Ohio
# Vocational Interest Survey

Ayres D'Costa

IN INTRODUCING THE OHIO VOCATIONAL INTEREST SURVEY (OVIS), I must go back before 1966 when I joined the Ohio Department of Education in a vocational interest measurement task that it had been engaged in since 1956. Its objective was to assist counselors helping students who were not planning to enter college. A checklist of job activities, similar to the U.S. Employment Service interest checklist had been developed in an attempt to get students to think about different kinds of vocational education courses on the basis of their interests. These data were also used to help administrators set priorities for establishing new vocational courses.

The idea of the Ohio Survey is the result of our desire to develop a guidance tool that would be psychometrically and scientifically sound. The OVIS has three main objectives. First, its goal is to work at the level of the students. It is concerned with what counselors do with a student's interest scores and, furthermore, with what students do with their own scores. Second, OVIS is concerned with the representativeness of what it measures as an instrument. Do interest measures really present the entire world of work to a student? And, if so, is the rationale behind the interest measures meaningful to a student? Third, can a student use the instrument and become a self-initiated explorer of the world of work?

## THE OVIS MODEL

Figure 7.1 presents the cubistic model of vocational interests (D'Costa and Winefordner, 1966) used in OVIS. This model should be explained

171

in detail because it is the most important concept counselors need to understand in order to interpret OVIS scores and use them in counseling. The OVIS authors use the data-people-things trichotomy as a basis for defining the world of work because research seems to suggest that it is the most meaningful model available. Roe (1957) utilized a "persons versus non-persons" approach to classify occupations, which we think can be represented as "persons versus things." Cooley and Lohnes (1968) created a career development tree model which focuses on the data-people-things trichotomy. The tree starts with a fork based on persons versus things and proceeds to develop a secondary fork constructed on a college versus non-college orientation, or high versus low data. Since this model is based on a random sample of 1000 Project TALENT students, it seems to give an empirical foundation for the data-people-things dimensions of work proposed in the OVIS model.

E. L. Thorndike has to be credited with pioneering this kind of approach when he defined intelligence as being *abstract, social,* and *mechanical* (Thorndike, 1921). These three components can be translated as data, people, and things. This trichotomy is also the basis for the worker trait groups defined in the 1965 *Dictionary of Occupational Titles* (DOT). The DOT assigns a six-digit code for every job. Thus 206.388

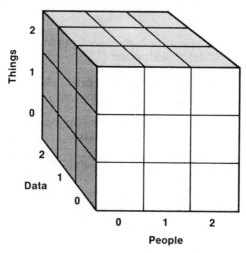

Figure 7.1. The data-people-things cube. (Reprinted from the *Manual for Interpreting, Ohio Vocational Interest Survey,* 1970, by special permission of Harcourt Brace Jovanovich, Inc.)

172

represents the job of file clerk. The three digits to the left of the decimal point, 206, identify its occupational category: it is broadly a clerical and sales occupation; specifically, it includes jobs in stenography, typing, filing, and related work; and more specifically, it is related to file clerks. The three digits to the right, 388, are the ones that define the data-people-things levels. The first digit gives the highest level of involvement with data, the second with people, and the third with things. The DOT has also taken the more than 20,000 jobs in the world of work and has grouped them on the basis of these three and other job characteristics into 114 homogeneous areas of work. These homogeneous areas are called "worker trait groups."

To simplify the data-people-things approach, OVIS took the three dimensions and sliced them into three levels each. This can be illustrated as a cube consisting of $3 \times 3 \times 3$ or 27 cells in all. Each of the 114 worker trait groups was plotted in the three-dimensional space or cube on the basis of the data, people, and things values that the DOT provides for each group. We found that the 114 worker trait groups are not uniformly distributed over the 27 cells of the cube, but that they form bigger clusters which appear to be psychologically meaningful areas of work. There is, for example, a cluster of "machine" work, "manual" work, and "medical" work.

In the development of a vocational interest inventory, the cubistic model of vocational interests offers a way to identify significant component areas of the world of work. The worker trait groups located in each area or cell in the cube and the jobs identified by the DOT for each worker trait group provide a rationale for developing items for each interest scale. Since OVIS items are based on the 114 worker trait groups, it too is a good representative of the world of work.

USING THE MODEL TO DEVELOP OVIS

The critical question that must be asked of the cubistic model is, How did it work out in practice? In Figure 7.2, the cube is divided into three slabs so that every cell can be seen. Each cell has been given an identifying code number. These numbers are not scaled measurements but ordered categories based on the nine hierarchial levels described by the DOT. In the DOT, a large number refers to a low level. In the OVIS system it is the reverse. The OVIS has three levels — 0, 1, 2 — as shown in Table 7.1. It seemed more convenient to use the largest number to refer

173

to the highest level. Thus a "2" or high level of data in the OVIS system corresponds to 0, 1, and 2 in the DOT system. The OVIS levels are cut off at logical points in the DOT system and are therefore uneven from one dimension to another. Note the cell in the lowest slab of Figure 7.2 (middle row, left-hand column) which is coded 001. This code represents work requiring a low level of involvement with data, a low level with people, and an average level with things.

Each OVIS scale corresponds to a cell in the cube. However, where no worker trait group was available for plotting in a cell, no OVIS scale was defined for that cell. Thus the first cell in the cube in which an OVIS scale is located has the code 001. The OVIS scale number for this cell is 1. The items written for OVIS scale 1 depict the four worker trait groups that have the OVIS code 001 to represent their level of involvement with data, people, and things. An examination of the four worker trait groups in this cluster suggested the name "manual work." (See Fig. 7.3 for a complete list of OVIS scales.) The jobs in the scale for manual work (scale 1) involve the unskilled use of tools and work done by hand. The corresponding levels in the DOT code for the things component in scale 1, which is the only significant component in this scale, indicate that it includes occupations involving manipulating, feeding, offbearing, handling, and tending.

OVIS scale 2 is located in the 002 cell of the cube. This means that

Table 7.1. OVIS Levels for Data, People, Things

| OVIS Rating | DOT Levels of Involvement and Functions | | | Level of Involvement |
| --- | --- | --- | --- | --- |
| | Data | People | Things | |
| High 2 | 0 Synthesizing<br>1 Coordinating<br>2 Analyzing | 0 Mentoring<br>1 Negotiating<br>2 Instructing<br>3 Supervising<br>4 Diverting | 0 Setting-up<br>1 Precision working<br>2 Operating-controlling<br>3 Driving-operating | Complex |
| Average 1 | 3 Compiling<br>4 Computing<br>5 Copying<br>6 Comparing | 5 Persuading<br>6 Speaking-<br>signaling<br>7 Serving | 4 Manipulating<br>5 Tending<br>6 Feeding-offbearing<br>7 Handling | ↑ |
| Low 0 | 7 No significant relationship<br>8 No significant relationship | 8 No significant relationship | 8 No significant relationship | Simple |

174

there is no significant involvement with data or people, but a high level of involvement with things. The corresponding worker activities defined in the DOT for this high things level are precision working, setting up, adjusting, operating or driving, and controlling. The worker trait groups in this cell suggested that the scale be labeled "machine work."

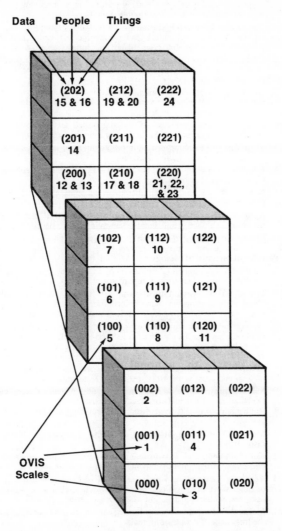

Figure 7.2. The OVIS scales. (Reproduced from the Ohio Vocational Interest Survey Test, copyright 1969 by Harcourt Brace Jovanovich, Inc. Reproduced by special permission of the publisher.)

1. **Manual Work** — Unskilled use of tools and routine work usually done by hand.
2. **Machine Work** — Operating and adjusting machines used in processing or manufacturing.
3. **Personal Services** — Providing routine services for people as a waiter, waitress, usher, household worker, etc.
4. **Caring for People or Animals** — Routine work related to the day-to-day needs of people or animals.
5. **Clerical Work** — Typing, recording, filing, IBM key punching, and other clerical or stenographic work.
6. **Inspecting and Testing** — Sorting, measuring, or checking products and materials; inspecting public facilities.
7. **Crafts and Precise Operations** — Skilled use of tools or other equipment as in the building trades, machine installation and repair, or the operation of trains, planes, or ships.
8. **Customer Services** — Conducting business relations with people as in retail selling, accepting reservations, receiving payments, or providing information.
9. **Nursing and Related Technical Services** — Providing services as a nurse, physical therapist, X-ray or medical laboratory technician, or dental hygienist.
10. **Skilled Personal Services** — Providing skilled services to people such as tailoring, cooking, barbering, or hairdressing.
11. **Training** — Instructing people in employment or leisure-time activities. Also includes animal training.
12. **Literary** — Writing novels, poetry, reviews, speeches or technical reports; editing, or translating.
13. **Numerical** — Using mathematics as in accounting, finance, data processing, or statistics.
14. **Appraisal** — Determining the efficiency of industrial plants and business, evaluating real estate, surveying land, or conducting chemical or other laboratory tests.
15. **Agriculture** — Farming, forestry, landscaping, or the related fields of botany and zoology.
16. **Applied Technology** — Application of engineering principles and scientific knowledge to the design of structures and machines.
17. **Promotion and Communication** — Advertising, publicity, radio announcing, journalism, news information service, interviewing, recruiting; also providing legal services as a judge or lawyer.
18. **Management and Supervision** — Administrative or supervisory positions, such as a shop foreman, supervisor, school administrator, police or fire chief, head librarian, executive, hotel manager, or union official. Includes owning or managing a store or business.
19. **Artistic** — Interior decorating, display work, photography, commercial and creative art work, or artistic restoration.
20. **Sales Representative** — Demonstrating and providing technical explanations of products or services to customers, selling and installing such products or services, and providing related technical assistance.
21. **Music** — Composing, arranging, conducting, singing, or playing instruments.
22. **Entertainment and Performing Arts** — Entertaining others by participating in dramatics, dancing, comedy routines, or acrobatics.
23. **Teaching, Counseling, and Social Work** — Providing instruction or other services to schools, colleges, churches, clinics, or welfare agencies. Includes instruction in art, music, ballet, or athletics.
24. **Medical** — Providing medical, surgical, or related services for the treatment of people or animals.

Figure 7.3. The OVIS interest scales. (Reproduced from the Ohio Vocational Interest Survey Test, copyright 1969 by Harcourt Brace Jovanovich, Inc. Reproduced by special permission of the publisher.)

The next slab of cells represents the "1" or average level of involvement with data. In the first column is the OVIS scale 5 with the identifying code 100. This signifies a moderate involvement with data and an insignificant involvement with people and things. The scale name corresponding to this cell is "clerical" and the jobs in it include filing, stenography, computing, recording, typing, and routine checking.

Scale 6 has average "things" content which involves checking, inspecting, and testing, but not the use of complex machines. Scale 7, crafts and precise operations, has an obvious machine element. The level of data remains the same, while the level of things increases as you move from scale 5 to scale 7 along this column.

The top slab relates to the highest level in the data dimension. Note that cell 200 has two scales in it (12 and 13). So far the cubistic model of vocational interests appears similar to Guilford's model for the structure of the intellect in that there is one scale for each cell. But the highest data slab is different because the higher level of the data dimension, the more complex the jobs become.[1] The split of cell 200 into scales 12 and 13 was not arbitrary. In these scales the people and things levels are low, and the data level is high. But the worker trait groups in this cell had to be divided, on the basis of the functions involved, into two groups — literary and numerical. OVIS 12 covers the worker trait groups of contract analysis, technical and creative writing, translating, and editing, while 13 includes auditing, mathematics, accounting, and physical sciences.

In this high data slab, the same phenomenon occurs in almost every one of the cells. The worker trait groups in each had to be assigned to more than one area or scale. Nevertheless, this does not change the basic data-people-things interpretation of the cells. In cells 210 and 220 there is increasing involvement with people as the level of involvement with data increases. In cell 210, scale 17 deals with promotion and communication, whereas scale 18 is concerned with management and supervision. In cell 220, there are three scales: scale 21 represents musical activities, scale 22 covers entertainment, which is broader than music alone, and scale 23 includes teaching, counseling, and social work.

The cubistic model has a logical organization that is reasonably symmetrical. In cell 011, scale 4 requires the lowest level of data and moderate levels of involvement with people and things. The type of work in-

1. Factor analysis of OVIS scores indicates that new factors or elements emerge as the data level is increased (D'Costa and Winefordner, 1966).

volves caring for people and animals. In a similarly located cell in the average data slab is scale 9, nursing and related technical services. Following this symmetrical trend, one might expect doctors in cell 211. However, physicians and surgeons are in cell 222 which requires the highest level of data, people, and things. Despite the multiple splitting of cells at the highest level of data, the interrelations between adjoining scales are remarkably meaningful.

The cubistic model of vocational interests provides a practical approach for the vocational counseling of young people. Roe's (1957) hypothesis that a people versus things orientation originates early in life does not violate the cubistic model. Perhaps this dichotomy should be used as a beginning vocational concept in elementary school. Then the data level should gradually be introduced in junior high or high school as developmental needs arise, for example, in deciding whether to continue in high school or in planning for post-high-school college, technical, or vocational training. Data, people, things thus become primary occupational concepts that are introduced on the basis of developmental needs and of how ready the individual is to understand certain ideas concerning future occupations. After learning to think in terms of data, people, and things, a child can begin to comprehend the twenty-four areas represented by the OVIS scales and from there the world of work through the 114 worker trait groups.

### THE DEVELOPMENT OF THE INSTRUMENT

OVIS has two parts — the interest inventory and the student information questionnaire. The interest inventory consists of 280 items. The same instrument is administered to males and to females. Only eleven items are scored for each of the twenty-four scales for either sex. A few items are intended specifically for males and are ignored in scoring females, whereas a few others are scored exclusively for females. In spite of these differences the interpretation of OVIS scales remains pretty much the same for males and for females.

The items in the interest inventory were developed from the job activities that were judged to be representative of the worker trait groups in each scale. We looked at typical jobs within each scale cluster and then went to volume I of the DOT for detailed descriptions of the job activities. In writing an item we modified the language so that it approximated the level of eighth graders. Item number 1 in the interest inventory portion of

OVIS is "Copy numbers or words neatly." This was taken from the work description for secretaries, typists, and other clerical persons.. Although we tried to keep the language at the eighth-grade level in every case, one might wonder whether we really managed to do this with some items. For example, item number 50 is "Diagnose hearing difficulties and recommend treatment." [2] We found that eighth graders think they understand this item. If a student finds the meaning unclear, we expect that he will be cautious and mark the item "neutral." As a student develops and grows in vocational maturity, we anticipate that he will be able to react with greater sensitivity to the inventory.

*Responses to inventory items.* The OVIS allows the subject to respond to each item independently of the other items. There are five modes of response — like very much, like, neutral, dislike, and dislike very much. No forced choice is involved in answering, for the purpose of the OVIS is to provide an inventory situation in which the student will feel comfortable and be willing to cooperate. We do expect an occasional uncooperative student and of course we do run into some problems, but the results for each student can be interpreted accordingly. Omission of items is not encouraged. If there is more than one item left blank in a scale, no score is reported for that scale.

*Inventory scales.* Each OVIS scale has been defined by worker trait groups that represent homogeneous job clusters. There is homogeneity in the worker trait groups in each OVIS scale based on factors other than data, people, and things. Using the DOT as our reference, we found that each OVIS scale tended to have a unique pattern of temperaments, interests, and aptitudes.

*The student information questionnaire.* This questionnaire tells what groups of school subjects a student likes best, what general program he is in, what further training is being planned, the kinds of vocational programs he would be interested in, and the type of work he would like to do. The responses to these questions are printed in the Student Report Folder and are summarized for an entire class or group to be used by school administrators for vocational planning.

The student information questionnaire provides the opportunity to secure additional local information. The counselor can slip in a short ques-

2. All items are reprinted from Ohio Vocational Interest Survey Test, copyright 1969 by Harcourt Brace Jovanovich, Inc. Reprinted by special permission of the publisher.

tionnaire of items of local importance. The responses are analyzed by computer along with the remaining OVIS questions and are printed in the profile. School-wide, system-wide, or state-wide summaries of these data can be obtained.

STANDARDIZATION

OVIS is not new. It has been used in Ohio since 1966 on some 100,000 high school students and in Florida on a research basis. A national standardization was conducted by Harcourt Brace Jovanovich, Inc., the publisher of OVIS, in ten different states. Distributions of OVIS scores are being studied by grade and sex. Percentiles and stanines are available. The distributions of scores for each OVIS scale are not perfectly normal, and thus they are skewed depending upon the scale. For example, most girls seem to prefer nursing over other careers, and therefore their scores on this scale are negatively skewed. The manual scale is one that is disliked by most girls, and so the skew is just the other way around. This aspect of OVIS is a real nuisance when normative comparisons, especially with stanines, have to be made. We suggest caution in the use of normative scores especially if the distributions are severely skewed.

Minor differences in scores on each scale between grades were found, but mean scores were very similar for each grade level. Sex differences were noticed very early in the development of the instrument and have been incorporated in the standardization sample.

Reliability measures have been obtained for the instrument at its different stages of development. These are of two kinds — internal consistency and test-retest. Internal consistency measures based on split half methods have yielded very high correlations, ranging from .75 to .95. We have also discovered that, with the exception of eighth graders, females are much more stable than males in their interest choices. Table 7.2 presents a summary of two-week test-retest reliability data by sex for grades 8 and 10.

The validity of OVIS scores is based upon their content or face validity and upon their power to discriminate among certain vocational groups. Content validity is provided by the cubistic model, the DOT, and the procedures used to derive items for each scale. Discriminant validity has been checked for an earlier version of OVIS in terms of vocational education groups (D'Costa, 1968) and in terms of academic programs. It has been found that not only do the scales discriminate certain vocational groups but they do so in meaningful ways. Thus the agriculture group was dis-

Table 7.2. Test-Retest Reliability Coefficients for the Twenty-four
OVIS Scales for Grade 8 and Grade 10 Samples

| Sample | N | Reliability Coefficients | |
|---|---|---|---|
| | | Range | Median |
| Grade 8 | | | |
| Males .............. | 644–652 | .72–.82 | .785 |
| Females ............ | 593–599 | .72–.84 | .775 |
| Grade 10 | | | |
| Males .............. | 566–570 | .75–.80 | .817 |
| Females ............ | 535–538 | .74–.90 | .848 |

SOURCE: *Manual for Interpreting, Ohio Vocational Interest Survey,*
copyright 1970 by Harcourt Brace Jovanovich, Inc. Reprinted by special permission of the publishers.

criminated by the OVIS scales for agriculture, care of people and animals,
and manual work.

## INTERPRETING AN OVIS PROFILE

Figure 7.4 presents a sample OVIS profile. Three kinds of scores are
presented — scale scores, percentiles, and stanines. The scale score is based
on a weight of 1 for "Dislike very much," 2 for "Dislike," 3 for "Neutral," 4 for "Like," and 5 for "Like very much." With eleven items in each
scale, an OVIS raw score can range from 11 to 55. The scale score is useful because it is simple and gives the student the opportunity to compare
his interests in one area with those in another. Scale scores are highlighted
by listing the OVIS scales in a student's profile not in serial order as defined in the cubistic model but in rank order based on raw scores. Thus,
the student can see the areas in which he has shown high interest and those
in which he has low interest.

Normative comparisons are supplied through the percentile equivalents
to each scale score. The OVIS was standardized on a representative national sample of about 47,000 high school students in grades 8 through
12. Stanine scores were developed from this same group. Stanines provide
steps of equal difficulty, each half a standard deviation, so that the difference between stanine 1 and 2, for instance, is the same as that between 4
and 5. This is not true of percentiles. The difference between percentile 1
and 2, or between 10 and 11, would be much greater than the difference
between 50 and 51. Percentiles tend to cluster in the center of the distribution, whereas stanines are evenly spread out.

The OVIS profile emphasizes the idiographic over the normative by

181

rank ordering the scales in the report by raw scores. The two approaches together offer a strong foundation of data to be used in counseling. For example, in Figure 7.4, Bruce Porter has a scale score of 49 and a stanine of 9 for his highest ranking score. This indicates that the interest scale or area Bruce likes best also stands pretty high when compared to the interests of other boys in the same grade.

The scale clarity index (SCI) is a novel feature of the OVIS. It is somewhat similar to a verification scale but it was not designed for that purpose. It measures consistency in responses. If a student dislikes an area, such as manual work, his responses to the items in this scale would probably average around a D response. If he is not certain how he feels toward, say, manual work, his responses would tend to vary since the items in the scale are homogeneous. The scale score alone would not reflect this variation because it is a sum of weights. The scale clarity index of H, F, or I, which stand for highly consistent, fairly consistent, or inconsistent respectively, is based on the deviation of his responses from his average response to the items in the scale. The cutoff limits for the scale clarity indices were arrived at by analyzing empirical data on all possible patterns of responses.

A mathematical basis for reporting the scale clarity indices is necessary since the mean and the standard deviation provide independent pieces of information. A lack of clarity in the responses of a student to any of the OVIS scales should be used by counselors as a valuable piece of information about the student, for it might reflect his vocational development.

The scale clarity concept depends upon the homogeneity of the twenty-four OVIS scales. Lack of homogeneity could introduce an artificial lack of clarity. The homogeneity of OVIS scales was checked carefully using factor analytic procedures similar to those utilized by Campbell, Borgen, Eastes, Johansson, and Peterson (1968) in developing the twenty-two basic interest scales for the SVIB. Incidentally there is a remarkable similarity between the Strong basic interest scales and the OVIS scales, even though the latter were derived from a theoretical model. The major difference between them is that the OVIS includes low-level work areas, such as manual work, personal service, and care of people and animals, and the SVIB does not.

## SOME ILLUSTRATIVE PROFILES

Information concerning Bruce's stronger and weaker interests is given in the rank order of his scores (see Fig. 7.4). Those at the top of the list

182

OVIS PROFILE CHART

Name   BRUCE                                    Date of Testing   FEBRUARY 11, 1969

Grade   9        Age  14 yrs.   7 mos.     Sex  M

NAT Reference Group    9th GRADE MALE

| Data–People–Things Code | Scale No. | Name | Scale Score | SCI | %ile Rank | Stanine |
|---|---|---|---|---|---|---|
| 200 | 13 | NUMERICAL | 49 | H | 96 | 9 |
| 022 | 2 | MACHINE WORK | 45 | F | 93 | 8 |
| 120 | 11 | TRAINING | 44 | H | 96 | 9 |
| 202 | 16 | APPLIED TECH | 42 | H | 75 | 6 |
| 102 | 7 | CRAFTS | 41 | F | 88 | 7 |
| 201 | 14 | APPRAISAL | 36 | F | 70 | 6 |
| 212 | 20 | SALES REPRESENT | 36 | F | 82 | 7 |
| 210 | 18 | MANAGEMENT | 35 | F | 62 | 6 |
| 220 | 22 | ENTERTAINMENT | 34 | H | 82 | 7 |
| 101 | 6 | INSPECT-TESTING | 33 | F | 89 | 8 |
| 220 | 23 | TEACH-COUNS-SOC W | 33 | F | 64 | 6 |
| 210 | 17 | PROMOTION-COMMU | 32 | F | 59 | 5 |
| 220 | 21 | MUSIC | 30 | I | 56 | 5 |
| 202 | 15 | AGRICULTURE | 29 | F | 54 | 5 |
| 110 | 8 | CUSTOMER SERVICE | 27 | F | 56 | 5 |
| 100 | 5 | CLERICAL WORK | 26 | I | 68 | 6 |
| 222 | 24 | MEDICAL | 26 | F | 63 | 6 |
| 112 | 10 | SKILLED PER SERV | 25 | I | 70 | 6 |
| 011 | 4 | CARE PEOPLE-ANIM | 24 | I | 49 | 5 |
| 111 | 9 | NURSING | 24 | H | 57 | 5 |
| 010 | 3 | PERSONAL SERVICE | 23 | H | 64 | 6 |
| 212 | 19 | ARTISTIC | 23 | F | 27 | 4 |
| 001 | 1 | MANUAL | 22 | H | 57 | 5 |
| 200 | 12 | LITERARY | 19 | H | 21 | 3 |

STUDENT QUESTIONNAIRE INFORMATION

1. Occupational Plans

   First   APPLIED TECH

2. Second  TRAINING

2. Best Liked Subjects

   First   MATHEMATICS

   Second  SOCIAL STUDIES

3. High School Program

   First   GENERAL

4. Post-High School Plans

   First   VOC-TECH SCHOOL

5. Interest in Vocational Programs

   INTERESTED

6. Vocational Program Choice

   First   ELECTRONICS

   Second  APPLIANCE REPAIR

7. Local Survey Information

| A | B | C | D | E | F | G | H |
|---|---|---|---|---|---|---|---|
| 3 | 6 | 3 | 4 | 9 | 1 | 5 | 2 |

Figure 7.4. Bruce's OVIS profile. (Reprinted with modifications from p. 7 of the *Manual for Interpreting, Ohio Vocational Interest Survey*, 1970, by special permission of Harcourt Brace Jovanovich, Inc.)

reflect his strongest likes and those at the bottom his weakest interests or dislikes. Discussion of Bruce's interests can be organized around these two clusters.[3]

Notice that scales 2, 16, and 17 are concerned with things: the third digit of the identifying code being 2. Four of the highest scales, 13, 2, 16, and 7, relate to work in which involvement with people is low. The second digit of these scales' data-people-things code is 0. Except for scale 2, all the highest ranks relate to jobs with moderate to high data involvement. Examination of the lowest ranking scales adds meaning to the high-

3. Discussion of this case and Sharon's has been adapted from the *Manual for Interpreting, Ohio Vocational Interest Survey*, by special permission of Harcourt Brace Jovanovich, Inc.

ranking ones. Scales 10, 4, 9, 3, and 19 all include jobs with average (level 1) involvement with people.

The scale clarity indices (SCI's) from Bruce's profile are another source for understanding his interests. Bruce's score on scale 13 is 49, and his scale clarity index is H, or highly consistent. Bruce must have responded either "Like" or "Like very much" to all the items in scale 13 in order to have scored 49. However, his score on scale 2, which is almost as high but which has a scale clarity index of F (fairly consistent), shows more varied responses on scale 2 than on scale 13.

Bruce's profile reveals another use of the scale clarity index. He earned a score of 30 on scale 21, music. This score suggests that his orientation for music is neutral. But his SCI of I (inconsistent) shows that some likes and some dislikes appeared in his responses. If one knows that music contains items from three different groups, instrumental, vocal, and creative, one may guess that he might like one set and dislike the other. Thus for Bruce, music may be a nonvocational interest or something he might want to explore further.

Additional details regarding Bruce Porter's case are provided in the OVIS *Manual*. Let us now look at a girl's profile and examine at the same time how the student questionnaire section can be combined with the interest inventory section of OVIS.

One immediately notices about Sharon's OVIS profile (Fig. 7.5) that she has many high scores reflecting many "like" responses. But there is a natural break in the rank ordered scale scores between 46 and 41, and she has high scale clarity indices for all the scales on which she scored 46 or higher. The work areas represented by her top scores usually require little training beyond high school. In the middle of the list Sharon's scales are not so high, but she has an SCI of I on most of them. This means she responded "Like" to some of the items in a scale and "Dislike" to others.

When Sharon's interests are compared to those of her norm group her scores tend to be high. More than half of her scales are scored at stanines of 7, 8, or 9. The scales in the lower half of the profile have stanine scores of 5, 6, and 7, indicating that although Sharon does not show much interest in these areas, she does not dislike them as much as the norm group of girls do.

It can be said that Sharon is interested in work that involves people and data more than things, for the scales on which she scores low are more concerned with things than with data or people. Also, her highest scales

184

have codes that indicate a moderate level of involvement: 1's predominate over 2's down to the break at Scale 10.

From Sharon's profile, it may be possible to say that her interests have not begun to arrange themselves in coherent patterns. She expresses more than an ordinary amount of liking for many different kinds and levels of work and rejects only mechanical or technical occupations.

More support for concern about Sharon's realism in choosing a career can be derived from an analysis of the student questionnaire information. Her occupational choices of clerical work and nursing are consistent with her highest interests, but her plans for education are confused. Plans to

OVIS PROFILE CHART

Name  SHARON                                    Date of Testing  FEBRUARY 16, 1970

Grade  10    Age  16  yrs.   3  mos.    Sex  F

NAT Reference Group    10th GRADE FEMALE

| Data-People-Things Code | Scale No. | Name | Scale Score | SCI | Stanine |
|---|---|---|---|---|---|
| 100 | 5 | CLERICAL WORK | 53 | H | 9 |
| 111 | 9 | NURSING | 52 | H | 9 |
| 011 | 4 | CARE PEOPLE-ANIMALS | 49 | H | 8 |
| 110 | 8 | CUSTOMER SERVICE | 47 | H | 9 |
| 220 | 22 | ENTERTAINMENT | 47 | H | 8 |
| 112 | 10 | SKILLED PER. SERV. | 46 | H | 8 |
| 222 | 24 | MEDICAL | 41 | I | 8 |
| 210 | 18 | MANAGEMENT | 39 | F | 8 |
| 010 | 3 | PERSONAL SERVICE | 39 | I | 6 |
| 212 | 19 | ARTISTIC | 38 | I | 6 |
| 212 | 20 | SALES REPRESENT. | 36 | I | 6 |
| 220 | 21 | MUSIC | 36 | I | 6 |
| 200 | 12 | LITERARY | 35 | F | 6 |
| 120 | 11 | TRAINING | 35 | I | 6 |
| 101 | 6 | INSPECT.-TESTING | 34 | I | 8 |
| 210 | 17 | PROMOTION-COMM. | 34 | I | 6 |
| 220 | 23 | TEACH.-COUNS.-SOC.W. | 32 | I | 5 |
| 200 | 13 | NUMERICAL | 30 | F | 6 |
| 201 | 14 | APPRAISAL | 29 | I | 7 |
| 202 | 16 | APPLIED TECHNOLOGY | 26 | I | 7 |
| 102 | 7 | CRAFTS | 22 | F | 6 |
| 001 | 1 | MANUAL | 13 | H | 3 |
| 202 | 15 | AGRICULTURE | 11 | H | 1 |
| 002 | 2 | MACHINE WORK | 11 | H | 2 |

ABILITY-ACHIEVEMENT RECORD (National Norms)

Otis Lennon Mental Ability Test
    1969 - Deviation 10.92
            Stanine 4

Stanford H.S. Achievement Test
    1969

English                 Stanine 2
Numerical Comprehension  Stanine 2
Reading                 Stanine 3
Spelling                Stanine 4

RANK IN CLASS:  554 in a class of 787

SCHOOL GRADES

Grade 10 (first semester)

English 10          D
Business Math       C
Typing 2            C
World History       D
Art 10              C

DAYS ABSENT:  Grade 9 - 10½

STUDENT QUESTIONNAIRE INFORMATION

1. Occupational Plans

   First Choice    CLERICAL

   Second Choice   NURSING

2. Best Liked Subjects

   First Choice    ART

   Second Choice   ENGLISH

3. High-School Program

   First Choice    GENERAL

4. Post-High School Plans

   First Choice    COLLEGE-UNIVERSITY

5. Interest in Vocational Programs
      INTERESTED

6. Vocational Program Choice

   First Choice    SECRETARIAL

   Second Choice   DENTAL ASSISTANT

7. Local Survey Information

A-3  (Father's Occupation)  CUSTOMER SERVICE

D-10 (Mother's Occupation)  HOUSEWIFE

E-5  (Brothers and Sisters) FIVE

F-8  (Self-estimate of Ability)
        ABOUT SAME AS GRADES I HAVE RECEIVED

G-4  (Self-estimate of Special Talent)
        CLERICAL

H-10 (Post-High School Plans)
        GRADUATION FROM A 4-YEAR COLLEGE

Figure 7.5. Sharon's OVIS profile. (Reprinted with modifications from p. 13 of the *Manual for Interpreting, Ohio Vocational Interest Survey*, 1970, by special permission of Harcourt Brace Jovanovich, Inc.)

185

attend college are inappropriate to a goal of clerical work. And if she expects to attend college, she should not choose the general curriculum in high school. Furthermore, she expresses interest in enrolling in a high school vocational course. Sharon's scholastic achievements are generally below the average of her peers. Therefore, college seems an unsuitable goal, but her estimate of her own capabilities is accurate, and her highest interests are congruent with them.

Because Sharon expresses so many differing interests, she might be assisted in crystallizing them around an appropriate goal by learning more about diverse clusters of work. She could be helped to discover that college is not likely to aid her in the type of job she is interested in. As she gathers more realistic information about jobs and work, she may be able to name one or two occupational areas compatible with her abilities and interests, and perhaps eventually begin to plan for a few specific jobs within those areas.

COUNSELING USES OF OVIS

The OVIS can be used in two ways: individual counseling to help the student to understand the meaning of his own profile and to utilize it for vocational planning and exploration; and curriculum planning.

The profile is useful in counseling with the individual student for a number of reasons. Through OVIS, the student might gain some insight into his general interest level with respect to the areas of work. On Bruce Porter's profile, for example, the highest five or six scales might be compared with the lowest scales. The rank order printout is designed to help in this. Another way of doing this is to consider scale scores above 40 and those below 26.

One can also look at the absolute level of interest on various scales. Bruce Porter's manual scale score is 22. If that total score is divided by the eleven items he answered, an average response of 2 is obtained, which is the equivalent of "dislike." With only this information at hand, one might say that Bruce dislikes manual work. But the stanine related to a score of 22 on this scale is 5, which is within a half standard deviation of the mean. Thus disliking manual work is the average response for boys of his age.

Counselors should also be particularly aware of the data-people-things emphasis noted in the high and low groups of scales. This is where the cubistic model becomes applicable in practice. Attention should be paid to the relative positions of the scales in the two groups in the cubistic space.

Scale clarity also merits close scrutiny. If the student is inconsistent, as Bruce is on the sample profile for the music scale, this could be the result of liking very much a specific job in the area covered by the scale, while not being attracted to the rest. As a student matures, he tends to narrow his choices and to become more specific about what he likes and dislikes. If the scale clarity approach were used for the OVIS inventories of college students, the specificity of vocational development might be a real problem, but for junior high and high school levels and for the current OVIS scales the scale clarity concept appears to work reasonably well.

The profile can be viewed in terms of the tendency of the person to like very much or dislike very much. At the same time one must consider scale clarity indices and note the consistency with which the responses have been made. Profiles with all 11's or all 55's with highly consistent scale clarity indices should be questioned.

The student information questionnaire can be used to check the compatibility of measured versus expressed interests and of academic versus vocational plans. The questionnaire also makes it possible to judge the consistency and realism of responses.

Group summaries of OVIS results may be beneficial in planning curriculum experiences such as group orientations. Thus if it is found that one or a few vocational occupations were chosen by large numbers of students, special group sessions might be held to explore other vocational areas. If a significant group does not have occupational plans, materials may be developed to stimulate vocational maturity. Since OVIS is linked to the *Dictionary of Occupational Titles*, it can be used as a starting point in exploring the world of work. It is also a link to the General Aptitude Test Battery because job clusters are described in the DOT in terms of their scores. These, in turn, are related to labor market information.

The Ohio Vocational Interest Survey approaches occupational planning through interests. Several jobs are suggested to the student under each scale. Furthermore, the detailed OVIS scale descriptions lead the student to other factors described in the DOT. Interests appear to be meaningful dimensions for vocational planning, and decisions made on the basis of interests can be lasting and stable.

187

# References

Campbell, D. P., F. H. Borgen, S. H. Eastes, C. B. Johansson, and R. A. Peterson. A set of basic interest scales for the Strong Vocational Interest Blank for men. *Journal of Applied Psychology*, 1968, 52, Pt. 2.

Cooley, W. W., and P. R. Lohnes. *Predicting development of young adults.* Palo Alto, Calif.: Project TALENT, American Institutes for Research and University of Pittsburgh, 1968.

D'Costa, A. The differentiation of high school students in vocational education areas using the Ohio Vocational Interest Survey. Ph.D. dissertation, Ohio State University, 1968.

————, and D. Winefordner. A cubistic model of vocational interests. *Vocational Guidance Quarterly*, 1969, 17, 242–249.

————, J. G. Odgers, and P. B. Koons. *Ohio Vocational Interest Survey.* New York: Harcourt Brace Jovanovich, 1969.

Roe, A. Early determinants of vocational choice. *Journal of Counseling Psychology*, 1957, 4, 212–217.

Thorndike, E. L. Intelligence and its measurements: A symposium. *Journal of Educational Psychology*, 1921, 12, 124–127.

United States Department of Labor, Bureau of Employment Security. *Dictionary of occupational titles.* Washington, D.C.: United States Government Printing Office, 1965.

188

# 8

# The Work Values Inventory

## Donald E. Super

HOW <u>DO</u> WE JUDGE WHAT PEOPLE WANT? WHAT <u>IS</u> MOTIVATION? Motivation is variously defined in terms of needs, personality traits, values, and interests. Defining each of these in turn is not easy, for the definitions often overlap. When one examines the instruments developed for assessing them, the constructs seem no more precise, for measures of needs contain items that resemble those found in tests of traits and values, and measures of interests often include items like those found in need, trait, and values inventories. Having worked sporadically over the past three decades at the development of one values inventory, I think I now have a somewhat clearer idea of the nature of these personal qualities, and I should like to begin pedantically, with definitions, for definitions in this domain are notoriously muddy.

A need is a lack of something which, if present, would contribute to the well-being of the individual and which is accompanied by a drive to do something about it. Concepts of needs sometimes focus on lacks such as nourishment, shelter, and love, and sometimes on drives such as achievement or the need to do something constructive.

Traits, values, and interests derive from needs. The need to have, to do, or even to be leads to action, and action leads to modes of behavior or traits that seek objectives formulated in generic terms (values) or in specific terms (interests). Traits are ways of acting to meet a need in a given

189

situation. Values are objectives that one seeks to attain to satisfy a need. Interests are the specific activities and objects through which values can be attained and needs met.

My focus on values is the result not of chance or of my own idiosyncratic interests, but of the hierarchical nature of needs, traits, values, and interests. It is the result of that hierarchical structure's effects on the relation between each of these human characteristics and behavior in education and in occupations. Studies on the relationships between personality and educational or vocational behavior have been generally unfruitful when personality has been defined as needs or traits. Those who assess these variables in educational or occupational counseling or selection do so more from blind belief in the importance of personality than from evidence that what they are assessing differentially affects choice or success. Needs are so fundamental, so far removed from specific activities and objects, that any one of them can be met in a great variety of ways. Traits are matters of style, also rather remote from specific activities and objects, so that any given role, educational or occupational, can be played with a variety of styles. Assessments of needs and traits may help us to understand the make-up of people, but they do not help us to predict educational or occupational behavior.

Values and interests, on the other hand, are closer to actual life. Values are the objectives sought in behavior, and interests are the activities in which the values are sought. A given value, like a given need, may be satisfied in more than one kind of activity, but the connection between goal and activity is closer for values than for needs, while not as close as that for interests. For example, the need for love may find outlets in many different kinds of life situations, both licit and illicit. The social values that derive from love preclude the seeking of certain kinds of relationships; they direct attention toward certain other kinds of activities such as volunteer community service, the ministry, social work, and education. Social service interests focus choice even more specifically on social work or on teaching.

It is therefore to values and to interests that educators and personnel workers must look if they want to attend to motivation in ways relevant to the choices and performances of their students and employees.

The Work Values Inventory (WVI) was developed to assess the various goals that motivate men to work. It is designed to measure the values *extrinsic to* as well as *intrinsic in* work, satisfactions which may be the by-products or the outcomes of work as well as those which men and women seek in their work activity. It attempts to measure these values in people at all age levels beginning with adolescence and at all educational and intelligence levels beginning with entry into junior high school. It is, both in the variety of values tapped and in the groups for which it is appropriate, a wide-ranging values inventory.

The intrinsic interest of work that is valued for its own sake has often been contrasted with work that is interesting largely because of what it makes possible, such as associating with people one likes. Work is seen, for many persons and particularly for those engaged in higher level occupations (Wrenn, 1964; Havighurst, 1964), as a means of self-actualization, of finding a life role (Friedmann and Havighurst, 1954), and of implementing one's self-concept (Super, 1951, 1963). For large numbers of others, particularly the semiskilled and unskilled in both blue- and white-collar categories, and also for many women at all occupational levels, work is seen as a means to other ends. For such people vocational interest inventories provide little in the way of useful data: their values and interests are not vocational. But work does have meaning to them, and its meaning should be realized.

Understanding the values of a student or a client in educational and vocational counseling or of an applicant for a position in business or industry is thus an important aid in clarifying goals and in determining the psychological appropriateness of a given type of education, training, or employment.

## DEVELOPMENT OF THE WVI

The Work Values Inventory has been tested in a variety of forms in research since 1951. First a series of items was selected from the published research on values and job satisfaction to be used in writing trial items (Super et al., 1957).

The refinement of items was done several times, in a series of tape-recorded interviews with eighth-grade boys concerning the meanings they saw in the items and essays by other junior high school pupils were used to write items in junior high school language. These students' essays showed that the constructs of a way of life, economic security, and surroundings need definition in order to have meaning, and that even then the first-named is not well handled by young boys and girls. Item refinement was also carried out in two series of experiments in which

191

items typed on $3 \times 5$ cards were sorted and labeled by young men, not college students or graduates, in order to ascertain the uniformity of understanding or the internal consistency of scales. Comparable work done with office clerks in India (Shah, 1969) gave similar results. Inventories made up of the seemingly best items were tried out, item analyzed, and examined for test-retest reliability. A forced-choice inventory was used with the Career Pattern Study subjects (Super et al., 1957), with other high school pupils (Hana, 1954), in a study on guidance counselors (Super and Kaplan, 1967), and in a number of other unpublished studies.

A forced-choice method, Cronbach (1969) has reported, differentiates better than a rating format. Normile (1967) has shown, with both forced-choice and rating forms of the WVI, that occupational groups are indeed somewhat better differentiated from each other by the forced-choice method. But the forced-choice format has two serious defects. It is found annoying by many subjects because of its seeming repetition of items, a major complaint with the early WVI. It is not as reliable as the rating form, as Cronbach has reported, and as found in a series of experiments with forced-choice, rank order, and rating forms of the WVI. I chose reliability, at the expense of some differentiating power and of some delay in publication. Thus, the WVI has evolved into a forty-five-item inventory responded to by rating each item on a five-point scale.

INTERPRETING VALUES INVENTORIES

The Work Values Inventory may be used with boys and girls in junior and senior high school, with college and university students, and with adults who have completed an elementary education. The vocabulary has been shown to be simple enough for seventh graders and is quite acceptable to graduate students and professional men and women. The constructs it measures have meaning for a wide variety of people at all socioeconomic and intellectual levels.

The meanings of values differ, however, from one intellectual, educational, or social level to another. For example, the phrase "lead the kind of life you most enjoy" means one thing to an intellectual, something else to a rake: their values are actually different. Independence, to an assembly worker, may signify only freedom from close supervision, whereas to a research biologist it may connote freedom to choose his own problems and to pursue them in his own way. Intellectual stimulation to the high-school-graduate office clerk may mean dealing with varied tasks rather

192

than following set routines, but to a graduate engineer it may mean being confronted with new situations for which novel solutions have to be developed.

The user of a values inventory must therefore avoid ascribing his own meanings to scores. Instead he must examine the profile to see, for example, (1) whether a high independence score is accompanied by high intellectual stimulation and creativity scores, suggesting that the student with whom he is dealing is a self-directing intellectual who might become a scientific researcher, or (2) whether the high independence score is associated with high variety and economic returns scores, indicating that the student's independence is of the entrepreneurial type which might lead to satisfaction in selling life insurance.

The two or three highly rated values, and the two or three on which scores are low, direct the counselor's attention to areas to be explored in an interview. The student can be asked to tell what, for example, he means by "lead the kind of life you enjoy," what constitutes variety, or what he finds intellectually stimulating. This kind of clinical interpretation of tests encourages the counselee to think and to talk rather than evoking only an "unh hunh" as he contemplates a percentile that compares him with other students or occupational groups.

Normative comparisons are of course helpful too. The current normative format of the WVI not only increases the reliability of scores, but makes legitimate the use of comparative data. National norms have been developed for each sex, grade, and curricular group of the six years of high school and will soon be available for junior colleges.

Sex differences do warrant separate norms for girls and boys in the twelfth grade, for girls at this age tend to value altruism more and independence less than boys; in the seventh grade, however, sex differences are negligible, as other data on development in boys and girls might suggest. Although grade differences are negligible from one year to the next, there is enough difference between junior and high school students to make it desirable to treat them separately. In the WVI *Manual*, grade norms for each sex are supplied, but use of them is not necessary. Curricular comparisons of high school students were made, but were not used, for no differences were found. At the college level, where curricular choices are more specialized and more meaningful, work with both the Allport-Vernon-Lindzey Study of Values (AVL) and the WVI shows that such norms are desirable. However, they are not yet available. Occu-

193

pational differences have been found with both the ipsative and the normative forms of the WVI. They will be discussed later.

## INDEPENDENCE OF THE VALUES SCALES

Scales that are developed on the basis of a logic derived from theory and research and refined by internal consistency methods, as were those of the WVI and the AVL, generally demonstrate a significant number of positive intercorrelations. This is especially true of scales that consist of rated rather than forced-choice items, for in ratings response sets tend to inflate the true correlations, while in forced choices the fact of preferring one alternative precludes making a response to the other option and lowers the obtained correlations.

For twelfth-grade boys the range of intercorrelations of the WVI scales is from −.07 for creativity and economic returns to .66 for economic returns and security; fifty of the correlations are equal to or above .30, and six are equal to or greater than .50. These six practically as well as significantly related scales are those loading on two factors that will be described later. For seventh-grade boys there are no correlations as high as .50, but there are forty-four equal to or exceeding .30. The data for girls are essentially the same.

There is considerable overlap between the economic returns, security, surroundings, and supervisory scales and between the intellectual stimulation and creativity scales. The amount of overlap is less in early adolescence than in later adolescence. Factor analytic studies of the WVI suggest the use of at least one of the scales loading on the material factor (e.g., economic returns), one loading on the self-expression factor (e.g., intellectual stimulation), and nine other scales that have lower correlations with these two clusters for a total of at least eleven of the fifteen scales. Valuing being respected by others (prestige), for example, is theoretically and empirically different enough from valuing income (economic returns) to warrant its retention as a separate scale despite the intercorrelation. For prediction studies, it is true, factor scores may well prove more effective.

## FACTORIAL STRUCTURE OF THE WVI

O'Connor and Kinnane (1961) used a form of the WVI that consisted of thirty items (two statements for each value) rated on a four-point scale, thus avoiding the correlational problems arising in the paired-comparison method and anticipating the present forty-five item, five-point scale form. They administered the Work Values Inventory to 191 male college students, computed correlations between items, and factored the matrix by the centroid method until six factors were extracted; these were rotated until a simple structure solution was achieved. An attempt was made to extract second-order factors, but none were found. The first-order factors appeared to be identifiable as security-economic-material, social-artistic, work conditions and associates, heuristic-creative, achievement-prestige, and independence-variety.

The current normative form of the WVI was administered twice with an interval of two weeks between testings to a sample of ninety-nine high school students, fifty-one boys and forty-eight girls. The results are shown in Table 8.1. A principal component analysis with varimax rotation was conducted for each of the four sets of data (test and retest for males and for females) to identify the basic dimensions of the inventory (Hendrix and Super, 1968). Results for boys are shown in Table 8.2 — results confirmed independently with 200 tenth-grade students in another study (Gable and Pruzek, 1969).

Table 8.1. Means, Standard Deviations, and Test-Retest Reliability
of Work Values Inventory Scales, Form A

| Scale | 51 Tenth-Grade Males | | 48 Tenth-Grade Females | | 99 Tenth Graders | | |
|---|---|---|---|---|---|---|---|
| | Mean[a] | S.D.[a] | Mean[a] | S.D.[a] | Mean[a] | S.D.[a] | Relia-bility[b] |
| 1. Altruism ..... | 10.61 | 3.12 | 12.19 | 2.61 | 11.13 | 3.34 | .83 |
| 2. Esthetics ..... | 7.76 | 3.08 | 7.56 | 3.05 | 7.52 | 3.19 | .82 |
| 3. Creativity .... | 10.06 | 2.81 | 9.29 | 2.49 | 9.43 | 2.95 | .84 |
| 4. Intellectual stimulation ... | 11.61 | 2.65 | 11.75 | 2.32 | 11.22 | 3.08 | .81 |
| 5. Independence . | 10.47 | 2.51 | 10.00 | 2.28 | 9.84 | 2.82 | .83 |
| 6. Achievement .. | 12.08 | 2.03 | 11.98 | 2.16 | 11.60 | 2.91 | .83 |
| 7. Prestige ...... | 11.49 | 2.17 | 11.29 | 2.19 | 11.05 | 2.81 | .76 |
| 8. Management .. | 9.80 | 2.44 | 9.48 | 2.74 | 9.38 | 2.94 | .84 |
| 9. Economic returns ....... | 12.84 | 2.12 | 11.63 | 2.57 | 11.88 | 3.03 | .88 |
| 10. Security ...... | 11.27 | 2.59 | 10.38 | 2.79 | 10.47 | 3.26 | .87 |
| 11. Surroundings .. | 10.94 | 2.51 | 11.31 | 2.25 | 10.76 | 2.94 | .82 |
| 12. Supervisory relations ...... | 10.92 | 2.54 | 10.73 | 2.66 | 10.64 | 2.98 | .83 |
| 13. Associates .... | 11.27 | 2.57 | 11.77 | 2.25 | 11.08 | 3.08 | .74 |
| 14. Variety ...... | 10.33 | 2.41 | 10.73 | 2.23 | 10.98 | 2.83 | .82 |
| 15. Way of life ... | 12.92 | 2.03 | 12.81 | 2.19 | 12.44 | 2.95 | .80 |

[a] Based on first administration of test.
[b] Based on retest after two weeks.

Table 8.2. Four Basic Dimensions[a] of the Work Values Inventory, Form A, for 51 Tenth-Grade Males

| I Material | II Goodness of Life | III Self-Expression | IV Behavior Control |
|---|---|---|---|
| | | *Test* | |
| 10 Security ....0.89 | 13 Associates ......0.87 | 3 Creativity ......0.74 | 5 Independence ..0.78 |
| 9 Economic returns ....0.88 | 1 Altruism ......0.71 | 14 Variety .........0.71 | 8 Management ...0.74 |
| 12 Supervisory relations .....0.75 | 11 Surroundings ...0.65 | 4 Intellectual stimulation ....0.61 | 7 Prestige ........0.60 |
| 11 Surroundings ...0.58 | | | |
| 15 Way of Life ....0.56 | | | |
| | | *Re-Test* | |
| 12 Supervisory relations ........0.86 | 1 Altruism ......0.85 | 14 Variety ........0.82 | 5 Independence ..0.81 |
| 10 Security ......0.86 | 2 Esthetics ......0.75 | 4 Intellectual stimulation ....0.77 | 8 Management ...0.74 |
| 11 Surroundings ...0.84 | 6 Achievement ...0.59 | 3 Creativity ......0.72 | |
| 9 Economic returns ......0.84 | | | |
| 13 Associates ......0.80 | | | |
| 7 Prestige ........0.74 | | | |
| 15 Way of life......0.71 | | | |

[a] In the first testing, a doubtful fifth factor had loadings on the esthetics and achievement scales.

196

It appears that for boys there are four separate dimensions underlying the Work Values Inventory. Two of these are quite distinct, whereas factors I and II are less stable and are related by the switching of certain values. The related factors I and II appear to consist respectively of material or situational (extrinsic) and goodness of life (intrinsic) work values. Factor III, self-expression, primarily includes occupationally related activities and, like factor II, may be closely connected to basic personality. Factor IV is one of autonomy or behavior control since it involves the direction of work and relationships with other persons. In girls, at least three distinct dimensions are exhibited, similar to those found in boys.

## VALIDITY

Since 1954, when the American Psychological Association's Committee on Test Standards published its landmark report, it has become customary to examine tests in the light of several different, well-defined aspects of validity, although as Loevinger (1957) has pointed out, content, concurrent, and predictive validity may be viewed as aspects of construct validity. One of the best proofs of the theoretical or construct validity of a test, for example, is that it does predict what the underlying theory says it should.

The construct validity of the WVI may be explored by asking whether the variables which the WVI seeks to measure are meaningful in terms of psychological theory. Some of the values tapped by the WVI are derived from Spranger's theory and from the AVL, which is based upon and has supported that theory. Spranger's theory is one of the sources of the altruism, esthetics, intellectual stimulation, prestige, and economic returns values, although some scales and constructs were modified as work progressed. The values assessed were also derived from research on job satisfaction and morale; work by Hoppock (1935), Centers (1948), and others led to the conclusion that there are many values associated with work that are not on Spranger's list. Theorizing by Darley and Hagenah (1955), Fryer (1931), Ginzberg (1951), and myself (Super, 1957), much of it based on pertinent research, provides further evidence of the relevance of the WVI to theory. This theory states that some values are intrinsic in the work activity itself (although not necessarily intercorrelated), that others are associated with it in various ways, and that still others are the results of work even though not necessarily related to any particular type of work.

Construct validity is often shown by how the test in question correlates with appropriate scales of other tests designed to assess the same or similar traits, e.g., the MVI with the AVL, the SVIB, and the Kuder Preference Record-Vocational (KPR-V). These correlations (Table 8.3) tend to be in expected directions, but are not substantial. Sometimes the changes made in the WVI constructs as a result of empirical item revision and sometimes the differences between values and interest seem to cause the low correlations. For example, the altruism scale correlates significantly, positively, and moderately with the social service scale of the Kuder and with the social scale of the AVL (.29), and to a much lesser extent with some other expected scales, but not with the YMCA key of the SVIB, which itself has a negligible correlation with the AVL social scale. Similarly, the creativity scale correlates moderately well with the artistic and scientific scales of the SVIB, with only the artistic and the literary scales of the Kuder, and with the AVL theoretical scale. Ivey (1963) has noted that it is the five WVI values which deal most with job-related activities (creative, esthetic, management, intellectual stimulation, and altruism) that *are* related to KPR-V scores. The remainder, which have more to do with rewards and concomitants, are appropriately *un*related to what might be called Kuder's intrinsic activity scales.

Content validity, too, is a concern. Since values are, by definition, goals or desired outcomes, there are three obvious ways by which values may be studied. One method is to observe what people seek and to infer values from their manifest behavior; this, however, is time-consuming and subject to errors of inference. The second is to secure a record from the subject of the choices he has made and to infer values from activities chosen; again there is the possibility of errors of inference, compounded by errors in self-reporting. The third is to ask the subject what he seeks; this method retains the error of self-report, but avoids errors of inference.

It is the self-report method which is used in the WVI. Social desirability, the major spoiler of self-report data, has been manipulated in experimentation with WVI items (Super and Mowry, 1962). It affects *only* the altruism and independence responses, the former scores being inflated and the latter deflated.

The statements used to express the fifteen values of the WVI were field tested in a variety of ways to ensure their comprehensibility and their adequacy in getting at the intended values. This objective seems to have been achieved, judging by the item-sorting and labeling experiments and by the

198

Table 8.3. Correlations of WVI Scales with Other Value and Interest Measures

| Values | WVI Form D and SVIB (52 Peace Corps Men)[a] | | | | | | | | WVI Form B and Kuder Preference Record Vocational Form CH (85 Boston University Freshmen)[b] | | | | | | | | | | WVI 1968–69 and AVL (304 Twelfth-Grade Boys)[c] | | | | | |
|---|---|---|---|---|---|---|---|---|---|---|---|---|---|---|---|---|---|---|---|---|---|---|---|---|
| | Artist | Physician | Engineer | Farmer | Y Secretary | Purchasing Agt. | Life Ins. Sales. | Lawyer | Outdoor | Mechanical | Computation | Scientific | Persuasive | Artistic | Literary | Musical | Social Service | Clerical | Theoretical | Economic | Esthetic | Social | Political | Religious |
| Altruism | 03 | -18 | -28 | -11 | 18 | -12 | 31 | 21 | -06 | -21 | -11 | -06 | -20 | -09 | -20 | -06 | 67 | -21 | -01 | -16 | -03 | 29 | -19 | 11 |
| Esthetics | 55 | 15 | -05 | -18 | 04 | -59 | -16 | 29 | 24 | -08 | -19 | -09 | -21 | 48 | -01 | 17 | 17 | -34 | -03 | -14 | 08 | 14 | -20 | 12 |
| Creativity | 24 | 21 | 25 | -27 | 11 | -29 | -19 | 21 | 23 | 14 | -01 | 02 | -23 | 37 | 35 | 04 | -32 | -26 | 17 | -11 | -07 | 03 | -06 | 05 |
| Intellectual stimulation | 11 | 09 | 06 | -29 | 02 | -20 | 07 | 33 | 29 | 19 | 21 | 34 | -31 | 07 | 03 | -06 | -11 | -19 | 23 | -05 | -10 | -09 | -04 | 05 |
| Independence | 02 | 10 | 05 | -12 | -10 | 09 | -06 | 15 | 06 | -02 | -12 | 02 | -13 | 06 | 08 | -01 | 03 | -07 | -03 | 05 | -06 | 00 | 10 | -04 |
| Achievement | 04 | 18 | -08 | 15 | 02 | -22 | 08 | -02 | -13 | -15 | 08 | -07 | 01 | 02 | 02 | -27 | 15 | 19 | 03 | -02 | -09 | 13 | 02 | -04 |
| Prestige | -24 | -25 | -25 | -03 | 27 | 11 | 29 | 08 | -10 | 15 | -12 | -16 | 09 | 10 | 10 | -10 | 04 | 09 | -06 | 09 | -17 | 05 | 14 | -02 |
| Management | -60 | -37 | -33 | -42 | 57 | 43 | 53 | 09 | -20 | 15 | 29 | 02 | 27 | -35 | 08 | -25 | -27 | 24 | 00 | 06 | -18 | -04 | 21 | -01 |
| Economic returns | -29 | -11 | 13 | 31 | -12 | 38 | -16 | -40 | 15 | 30 | -01 | 14 | 22 | -11 | 00 | -08 | -36 | -01 | -11 | 24 | -12 | -13 | 24 | -10 |
| Security | -03 | 07 | 10 | 36 | -18 | 22 | -18 | -28 | -07 | 15 | 08 | 12 | 16 | -24 | -09 | -07 | -11 | 16 | -06 | 13 | -11 | -01 | 13 | -05 |
| Surroundings | 05 | 16 | 27 | 49 | -32 | 08 | -43 | -40 | -09 | -17 | -03 | -11 | 08 | -08 | -15 | 17 | -01 | 24 | -07 | 09 | -13 | 03 | 04 | 05 |
| Supervisory relations | -08 | 13 | 21 | 02 | -17 | 13 | -22 | -28 | -17 | 08 | 02 | 07 | 06 | -19 | -20 | 14 | 00 | 17 | -06 | 03 | -05 | -01 | 02 | 06 |
| Associates | -06 | -08 | -04 | 31 | 03 | 13 | 02 | -21 | -14 | -13 | -01 | -03 | 01 | -20 | -16 | 24 | 18 | 10 | -05 | 08 | -10 | 15 | -08 | 02 |
| Variety | 15 | 01 | -05 | 05 | -16 | 07 | 08 | 12 | -06 | -19 | 12 | 24 | 11 | 01 | -07 | 05 | 07 | 08 | 05 | 00 | -06 | 01 | -01 | 03 |
| Way of life | 05 | 02 | 09 | 03 | -07 | -14 | -22 | 05 | 00 | -08 | -19 | -05 | 11 | 19 | 19 | 02 | -14 | -02 | -09 | 13 | -07 | -03 | 08 | -01 |

[a] r = .23, p = .05 one-tailed; r = .27, p = .05 two-tailed.
[b] r = .18, p = .05 one-tailed; r = .21, p = .05 two-tailed.
[c] r = .055, p = .05 one-tailed; r = .11, p = .05 two-tailed.

essays written about the items by junior high school pupils. In the process of refining statements, however, the original nature of the item was in a few instances changed. What started out as an item to assess Spranger's theoretical value, the desire to understand, became intellectual stimulation, a rather less abstract desire to use one's intelligence. This is suggested by the current phrasing (e.g., "have to keep solving new problems") and by the fact that the scale has only a low positive correlation (.23) with the theoretical scale of the AVL. The achievement scale, designed to assess the seeking of satisfaction in mastery, involves more interest in tangible than in intangible outcomes. The prestige scale, intended to appraise political or power-seeking values, developed into a respect-seeking scale, as shown by its content and by its negligible, even though significant, positive correlation (.14) with the seemingly appropriate AVL scale. The low intercorrelations of apparently similar scales is, of course, a common phenomenon. Finally, the way of life scale, intended to assess a type of value that emerges in many interview studies as being important to many people today, seems more than other scales to have different meanings for people at different ages and at different intellectual and social levels; it correlates with virtually nothing.

The case for the content validity of the WVI rests, then, on the phrasing of items on the basis of a study of the literature on values, and on the revamping of the items in the light of their comprehension by teenagers and young adults of average ability.

The concurrent validity of value measures may be examined by their intercorrelation with personality measures. Values are often thought of as manifestations of personality traits and adjustment. For this reason the first kind of theoretically based concurrent validation to examine is the intercorrelations of WVI and personality and adjustment scales.

Few significant relationships, and these puzzling, were found in one study of ninth-grade boys (Super, 1962). Perhaps the safest conclusion is that work values, like most measurable variables, are not appreciably related to personality traits. Perhaps values are better defined by the activities in which they may be achieved than by the behavioral traits or styles exhibited in the process. Experience and status variables of other types, reflecting ability and school achievement, have therefore been studied in relation to the Work Values Inventory (Super, 1962; Ivey, 1963) with results which are also generally negative.

Curricular differences, too, have been studied. Although it has been shown that choice of curriculum in junior and even senior high school is determined largely by sex, socioeconomic status, and intellectual level, it seems likely that values are part of the same complex constellation of determinants. Many boys and girls change curricula during the course of secondary and higher education, and many make changes of field after leaving school or college, but the directional decisions they make in high school are nevertheless significant aspects of their careers.

Curricular differences in grades 7 through 12 are in most instances no greater than one raw score point or one-half of a standard deviation. The slight differences that do appear are such as might be expected: boys in the college preparatory curriculum have slightly higher mean scores on intellectual stimulation values than do boys in commercial and vocational curricula and somewhat lower means on economic returns than commercial pupils, while vocational students are a little higher on esthetic values. These and other differences at the high school level, which appear to contribute to the construct validity of the WVI, are not great enough to be of practical value in counseling or in personnel selection.

Curricular differences at higher educational levels may well prove significant, for studies of the AVL have frequently found them, and the existence of occupational differences with the WVI also supports this expectation. Post-high-school data with earlier forms of the WVI do show differences between various types of professional, technical, and business institute students, and the current form should do so too.

Grade differences can be expected to reflect whatever age differences might exist. Hana (1954) used the WVI to demonstrate a lack of age and grade differences in values during the junior and senior high school years. In the national sample on which the present form was standardized, the differences are also of no practical significance. Boys appear to show some slight decrease in altruism scores as they progress from grade 7 to grade 12 (or the schools tend to discourage and lose the more altruistic boys, which does not seem likely); a similar decrease in esthetics scores is noticeable. Girls show grade changes in values which are generally similar to those in boys.

Sex differences in values have frequently been observed. They are found also with the WVI, but only after the middle teens. Girls in the twelfth grade tend to make slightly higher scores on the altruism scale than do boys. Girls in the seventh grade differ less if at all from their male peers; at this level sex differences in values are truly negligible. Boys tend to make higher scores on the independence scale in twelfth grade, but again, the difference in the seventh grade is small.

One of the most important kinds of data for establishing the validity of an instrument for vocational use is its ability to differentiate people in various occupations. In the long run it is, of course, the ability to predict occupational choice, stability, satisfaction, or success that is significant but while longitudinal data on predictive validity are maturing, data on concurrent validity are helpful. In the case of a self-descriptive inventory, observed differences in traits *may* be the results of experience in the occupation rather than its cause. But at least in the case of the SVIB (1943, 1955), it has been demonstrated that differences found in members of an occupation exist before occupational entry or even training. This being true of interests, it may be expected to be true of values.

Earlier forms of the WVI have been used with several occupational groups, both advanced trainees and experienced workers. Sample results for two values illustrate the kinds of differences observed. Altruism is particularly characteristic of teachers and school counselors, of priests, and to a lesser extent business and clerical workers. Most occupational groups tend to make at least moderate scores on this value, which is one of two shown to be affected by social desirability. Engineers, however, give it little stress. Similarly, creativity values are high in teachers in the Peace Corps, in psychologists, and also in engineers; of the groups studied, electronics students and office workers are particularly low.

Four occupational studies may briefly be cited. Normile (1967) administered both ipsative and normative forms of the WVI to men employed in seven professions in the Baltimore area and found significant differences even in this group of high-level occupations. Psychiatrists, lawyers, and engineers valued intellectual stimulation more than did teachers; teachers valued economic security more than did psychiatrists and psychologists; priests were highest on altruism and lowest in their valuation of economic returns. In one of my unpublished studies, Peace Corps teacher trainees attached most importance to altruism, esthetics, creativity, intellectual stimulation, variety, and way of life, scoring low on economic returns, security, and surroundings. In another study (Super and Kaplan, 1967), school counselors attending summer NDEA Guidance Institutes were high on altruism, but also on economic returns and prestige, and low on esthetics — findings on the nature of those being trained for school counselors which some have found not altogether reassuring. Disadvantaged persons selected for clerical training in a New York bank were found to resemble the bank's regular newly hired clerical workers (Gapas, 1970).

Data on the occupational predictive validity of the WVI are now being collected on people working in the First National City Bank of New York, in three General Electric Company divisions, and in one IBM division. In due course, such data will, it is hoped, be much more extensive than the validity data available for any current values inventory.

CONCLUSIONS

I have gone into some detail on the differences between interests and values, seeking to clarify a distinction that has often been left unclarified and even muddy. I have pointed out why, if we are to measure motivation in education and in work (and we sorely need to), it will probably be by means of interest and values inventories. Some of the main characteristics of values inventories have been discussed in detail. This focus on values is doubly warranted because interest inventories are now widely known and used, whereas values inventories have been little known and used in the practice of counseling. I hope the WVI, on the basis of its merits, will stimulate more such use, and that my discussion will prove to be more than a bit of bragging by a new father.

## References

Allport, G. W., P. E. Vernon, and G. A. Lindzey. *A study of values* (rev. ed.). Boston: Houghton Mifflin, 1960.

Centers, R. Motivational aspects of occupational stratification. *Journal of Social Psychology*, 1948, 28, 187–217.

———, and D. E. Bugental. Intrinsic and extrinsic job motivation among different segments of the working population. *Journal of Applied Psychology*, 1966, 50, 193–197.

Crites, J. O. Factor analytic dimensions of vocational motivation. *Journal of Applied Psychology*, 1961, 45, 330–337.

Cronbach, L. J. *Essentials of psychological testing.* New York: Harper and Row, 1960.

Darley, J. G., and T. Hagenah. *Vocational interest measurement: Theory and practice.* Minneapolis: University of Minnesota Press, 1955.

Dipboye, W. J., and W. F. Anderson. The ordering of occupational values by high school freshmen and seniors. *Personnel and Guidance Journal*, 1959, 38, 121–124.

Dukes, W. F. Psychological studies of values. *Psychological Bulletin*, 1955, 52, 29–50.

English, H. B., and A. C. English. *Comprehensive dictionary of psychological and psychoanalytical terms.* New York: Longmans Green, 1958.

Friedmann, E. A., and R. J. Havighurst. *The meaning of work and retirement.* Chicago: University of Chicago Press, 1954.

Fryer, D. *The measurement of interests in relation to human adjustment.* New York: Holt, 1931.

Gable, R. K., and R. M. Pruzek. Super's Work Values Inventory: Two multivariate studies of interitem relationships. Albany: State University of New York. Mimeographed, 1969.

Gapas, G. Dissertation in process in the School of Education, New York University. Data from personal communication with Mr. Robert Weiss, Mgr., Personnel Research, First National City Bank, New York. July 17, 1970.

Ginzberg, E., S. Ginsburg, S. Axelrad, and J. Herma. *Occupational choice.* New York: Columbia University Press, 1951.

Hana, M. Work values in relation to age, intelligence, socio-economic level, and occupational interest level. Ph.D. dissertation, Teachers College, Columbia University, 1954.

Havighurst, R. J. Youth in exploration and man emergent. In H. Borow (ed.), *Man in a world at work.* Boston: Houghton Mifflin, 1964.

Hendrix, V. L., and D. E. Super. Factor dimension and reliability of the Work Values Inventory. *Vocational Guidance Quarterly*, 1968, 17, 269–274.

Hoppock, R. *Job satisfaction.* New York: Harper and Row, 1935.

Ivey, A. E. Interest and work values. *Vocational Guidance Quarterly*, 1963, 7, 121–124.

Jacob, P. E. *Changing values in college: An exploratory study of the impact of college teaching.* New York: Harper and Row, 1957.

Katzell, R. A. Personal values, job satisfaction and job behavior. In H. Borow (ed.), *Man in a world at work.* Boston: Houghton Mifflin, 1964.

Kelly, E. L., and D. W. Fiske. *The prediction of performance and clinical psychology.* Ann Arbor: University of Michigan Press, 1951.

Kinnane, J. F., and J. R. Gaubinger. Life values and work values. *Journal of Counseling Psychology*, 1963, 10, 366–367.

Kinnane, J. F., and M. W. Pable. Family background and work value orientation. *Journal of Counseling Psychology*, 1962, 9, 320–325.

Kinnane, J. F., and A. Suziedelis. Work values orientation and inventoried interest. *Journal of Counseling Psychology*, 1962, 9, 144–147.

Loevinger, J. Objective tests as instruments of psychological theory. *Psychological Reports*, 1957, 3, 635–694.

Morris, C. *Varieties of human value.* Chicago: University of Chicago Press, 1956.

Normile, R. H. Differentiating among known occupational groups by means of the WVI. Ph.D. dissertation, Catholic University, 1967.

O'Connor, J. P., and J. F. Kinnane. A factor analysis of work values. *Journal of Counseling Psychology*, 1961, 8, 263–267.

O'Hara, R. P., and D. V. Tiedeman. Vocational self-concepts in adolescence. *Journal of Counseling Psychology*, 1959, 6, 292–301.

Olive, L. E. Relationship of values to the perception of activities involved in an occupation. *Journal of Counseling Psychology*, 1964, 11, 262–266.

Raylesberg, D. D. *Personal values in the perceptions of an occupation.* New York: Privately published, 1949.

Rokeach, M. *Beliefs, attitudes and values.* San Francisco: Jossey-Bass, 1968.

Rosenberg, M. *Occupations and values.* Glencoe, Ill.: Free Press, 1957.

Schwarzweller, H. K. Values and occupational choice. *Social Forces*, 1960, 39, 126–135.

Shah, U. Work values and job satisfaction. Ph.D. dissertation, Teachers College, Columbia University, 1969.

Singer, S. A., and B. Stefflre. The relationship of job values and desires to vocational aspirations of adolescents. *Journal of Applied Psychology*, 1954, 38, 419–422.

Stefflre, B. Construct validity of vocational values inventory. *Journal of Educational Research*, 1959, 52, No. 9, 339–341.

Strong, E. K., Jr. *Vocational interests of men and women*. Stanford: Stanford University Press, 1943.

———. *Vocational interests 18 years after college*. Minneapolis: University of Minnesota Press, 1955.

Super, D. E. Vocational adjustment: Implementing a self-concept. *Occupations*, 1951, 30, 88–92.

———. The structure of work values in relation to status, achievement, interests and adjustment. *Journal of Applied Psychology*, 1962, 46, 234–239.

———. Self-concepts in vocational development. In D. E. Super, R. Starishevsky, N. Matlin, and J. P. Jordaan (eds.), *Career development: Self-concept theory*. New York: College Entrance Examination Board, 1963.

———, and J. O. Crites. *Vocational development: A framework for research*. New York: Teachers College Press, 1957.

———, R. Hummel, H. Moser, P. Overstreet, and C. Warnath. *The psychology of careers*. New York: Harper and Row, 1957.

Super, D. E., and H. Kaplan. Work values of school counselors attending NDEA summer guidance institutes. *Personnel and Guidance Journal*, 1967, 46, 27–31.

Super, D. E., and J. G. Mowry. Social and personal desirability in the assessment of work values. *Educational and Psychological Measurement*, 1962, 22, 715–719.

Super, D. E., and P. L. Overstreet. *The vocational maturity of ninth-grade boys*. New York: Teachers College Press, 1960.

Vroom, V. H. *Work and motivation*. New York: Wiley, 1964.

Woodbury, R. W. Sex differences, parental occupational level, and intelligence as measured by Super's WVI on 379 southern rural, caucasian, protestant 9th graders of North Carolina. M.A. thesis, North Carolina State University, 1966.

Wrenn, C. G. Human values and work in American life. In H. Borow (ed.), *Man in a world at work*. Boston: Houghton Mifflin, 1964.

# 9

# Illustrative Interpretations of Inventories

THE MATERIAL IN this chapter is adapted from a panel discussion on all the inventory profiles for three different persons (see the reproductions of the profiles on the following pages). The discussion took place at a workshop conducted at Stevens Institute of Technology by Dr. Karl Springob in January 1971. The discussants were all the contributors to this volume, with the exception of Dr. David Campbell. Dr. David Weiss was not present at the workshop but has added comments on the three MIQ profiles. Sufficient changes have been made in the information given to preserve the privacy of those individuals whose profiles were used.

It should be noted that the sequential order of the participants' discussions has the disadvantage that the interpretation of each is likely to be influenced by the one preceding it. The interpretations also might differ from those that would be presented to the subjects because they were not there to interact with, validate, or emphasize what the discussants said.

## Robert's Profile

BACKGROUND INFORMATION

Robert is sixteen years old and is in the eleventh grade. He is the older of two boys in the family. His father is employed by a company with many branch locations, and Robert has lived in a number of cities and has gone to several different schools. They presently live in a suburban community near a moderate sized city. He is in the third year of his present high

206

school from which he expects to graduate. His grade average is below C, and he ranks in the lowest quartile of his class. Nationally standardized tests of achievement in the past two years have ranked him no lower than the 70th percentile in any area except reading natural science. He says he likes history, business law, and literature, the last because he has a toler-

**VIS PROFILE CHART**

Date of Testing  DECEMBER 18, 1970

Grade 11  Age 16  yrs. 6 mos.  Sex

NAT  Reference Group 11TH GRADE MALE

| Name | ROBERT |
|---|---|
| School | IOWA ST U |
| Counselor | |

| Scale Number | Scale Name | Scale Score | %ile Rank | Stanine Profile Low 1 2 3 | Average 4 5 6 | High 7 8 9 | Scale Clarity Index |
|---|---|---|---|---|---|---|---|
| 18 | MANAGEMENT | 43 | 92 | | | 8 | H |
| 17 | PROMOTION-COMMU | 39 | 88 | | | 7 | F |
| 15 | AGRICULTURE | 37 | 78 | | | 7 | F |
| 4 | CARE PEOPLE-ANIM | 31 | 79 | | | 7 | I |
| 22 | ENTERTAINMENT | 31 | 76 | | 6 | | F |
| 21 | MUSIC | 30 | 59 | | 5 | | F |
| 20 | SALES REPRESENT | 29 | 54 | | 5 | | F |
| 2 | MACHINE WORK | 28 | 44 | | 5 | | H |
| 11 | TRAINING | 28 | 31 | 4 | | | H |
| 7 | CRAFTS | 26 | 30 | 4 | | | H |
| 16 | APPLIED TECH | 26 | 20 | 3 | | | H |
| 23 | TEACH-COUN-SOC W | 26 | 41 | | 5 | | H |
| 13 | NUMERICAL | 25 | 37 | 4 | | | H |
| 14 | APPRAISAL | 24 | 20 | 3 | | | H |
| 19 | ARTISTIC | 24 | 35 | 4 | | | H |
| 5 | CLERICAL WORK | 23 | 49 | | 5 | | H |
| 6 | INSPECT-TESTING | 23 | 44 | | 5 | | H |
| 8 | CUSTOMER SERVICE | 23 | 37 | 4 | | | H |
| 9 | NURSING | 22 | 44 | | 5 | | H |
| 3 | PERSONAL SERVICE | 21 | 54 | | 5 | | H |
| 12 | LITERARY | 21 | 31 | 4 | | | H |
| 24 | MEDICAL | 21 | 38 | 4 | | | H |
| 10 | SKILLED PER SERV | 20 | 40 | | 5 | | H |
| 1 | MANUAL WORK | 16 | 24 | 4 | | | H |

**Student Questionnaire Information**

1. Occupational Plans

First Choice  MANAGEMENT

Second Choice PROMOTION-COMMU

2. Best Liked Subjects

First  SOCIAL STUDIES

Second ENGLISH

3. High School Program

First  GENERAL

4. Post-High School Plans

First  UNDECIDED

5. Interest in Vocational Programs

NOT INTERESTED

6. Vocational Program Choice

First

Second

7. Local Survey Information

A  B  C  D  E  F  G  H

— — — — — — — —

Figure 9.1a. Robert's OVIS profile. (Reproduced from the Ohio Vocational Interest Survey Test, copyright 1969 by Harcourt Brace Jovanovich, Inc. Reproduced by special permission of the publisher.)

NAME

# MINNESOTA VOCATIONAL INTEREST INVENTORY

| | OCCUPATIONAL SCALES | STD. SCORE [a] |
|---|---|---|
| 1 | BAKER | 63 |
| 2 | FOOD SERVICE MANAGER | 40 |
| 3 | MILK WAGON DRIVER | 43 |
| 4 | RETAIL SALES CLERK | 36 |
| 5 | STOCK CLERK | 56 |
| 6 | PRINTER | 45 |
| 7 | TAB. MACHINE OPERATOR | 36 |
| 8 | WAREHOUSEMAN | 57 |
| 9 | HOSPITAL ATTENDANT | 36 |
| 10 | PRESSMAN | 34 |
| 11 | CARPENTER | 36 |
| 12 | PAINTER | 32 |
| 13 | PLASTERER | 15 |
| 14 | TRUCK DRIVER | 47 |
| 15 | TRUCK MECHANIC | 23 |
| 16 | INDUSTRIAL EDUC. TEACHER | 17 |
| 17 | SHEET METAL WORKER | 23 |
| 18 | PLUMBER | 24 |
| 19 | MACHINIST | 10 |
| 20 | ELECTRICIAN | 16 |
| 21 | RADIO-TV REPAIRMAN | 26 |
| 22 | | |
| 23 | | |
| 24 | | |
| 25 | | |

(Scale axis: 0, 10, 20, 30, 40, 50, 60)

a. SCORES ABOVE 60 ARE PLOTTED AS 60.
NEGATIVE SCORES ARE PLOTTED AS ZERO.

| AREA SCALES | STD. SCORE |
|---|---|
| H-1 MECHANICAL | 49 |
| H-2 HEALTH SERVICE | 45 |
| H-3 OFFICE WORK | 53 |
| H-4 ELECTRONICS | 44 |
| H-5 FOOD SERVICE | 61 |
| H-6 CARPENTRY | 45 |
| H-7 SALES-OFFICE | 69 |
| H-8 "CLEAN HANDS" | 60 |
| H-9 OUTDOORS | 48 |

STANDARD SCORES (20, 30, 40, 50, 60, 70, 80)

SEE OTHER SIDE FOR EXPLANATION

Figure 9.1b. Robert's MVII profile. (Reproduced by permission. Copyright © 1965 by The Psychological Corporation, New York, N.Y. All rights reserved.)

208

# NCS PROFILE — STRONG VOCATIONAL INTEREST BLANK — FOR MEN

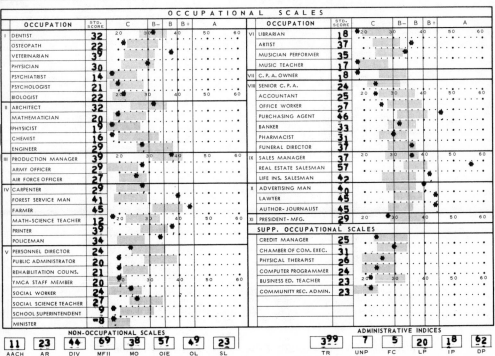

## BASIC INTEREST SCALES

| SCALE | STD. SCORE |
|---|---|
| PUBLIC SPEAKING | 51 |
| LAW/POLITICS | 63 |
| BUSINESS MANAGEMENT | 43 |
| SALES | 49 |
| MERCHANDISING | 36 |
| OFFICE PRACTICES | 35 |
| MILITARY ACTIVITIES | 47 |
| TECHNICAL SUPERVISION | 58 |
| MATHEMATICS | 25 |
| SCIENCE | 28 |
| MECHANICAL | 36 |
| NATURE | 52 |
| AGRICULTURE | 56 |
| ADVENTURE | 76 |
| RECREATIONAL LEADERSHIP | 52 |
| MEDICAL SERVICE | 47 |
| SOCIAL SERVICE | 37 |
| RELIGIOUS ACTIVITIES | 40 |
| TEACHING | 45 |
| MUSIC | 36 |
| ART | 40 |
| WRITING | 38 |

DOUBLE LINE = AVERAGE SCORE FOR 650 52 YEAR OLD MEN. SINGLE LINE = AVERAGE SCORE FOR SAME MEN WHEN 16 YEARS OLD.

## OCCUPATIONAL SCALES

| OCCUPATION | STD. SCORE |  | OCCUPATION | STD. SCORE |
|---|---|---|---|---|
| I DENTIST | 32 |  | VI LIBRARIAN | 18 |
| OSTEOPATH | 22 |  | ARTIST | 37 |
| VETERINARIAN | 39 |  | MUSICIAN PERFORMER | 35 |
| PHYSICIAN | 30 |  | MUSIC TEACHER | 17 |
| PSYCHIATRIST | 14 |  | VII C. P. A. OWNER | 18 |
| PSYCHOLOGIST | 21 |  | VIII SENIOR C. P. A. | 24 |
| BIOLOGIST | 22 |  | ACCOUNTANT | 25 |
| II ARCHITECT | 32 |  | OFFICE WORKER | 27 |
| MATHEMATICIAN | 20 |  | PURCHASING AGENT | 46 |
| PHYSICIST | 19 |  | BANKER | 33 |
| CHEMIST | 16 |  | PHARMACIST | 31 |
| ENGINEER | 29 |  | FUNERAL DIRECTOR | 37 |
| III PRODUCTION MANAGER | 39 |  | IX SALES MANAGER | 37 |
| ARMY OFFICER | 29 |  | REAL ESTATE SALESMAN | 57 |
| AIR FORCE OFFICER | 27 |  | LIFE INS. SALESMAN | 42 |
| IV CARPENTER | 29 |  | X ADVERTISING MAN | 40 |
| FOREST SERVICE MAN | 41 |  | LAWYER | 45 |
| FARMER | 45 |  | AUTHOR- JOURNALIST | 45 |
| MATH-SCIENCE TEACHER | 12 |  | XI PRESIDENT- MFG. | 29 |
| PRINTER | 39 |  | SUPP. OCCUPATIONAL SCALES | |
| POLICEMAN | 34 |  | CREDIT MANAGER | 25 |
| V PERSONNEL DIRECTOR | 24 |  | CHAMBER OF COM. EXEC. | 31 |
| PUBLIC ADMINISTRATOR | 20 |  | PHYSICAL THERAPIST | 26 |
| REHABILITATION COUNS. | 21 |  | COMPUTER PROGRAMMER | 24 |
| YMCA STAFF MEMBER | 20 |  | BUSINESS ED. TEACHER | 23 |
| SOCIAL WORKER | 24 |  | COMMUNITY REC. ADMIN. | 23 |
| SOCIAL SCIENCE TEACHER | 27 |  |  |  |
| SCHOOL SUPERINTENDENT | 9 |  |  |  |
| MINISTER | -8 |  |  |  |

## NON-OCCUPATIONAL SCALES

| AACH | AR | DIV | MFII | MO | OIE | OL | SL |
|---|---|---|---|---|---|---|---|
| 11 | 23 | 44 | 69 | 38 | 51 | 49 | 23 |

## ADMINISTRATIVE INDICES

| TR | UNP | FC | LP | IP | DP |
|---|---|---|---|---|---|
| 399 | 7 | 5 | 20 | 18 | 62 |

Figure 9.1c. Robert's SVIB profile

ant teacher. He likes to read, has attempted unsuccessfully to make the baseball team, but otherwise is not particularly interested in school.

When Robert turned sixteen, he sought a job with a neighbor who owns a service station. After about six months of part-time employment, he has progressed to the point where he is trusted to run the station by himself, arrange service for regular customers, and handle the bookkeeping involved in closing the station. He is pleased to have the job and says he likes the responsibility it entails compared to, say, working as a carry-out boy in a grocery store. Robert regards the college students with whom he works as his friends, and prefers to talk with his high school counselor and his employer about his problems rather than with his family.

## Report of Scores  Kuder Occupational Interest Survey  (Form DD)

NAME ROBERT  1 LOCATION  000-38618  DATE OF SURVEY 12-21-70

| OCCUPATIONAL SCALES WOMEN | | COLLEGE MAJOR SCALES, WOMEN | OCCUPATIONAL SCALES MEN | | | | COLLEGE MAJOR SCALES MEN | |
|---|---|---|---|---|---|---|---|---|
| Accountant | Nurse | Art & Art Education | Acc't, Certified Public .37 | Engineer, Electrical .31 | Optometrist .30 | Psychology Professor .22 | Agriculture .41 | Foreign Languages .31 |
| Bank Clerk | Nutritionist | Biological Sciences .33 | Architect .33 | Engineer, Heating/ Air Cond. .32 | Osteopath .26 | Radio Station Manager .33 | Animal Husbandry .41 | Forestry .41 |
| Beautician | Occupational Therapist | Business Ed & Commerce | Automobile Mechanic .28 | Engineer, Industrial .32 | Painter, House .33 | Real Estate Agent .35 | Architecture .39 | History .32 |
| Bookkeeper | Office Clerk | Drama | Automobile Salesman .35 | Engineer, Mechanical .34 | Pediatrician .26 | Sales Eng, Heating/Air Cond. 34 | Art & Art Education .32 | Law (Grad School) .39 |
| Bookstore Manager | Physical Therapist | Elementary Education | Banker | Engineer, Mining & Metal .32 | Personnel Manager .34 | Science Teacher, High School .26 | Biological Sciences .30 | Mathematics .35 |
| Computer Programmer | Primary School Teacher | English | Bookkeeper .32 | Farmer .32 | Pharmaceutical Salesman .31 | School Superintendent .32 | Business Acc't & Finance .41 | Music & Music Ed .30 |
| Counselor, High School | Psychologist | Foreign Languages | Bookstore Manager .33 | Florist .40 | Pharmacist .30 | Social Caseworker .30 | Business & Marketing .41 | Physical Education .45 |
| Dean of Women | Psychologist, Clinical | General Social Sciences | Bricklayer .35 | Forester .39 | Photographer .37 | Social Worker, Group .28 | Business Management .43 | Physical Sciences .30 |
| Dental Assistant | Religious Education Director | Health Professions | Building Contractor .34 | Insurance Agent .35 | Physical Therapist .30 | Social Worker, Psychiatric .28 | Economics .40 | Political Science & Gov't .36 |
| Department Store Saleswoman | Science Teacher, High School | History | Buyer .35 | Interior Decorator .28 | Physician .25 | Statistician .27 | Elementary Education .40 | Premed, Pharm & Dentistry .29 |
| Dietitian, Administrative | Secretary | Home Economics Education | Carpenter .30 | Journalist .32 | Plumber .33 | Supv/Foreman, Industrial .29 | Engineering, Chemical .35 | Psychology .33 |
| Dietitian, Public School | Social Caseworker | Mathematics .25 | Chemist .29 | Lawyer | Plumbing Contractor .34 | Travel Agent .38 | Engineering, Civil .41 | Sociology .36 |
| Florist | Social Worker, Group | Music & Music Education .35 | Clothier, Retail .27 | Librarian | Podiatrist .24 | Truck Driver .28 | Engineering, Electrical .35 | U.S. Air Force Cadet .43 |
| Home Demonstration Agent | Social Worker, Medical | Nursing | Computer Programmer .35 | Machinist .30 | Policeman .39 | Television Repairman .30 | Engineering, Mechanical .39 | U.S. Military Cadet .43 |
| Home Ec Teacher, College | Social Worker, Psychiatric | Physical Education | Counselor, High School .33 | Mathematician .27 | Postal Clerk .33 | University Pastor .25 | English .26 | |
| Interior Decorator | Social Worker, School | Political Science | County Agricultural Agent .33 | Math Teacher, High School .28 | Printer .32 | Veterinarian .30 | | |
| Lawyer | Stenographer | Psychology | Dentist .29 | Meteorologist .31 | Psychiatrist .24 | Welder .30 | | |
| Librarian | X-Ray Technician | Sociology .32 | Electrician | Minister .24 | Psychologist, Clinical .26 | X-Ray Technician .27 | | |
| Math Teacher, High School | | Teaching Sister, Catholic .37 | Engineer, Civil .41 | Nurseryman .41 | Psychologist, Counseling .26 | YMCA Secretary .29 | | |
| | | | | | Psychologist, Industrial .29 | | | |

| OCCUPATIONAL SCALES WOMEN | | COLLEGE MAJOR SCALES WOMEN | | OCCUPATIONAL SCALES MEN | | COLLEGE MAJOR SCALES MEN | |
|---|---|---|---|---|---|---|---|
| Title | Score | Title | Score | Title | Score | Title | Score |
| | | | | NURSERYMAN | .41 | PHYSICAL EDUC | .45 |
| | | | | FLORIST | .40 | BUS MANAGEMENT | .43 |
| | | | | FORESTER | .39 | AIR FORCE CADET | .43 |
| | | | | POLICEMAN | .39 | MILITARY CADET | .43 |
| | | | | TRAVEL AGENT | .38 | AGRICULTURE | .41 |
| | | | | ACCT,CERT PUBLIC | .37 | ANIMAL HUSBANDRY | .41 |
| | | | | ENGINEER, CIVIL | .37 | BUS ACCT AND FIN | .41 |
| | | | | PHOTOGRAPHER | .37 | BUS & MARKETING | .41 |
| | | | | AUTO SALESMAN | .35 | ENGINEERNG,CIVIL | .41 |
| | | | | BRICKLAYER | .35 | FORESTRY | .41 |

V  46

M  .36  S  .40
MBI  .04  F  .35
W  .22  D  .25
WBI  .05  MO  .17

Figure 9.1d. Robert's KOIS profile. (From *Kuder Occupational Interest Survey — Form DD* by G. Frederic Kuder. Copyright © 1965, 1968, 1970, Science Research Associates, Inc. Reproduced by permission of the publisher.)

About his future plans, Robert says that he will attend a junior college because he is not qualified to enter a four-year school. He hopes to transfer to a four-year college and then go to law school. This will be preparation for joining the FBI. If anything fails in this plan, he thinks that he would enjoy being a small business owner. He expects that these plans will afford opportunities for outside work, autonomy, and perhaps exciting kinds of work.

## OVIS

*Ayres D'Costa:* The way to begin to interpret an OVIS profile is to look at high interest areas and compare them with the low interest areas.

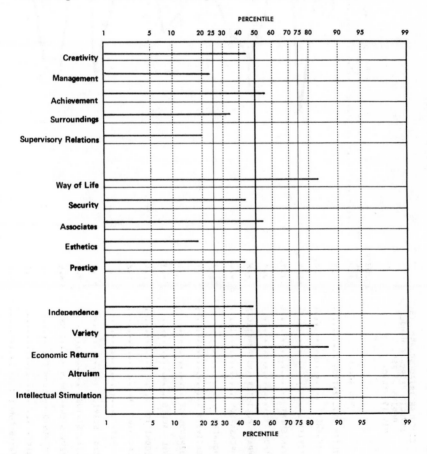

Figure 9.1e. Robert's WVI profile

211

REPORT ON THE MINNESOTA IMPORTANCE QUESTIONNAIRE
(MIQ)
1967 REVISION

CIRCULAR TRIAD SCORE= 15
INVALID RESPONSE RANGE
BEGINS AT 255.
MIQ IS VALID.

| MIQ SCALE | ADJUSTED SCALE VALUE |
|---|---|
| ABILITY UTILIZATION ........... | .2 |
| ACHIEVEMENT ............... | 1.0 |
| ACTIVITY ............... | -1.8 |
| ADVANCEMENT ............... | 1.7 |
| AUTHORITY ............... | 0.0 |
| COMPANY POLICIES AND PRACTICES | -.8 |
| COMPENSATION ............... | -.4 |
| COWORKERS ............... | .3 |
| CREATIVITY ............... | .7 |
| INDEPENDENCE ............... | .1 |
| MORAL VALUES ............... | -.3 |
| RECOGNITION ............... | 1.4 |
| RESPONSIBILITY ............... | 1.2 |
| SECURITY ............... | .2 |
| SOCIAL SERVICE ............... | -1.0 |
| SOCIAL STATUS ............... | 2.2 |
| SUPERVISION—HUMAN RELATIONS . | -.8 |
| SUPERVISION—TECHNICAL ....... | -.8 |
| VARIETY ............... | .7 |
| WORKING CONDITIONS ........... | .7 |

CORRESPONDENCE BETWEEN OCCUPATIONAL REINFORCER PATTERNS AND MIQ SCALE VALUES FOR ROBERT

81 OCCUPATIONS LISTED IN DECREASING ORDER OF CORRESPONDENCE, USING D-SQUARED INDEX.
OCCUPATIONS AT THE TOP OF THIS LIST ARE THOSE IN WHICH THIS INDIVIDUAL IS MOST LIKELY TO BE SATISFIED.
OCCUPATIONS AT THE BOTTOM OF THE LIST ARE THOSE IN WHICH HE(SHE) IS LEAST LIKELY TO BE SATISFIED.

| OCCUPATION | CLUSTER | D-SQUARED | PREDICTION OF SATISFACTION |
|---|---|---|---|
| PROGRAMMER (BUSINESS,ENGINEERING AND SCIENCE) | 2 | 23.65 | NOT LIKELY SATISFIED |
| ENGINEER, MECHANICAL | 1 | 23.88 | NOT LIKELY SATISFIED |
| DRAFTSMAN, ARCHITECTURAL | 9 | 25.09 | NOT LIKELY SATISFIED |
| WELDER, COMBINATION | 9 | 25.11 | NOT LIKELY SATISFIED |
| COMMERCIAL ARTIST, ILLUSTRATING | - | 25.29 | NOT LIKELY SATISFIED |
| COOK(HOTEL-RESTAURANT) | - | 25.84 | NOT LIKELY SATISFIED |
| STATISTICIAN, APPLIED | 2 | 25.84 | NOT LIKELY SATISFIED |
| ELECTRICIAN | 9 | 26.11 | NOT LIKELY SATISFIED |
| HEAVY EQUIPMENT OPERATOR(CONSTRUCTION) | 7 | 26.33 | NOT LIKELY SATISFIED |
| SALESPERSON, SHOE | 2 | 26.34 | NOT LIKELY SATISFIED |
| ACCOUNTANT, COST | 2 | 26.36 | NOT LIKELY SATISFIED |
| ENGINEER, TIME STUDY | 1 | 26.41 | NOT LIKELY SATISFIED |
| TEACHER, SECONDARY SCHOOL | 4 | 26.78 | NOT LIKELY SATISFIED |
| PIPEFITTER | 7 | 26.98 | NOT LIKELY SATISFIED |
| FIRE FIGHTER | - | 27.24 | NOT LIKELY SATISFIED |
| EMBALMER | 6 | 27.36 | NOT LIKELY SATISFIED |
| SHEET METAL WORKER | 9 | 27.70 | NOT LIKELY SATISFIED |
| MACHINIST | 9 | 27.74 | NOT LIKELY SATISFIED |
| TRUCK DRIVER | - | 32.81 | NOT LIKELY SATISFIED |
| AUTOMOBILE MECHANIC | 9 | 33.16 | NOT LIKELY SATISFIED |
| WAITER-WAITRESS | 6 | 33.39 | NOT LIKELY SATISFIED |
| LIBRARIAN | 4 | 33.53 | NOT LIKELY SATISFIED |
| MARKER | 8 | 33.90 | NOT LIKELY SATISFIED |
| MEAT CUTTER | 8 | 34.06 | NOT LIKELY SATISFIED |
| BUS DRIVER | - | 34.29 | NOT LIKELY SATISFIED |
| TYPIST, CIVIL SERVICE | 5 | 34.52 | NOT LIKELY SATISFIED |
| OFFICE-MACHINE SERVICEMAN | 9 | 34.77 | NOT LIKELY SATISFIED |
| NURSE, PROFESSIONAL | - | 34.80 | NOT LIKELY SATISFIED |
| NURSE, LICENSED PRACTICAL | 6 | 35.28 | NOT LIKELY SATISFIED |
| AIRPLANE STEWARDESS | - | 35.94 | NOT LIKELY SATISFIED |
| CASEWORKER | 4 | 36.72 | NOT LIKELY SATISFIED |
| NURSE AID | 6 | 37.43 | NOT LIKELY SATISFIED |
| CASHIER-CHECKER | - | 37.94 | NOT LIKELY SATISFIED |
| ORDERLY | 6 | 39.85 | NOT LIKELY SATISFIED |

9 OCCUPATIONAL FAMILIES LISTED IN DECREASING ORDER OF CORRESPONDENCE, USING D-SQUARED INDEX

| | | |
|---|---|---|
| CLUSTER 2 | -- TECHNICAL OCCUPATIONS, SEMI-PROFESSIONAL | 25.53 |
| CLUSTER 1 | -- TECHNICAL OCCUPATIONS, PROFESSIONAL | 25.55 |
| CLUSTER 7 | -- MANUAL OCCUPATIONS, BUILDING TRADES | 27.69 |
| CLUSTER 9 | -- MANUAL OCCUPATIONS, SERVICE-MAINTENANCE | 28.27 |
| CLUSTER 3 | -- SALES OCCUPATIONS, SERVICE | 29.24 |
| CLUSTER 5 | -- SERVICE OCCUPATIONS, BUSINESS DETAIL | 30.12 |
| CLUSTER 8 | -- MANUAL OCCUPATIONS, MANUFACTURING | 30.74 |
| CLUSTER 4 | -- SERVICE OCCUPATIONS, SOCIAL-EDUCATIONAL | 30.99 |
| CLUSTER 6 | -- SERVICE OCCUPATIONS, PERSONAL | 31.61 |

Figure 9.1f. Robert's MIQ profile. (Solid line above indicates that items have been dropped for reasons of space.)

*The Manual for Interpreting OVIS* indicates a raw score of 40 as a cutoff for high interest. Robert has scored "high" in one scale only, namely management (see Fig. 9.1a). However, on at least two other scales the raw scores are close to high — promotion and communication (scale 17) and agriculture (scale 15). A break occurs at this point: the raw score on the care of people and animals scale is 31 whereas the agriculture scale has a score of 37. At the bottom of the list of scales in the profile are the low interest areas. *The Manual for Interpreting OVIS* indicates a raw score cutoff of 26. Several scales have low scores.

His high interest in the management and the promotion and communications scales is corroborated by the satisfaction he derives from the management aspects of his current job at the gas station. There is also significance in his interest in going to law school, joining the FBI, or becoming a small business owner. One common element that highlights his current interests is independent outdoor work. This also has been brought out in the four OVIS scales in which he has expressed high interest.

Robert's expressed vocational plans and inventoried interests are consistent. This should be brought to his attention. Counselors should note that discrepancies also occur and suggest the need for counseling.

The OVIS provides other information. The top four scales in the profile indicate a high level of data. Robert's interest in things or in people is not high. The scales at the bottom of the list in the profile corroborate this. Note the dislike for scales with high things involvement. The highly liked scales have low levels of things whereas the disliked scales have high levels of things.

The OVIS is unique in that it lets one look at the consistency with which the subjects respond to the job activities in each scale. This information is provided in the scale clarity indices presented for each scale in terms of high, fair, or inconsistent. Robert has a high scale clarity index for all the low interest scales. The scale clarity in the top scales is not as high. Scale 4, which is care of people and animals, stands out as the only one with an inconsistent response pattern. One wonders if perhaps he does like people only, or animals only, but not both. Since he shows high interest in agriculture, one might guess that he probably likes animals but not people. Such an inference could be discussed in a counseling situation, which might provide some useful information. Further, Robert should be helped to understand that a law degree requires good schoolwork and that his undecided vocational plans need attention.

214

*Question:* Some other inconsistencies appear in the profile. He says that he likes reading and the highest scales all need higher education, yet the rank of his literary scale is low. Wouldn't that be contradictory to pursuing higher education?

*Dr. D'Costa:* Yes, the literary scale score is low and does contradict his plan for higher education. He says he likes his school work in literature because he has a tolerant teacher. This may be important for his counselor to explore further.

## MVII

*W. Leslie Barnette:* I would not take too seriously his plans concerning transfer to a four-year college and the ultimate goal of the FBI; his alternate plan of small business makes more sense. I think the area scales are most relevant to this latter plan. He is highest in sales-office, next highest in food service and clean hands, all of which points to interest in small business management. He rejects the technical and manual areas. At the top of the profile his highest occupational scale score is baker; also very high are stock clerk and warehouseman (see Fig. 9.1b). I don't think that means he ought to buy a bakery necessarily, but his profile does suggest small business sales. I would be inclined to encourage him to seek out the general business program in his junior college. I might also comment that the high on truck driver represents an adolescent desire to be independent and outdoors, which Dr. D'Costa mentioned.

*Question:* Would you consider this boy's food service and to some extent the office worker interests to be feminine?

*Dr. Barnette:* That is not enough information to reach such a conclusion. Both acceptance of the food sales, clerical, and hospital attendant scales and rejection of the building trades, electronic, technical, and the like are indicative of feminine (as culturally defined) interests. On this boy's profile the scores for the latter scales are actually fairly close to the men-in-general bars rather than on the extreme left, and although one of the food service scales is high, only one out of the seven office scores is high and he has a chance-level score on hospital attendant. I don't see that as very feminine.

## SVIB

*Lenore Harmon:* I examined the profiles before I read the background information, and I would like to tell you what my first impression was. I

215

have advised looking at the administrative indices first, but in this case, I looked at the extremely high score on the adventure scale (Fig. 9.1c), and thought, "How old is this person?" Then I looked down at the academic achievement and age related scales and decided that he must be very young; therefore I would be very cautious about interpreting this profile at all. Strong's original research on the earliest form of the men's SVIB suggests that the greatest changes in occupational scale scores occur between the ages of sixteen and twenty-five. Although the SVIB has been helpful in identifying interest patterns of mature high school students, it is generally used with caution for students of sixteen. I have a feeling that this young man's profile may change with age.

On the basis of his high score on the purchasing agent scale, I think he may well find himself in the business world. I would be more likely to bet on sales than on administration. Despite his low academic achievement score, I wonder if he won't go to college because low academic achievement scores are associated with business interests. However, I would interpret the profile with extreme caution because of his age.

*Question:* What do you think of his MF score of 69?

*Dr. Harmon:* Look at the level of his adventure score on the basic interest scales. Note his high scores on forest service man, farmer, and the sales scales, all traditionally men's occupations. There is nothing feminine about this profile. Perhaps you were thinking that a 69 is in the feminine direction. Remember that on the MFII scale (on both the men's and women's forms) most people find low scores threatening.

## KOIS

*Donald Zytowski:* My conclusions concerning the KOIS are very similar to Dr. Harmon's. This is a very young person, and his scores should be interpreted rather tentatively. The V score is just one point higher than the usual minimum (see Fig. 9.1d). Moreover, his M score is only 36, and the difference between this score and the average of the highest occupational scores in the ranks is very slight. This suggests that interpretation of the occupational scores should proceed cautiously, if at all. There are few scores over 32, and none over 41. I think this reflects immature, more or less "unformed" occupational interests.

Average scores for the college major scales are slightly higher than those on the occupational scales, and perhaps he truly will be able to carry through on his plans to begin with junior college and continue at a four

216

year school. I would focus on the adventure score from the SVIB as the source of high similarities with such outdoor occupational and college major scales as physical education, air force, military, agriculture, nurseryman, florist, and forester. This inventory was given too soon; Robert is not old enough to obtain reliable scores. I would not venture to interpret his inventory in any depth or with much confidence. Instead, he might benefit more from learning about his interests as reflected in homogeneous scales.

## WVI

*Donald Super:* In studying this profile, I first reviewed the highs — economic returns, intellectual stimulation, variety and way of life — and then contrasted them with the lows (see Fig. 9.1e). None were really very low except altruism and perhaps esthetics. Then I looked for a kind of internal consistency in the profile to see whether he had a well-organized set of values or whether his values seemed disorganized. The fact that intellectual stimulation was high, esthetics low, and creativity average struck me as being inconsistent. Those values do tend to go together, although the correlations are not perfect. Looking at somewhat related but generally independent scales can tell one something.

I was surprised too that economic returns is high, but security is only average. Also variety is high, but independence is just average. My notation made before this discussion agrees with something arising from the KOIS interpretation. My notation is "immature, uncrystallized." The pattern doesn't make sense psychologically. I would not want to make any specific recommendations regarding occupational choices on the basis of the Work Values Inventory, and I would be inclined to be equally cautious about interest inventories in view of these inconsistencies. Since these notes were made before the other interpretations were given, this is a consensual validation in what we have been saying.

In counseling then, I would look in greater depth at Robert's values, at what he wants out of life. I would encourage him to examine and to think through these apparent inconsistencies. I would engage him not in occupational counseling, but in personal counseling of the value orientation type. After trying to help him clarify values and objectives, I would not be at all eager to assist him in making directional, vocationally relevant decisions. Of course, he can't mark time while he thinks through his values, so

I would consider what kinds of exploratory experiences in addition to counseling would be helpful to him in self-clarification.

*Question:* What is an example of an item on the intellectual stimulation scale?

*Dr. Super:* Having to solve problems. People at different intellectual levels find different things intellectually stimulating. I would want to know what he finds stimulating; it might not be thinking or cognitive problems, but it could be mechanical or human relations problems. In this case, it apparently is not linked with creativity, in the sense of inventing something or writing a book; it is not esthetics, in the sense of making beautiful things; perhaps it is solving management problems because he is high on economic returns. This could fit the interpretation of the MVII.

*Question:* Doesn't the profile present a picture of a person who is pleasure oriented? Doesn't he want variety, money, to do his own kind of thing, and maybe study only what he likes?

*Dr. Super:* I think this is a possibility, for way of life is high and the achievement and security scores are average. But the average independence would bother me a little; I'd expect a little more independence if what you're saying is correct.

## MIQ

*David Weiss:* Robert's MIQ profile shows "high" needs for social status and activity and "moderate" needs for recognition, responsibility, and achievement (see Fig. 9.1f). Because of a relatively large proportion of "neutral," "low," and "very low" needs, the $D^2$ comparison of Robert's MIQ profile with the eighty-one ORP profiles gives a prediction of "not likely satisfied" for all eighty-one occupations. In interpreting a low profile of this kind, the counselor needs to make further comparisons of Robert's preferences with available Occupational Reinforcer Pattern (ORP) information.

Robert's highest need is for social status. The ORP *Manual* (Borgen et al., 1968, p. 234) lists only one occupation — securities salesman — that has an ORP scale value in the moderate to high range (greater than 1.0). The securities salesman ORP profile also shows high or moderate scale values for all of Robert's other high and moderate MIQ scales — advancement, recognition, responsibility, and achievement. Thus, although the total securities salesman ORP profile configuration is not highly similar to Robert's MIQ profile, a matching of high points reflects some similarity.

Analogous high-point matchings using the advancement, recognition, responsibility, and achievement scales, in that order, uncover other occupations with ORP profiles that match Robert's MIQ high and moderate scale values. These include three engineering occupations — time study, civil, and mechanical engineer — screw-machine operator, office machine serviceman, cost accountant, programmer, technical writer, claim examiner, commercial artist, electrician, and shoe salesman. For most of these occupations the four MIQ high-point codes match the ORP high scales; for a few occupations there is a three- or two-scale high-point match. These occupational possibilities would provide the counselor not with specific predictions of satisfaction, but with suggestions for further discussion with Robert and for integration with the other interest, ability, and personality information available.

## Doug's Profile

BACKGROUND INFORMATION

In his third year of college, and at the age of twenty-one, Doug "flunked out" of school, with his third consecutive quarter of grades averaging a hair below C. Doug's average would have been above C, but he received incompletes in the two courses he was doing best in, and those remaining included the D which put him out of school.

Doug is the fourth of six children, born over a span of some twenty-five years. To him, this meant that he pretty much grew up by himself, since his older brother was five years ahead of him, and the next child five years behind him. He has always lived on a farm, somewhat removed from the county seat where his father operates a prosperous management business. Doug's oldest brother has joined the father in the operation of the business, and his next brother is studying business in graduate school. Doug does odd jobs for his father's business, but hasn't any intention of joining the firm.

As an elementary and junior high school student, Doug was always the outstanding achiever. In high school his standing began to slip, but his college admission tests virtually topped the norm group. In high school he was interested in science, music, and dramatics. He says he didn't "run around a lot," and he continues even now to be somewhat uninterested in girls.

He describes himself as "not too fired up about anything," although he

219

has participated persistently in vocal and instrumental performance groups in college. He has always earned incompletes. He never has declared a major, but has amassed credits in music, art, and botany. His vision of what he wants to do with himself has been clouded by his ability to see too many different possibilities. He says about himself, "I don't seem to put any effort with my intentions."

## OVIS

*Ayres D'Costa:* The OVIS profile does not show any stanines because no norms are currently available for college groups. Grade 12 norms can be used. Looking at his high interests one notices the top four to seven scales, depending upon where a cutoff is drawn (see Fig. 9.2a). These scales all involve high data levels except care of people and animals, which might reflect the fact that he lives on a farm. The scales also indicate that Doug is interested in working with people or in the humanities. His low things orientation can be seen in the interest scales at the bottom of the list. Notice the dislike for high things scales. His vocational plans are consistent with his measured interests. Music or art teaching should be areas to explore.

The high scale clarity indices coupled with the restricted range of scale scores, 25 to 44 instead of the possible 11 to 55, suggest that his responses were typically nonextreme. This should be explored in terms of the observation that he is "not fired up about anything." He could lack family support for his interest in music and art. His high measured interest in the agriculture scale appears inconsistent with his dislike for things and may reflect an attempt to please his family. His inconsistency in vocational plans may be the place at which to begin counseling with him.

## KOIS

*Donald Zytowski:* The V score is 50, which is solid support for the profile. This young man's M score is similar in level to Robert's but the range of the top ten or so occupational scores is considerably higher (see Fig. 9.2b). The difference between the two levels indicates some distinct similarities with the interests of some occupations. The W score exceeds the M score. This is fairly unusual and it signifies that he has interests similar to those stereotypically described as women's occupations. The peculiar thing is that this is not reflected in his occupational scores, but it is to an extent in his college major scores.

The ranking of occupational scores brings to mind the sensitivity of the social service scale on the Kuder Preference Record to psychiatric disorders. Doug's profile is a similar situation; it is not psychiatric in nature, but his strong similarity to psychiatrists, pediatricians, clinical psychologists, and social workers especially says that his interests are organized

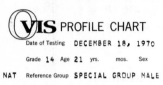 **VIS** PROFILE CHART

Date of Testing **DECEMBER 18, 1970**

Grade **14** Age **21** yrs.　　mos.　Sex

**NAT**　Reference Group **SPECIAL GROUP MALE**

| Name | **H** | **DOUGLAS** |
|---|---|---|
| School | | **IOWA ST U** |
| Counselor | | |

| Scale Number | Scale Name | Scale Score | %ile Rank | Low 1 2 3 | Average 4 5 6 | High 7 8 9 | Scale Clarity Index |
|---|---|---|---|---|---|---|---|
| 21 | MUSIC | 44 | | | | | H |
| 23 | TEACH-COUN-SOC W | 43 | | | | | H |
| 12 | LITERARY | 40 | | | | | H |
| 15 | AGRICULTURE | 40 | | | | | H |
| 4 | CARE PEOPLE-ANIM | 39 | | | | | H |
| 19 | ARTISTIC | 39 | | | | | H |
| 11 | TRAINING | 38 | | | | | H |
| 17 | PROMOTION-COMMU | 36 | | | | | H |
| 14 | APPRAISAL | 34 | | | | | H |
| 18 | MANAGEMENT | 34 | | | | | H |
| 13 | NUMERICAL | 33 | | | | | H |
| 7 | CRAFTS | 32 | | | | | H |
| 16 | APPLIED TECH | 31 | | | | | F |
| 22 | ENTERTAINMENT | 31 | | | | | H |
| 24 | MEDICAL | 31 | | | | | H |
| 5 | CLERICAL WORK | 30 | | | | | F |
| 9 | NURSING | 30 | | | | | H |
| 10 | SKILLED PER SERV | 30 | | | | | F |
| 6 | INSPECT-TESTING | 28 | | | | | H |
| 20 | SALES REPRESENT | 28 | | | | | H |
| 2 | MACHINE WORK | 27 | | | | | H |
| 1 | MANUAL WORK | 26 | | | | | H |
| 3 | PERSONAL SERVICE | 25 | | | | | H |
| 8 | CUSTOMER SERVICE | 25 | | | | | H |

**Student Questionnaire Information**

1. Occupational Plans

　First Choice **AGRICULTURE**

　Second Choice **MUSIC**

2. Best Liked Subjects

　First **MUSIC**

　Second **ART**

3. High School Program

　First **COLLEGE PREP.**

4. Post-High School Plans

　First **COLLEGE-UNIVERSITY**

5. Interest in Vocational Programs

　　**NOT INTERESTED**

6. Vocational Program Choice

　First

　Second

7. Local Survey Information

　A　B　C　D　E　F　G　H

　— — — — — — — —

Figure 9.2a. Doug's OVIS profile. (Reproduced from the Ohio Vocational Interest Survey Test, copyright 1969 by Harcourt Brace Jovanovich, Inc. Reproduced by special permission of the publisher.)

around the need eventually to solve the problem of his identity or to express it in social roles. He is a person who needs counseling directed toward his personal view of himself. Much of his occupational profile is invalid in the light of what he says his interests are. Perhaps, but very warily, the minister and librarian scales indirectly express cultural interests, which he states through his interest in art. Comparing Doug's KOIS with his other profiles, I must say that it is a surprise to me, one which I did not expect to emerge.

## Report of Scores — Kuder Occupational Interest Survey (Form DD)

NAME  H    DOUGLAS                    LOCATION                    000-38602  DATE OF SURVEY  11-30-70

| OCCUPATIONAL SCALES WOMEN | COLLEGE MAJOR SCALES, WOMEN | OCCUPATIONAL SCALES MEN | | COLLEGE MAJOR SCALES MEN |
|---|---|---|---|---|
| 1. Accountant  20. Nurse | 1. Art & Art Education | 1. Acc't, Certified Public .30  20. Engineer, Electrical .32 | 39. Optometrist .35  59. Psychology Professor .47 | 1. Agriculture .34  16. Foreign Languages .48 |
| 2. Bank Clerk  21. Nutritionist | 2. Biological Sciences | 2. Architect .42  21. Engineer, Heating/Air Cond .31  40. Osteopath .35 | 41. Painter, House .23  60. Radio Station Manager .31  61. Real Estate Agent .26 | 2. Animal Husbandry .36  17. Forestry .37 |
| 3. Beautician  22. Occupational Therapist | 3. Bus Ed & Commerce | 3. Automobile Mechanic .19  22. Engineer, Industrial .29 | 42. Pediatrician .46  62. Sales Eng, Heating/Air Cond .24 | 3. Architecture .36  18. History .44 |
| 4. Bookkeeper  23. Office Clerk | 4. Drama | 4. Automobile Salesman .19  23. Engineer, Mechanical .35 | 43. Personnel Manager .35  63. Sci Teacher, High School .40 | 4. Art & Art Education .37  19. Law (Grad School) .40 |
| 5. Bookstore Manager  24. Physical Therapist | 5. Elementary Education | 5. Banker .28  24. Engineer, Mining & Metal .37 | 44. Pharmaceutical Salesman .27  64. School Superintendent .35 | 5. Biological Sciences .42  20. Mathematics .38 |
| 6. Computer Programmer  25. Primary School Teacher | 6. English | 6. Bookkeeper .25  25. Farmer .31 | 45. Pharmacist .30  65. Social Case worker .46 | 6. Business: Acc't & Finance .24  21. Music & Music Ed .47 |
| 7. Counselor, High School  26. Psychologist | 7. Foreign Languages | 7. Bookstore Manager .38  26. Florist .27 | 46. Photographer .27  66. Social Worker, Group .47 | 7. Business & Marketing .20  22. Physical Education .28 |
| 8. Dean of Women  27. Psychologist, Clinical | 8. General Social Sciences | 8. Bricklayer .24  27. Forester .35 | 47. Physical Therapist .36  67. Social Worker, Psychiatric .44 | 8. Business Management .25  23. Physical Sciences .42 |
| 9. Dental Assistant  28. Religious Educ Director | 9. Health Professions | 9. Building Contractor .27  28. Insurance Agent .25 | 48. Physician .36  68. Statistician .46 | 9. Economics .31  24. Political Science & Gov't .41 |
| 10. Department Store Saleswoman  29. Sci Teacher, High School | 10. History | 10. Buyer .29  29. Interior Decorator .33 | 49. Plumber .22  69. Supv/Foreman, Industrial .27 | 10. Elementary Education .44  25. Premed, Pharm & Dentistry .36 |
| 11. Dietitian, Administrative  30. Secretary | 11. Home Economics Education | 11. Carpenter .21  30. Journalist .39 | 50. Plumbing Contractor .21  70. Travel Agent .32 | 11. Engineering, Chemical .32  26. Psychology .38 |
| 12. Dietitian, Public School  31. Social Case worker | 12. Mathematics | 12. Chemist .44  31. Lawyer .44 | 51. Podiatrist .33  71. Truck Driver .21 | 12. Engineering, Civil .30  27. Sociology .45 |
| 13. Florist  32. Social Worker, Group | 13. Music & Music Education | 13. Clothier, Retail .25  32. Librarian .49 | 52. Policeman .27  72. Television Repairman .26 | 13. Engineering, Electrical .33  28. U.S. Air Force Cadet .36 |
| 14. Home Demonstration Agent  33. Social Worker, Medical | 14. Nursing | 14. Computer Programmer .41  33. Machinist .22 | 53. Postal Clerk .26  73. University Pastor .49 | 14. Engineering, Mechanical .27  29. U.S. Military Cadet .30 |
| 15. Home Ec Teacher, College  34. Social Worker, Psychiatric | 15. Physical Education | 15. Counselor, High School .42  34. Mathematician .45 | 54. Printer .31  74. Veterinarian .34 | 15. English .42 |
| 16. Interior Decorator  35. Social Worker, School | 16. Political Science | 16. County Agricultural Agent .34  35. Math Teacher, High School .34 | 55. Psychiatrist .47  75. Welder .22 | |
| 17. Lawyer  36. Stenographer | 17. Psychology | 17. Dentist .34  36. Meteorologist .39 | 56. Psychologist, Clinical .46  76. X-Ray Technician .33 | |
| 18. Librarian  37. X-Ray Technician | 18. Sociology | 18. Electrician .21  37. Minister .51 | 57. Psychologist, Counseling .44  77. YMCA Secretary .40 | |
| 19. Math Teacher, High School | 19. Teaching Sister, Catholic | 19. Engineer, Civil .36  38. Nurseryman .34 | 58. Psychologist, Industrial .36 | |

| OCCUPATIONAL SCALES WOMEN | | | COLLEGE MAJOR SCALES WOMEN | | | OCCUPATIONAL SCALES MEN | | | COLLEGE MAJOR SCALES MEN | | |
|---|---|---|---|---|---|---|---|---|---|---|---|
| Rank | Scale | Score | Rank | Scale | Score | Rank | Scale | Score | Rank | Scale | Score |
| 1. | 6. | | 1. | | | 1. 37 .51  6. 66 .47 | | | 1. 16 .48  6. 05 .42 | | |
| 2. | 7. | | 2. | | | 2. 32 .49  7. 42 .46 | | | 2. 21 .47  7. 15 .42 | | |
| 3. | 8. | | 3. | | | 3. 73 .49  8. 56 .46 | | | 3. 27 .45  8. 23 .42 | | |
| 4. | 9. | | 4. | | | 4. 55 .47  9. 65 .46 | | | 4. 10 .44  9. 24 .41 | | |
| 5. | 10. | | 5. | | | 5. 59 .47  10. 68 .46 | | | 5. 18 .44  10. 19 .40 | | |

V ____ 50

| | | | |
|---|---|---|---|
| M | .33 | S | .27 |
| MBI | .25 | F | .34 |
| W | .36 | D | .29 |
| WBI | .29 | Mo | .32 |

Figure 9.2b. Doug's KOIS profile. (From *Kuder Occupational Interest Survey — Form DD* by G. Frederic Kuder. Copyright © 1965, 1968, 1970, Science Research Associates, Inc. Reproduced by permission of the publisher.)

222

## WVI

*Donald Super:* Again, I think it is appropriate to identify the highs: intellectual stimulation and esthetics, which are high within the context of his general level of scores (see Fig. 9.2c). (Remember that WVI scales are not ipsative — that a high score on one scale does not require a corresponding reduction spread over the remaining scales.) Looking at the lows, economic returns, security, surroundings, and achievement, I am struck by the fact that, with the exception of creativity, he tends to be high on the scales of the self-expressive factor and low on the material. From this point of view he appears internally consistent and well organized. From the blind analysis of the profile, I felt reasonably comfortable about

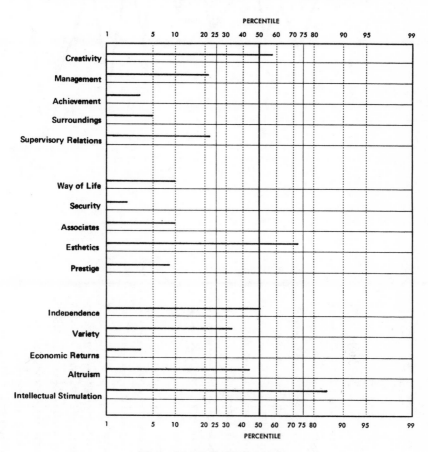

Figure 9.2c. Doug's WVI profile

REPORT ON THE MINNESOTA IMPORTANCE QUESTIONNAIRE
(MIQ)
1967 REVISION

CIRCULAR TRIAD SCORE= 30
INVALID RESPONSE RANGE
BEGINS AT 255.
MIQ IS VALID.

| MIQ SCALE | ADJUSTED SCALE VALUE |
|---|---|
| ABILITY UTILIZATION | 1.2 |
| ACHIEVEMENT | .2 |
| ACTIVITY | -.8 |
| ADVANCEMENT | 0.0 |
| AUTHORITY | -.5 |
| COMPANY POLICIES AND PRACTICES | 1.5 |
| COMPENSATION | .1 |
| COWORKERS | -.4 |
| CREATIVITY | 1.0 |
| INDEPENDENCE | -.1 |
| MORAL VALUES | 2.0 |
| RECOGNITION | -.5 |
| RESPONSIBILITY | .6 |
| SECURITY | -1.5 |
| SOCIAL SERVICE | .6 |
| SOCIAL STATUS | -.5 |
| SUPERVISION—HUMAN RELATIONS | -1.2 |
| SUPERVISION—TECHNICAL | -1.5 |
| VARIETY | .6 |
| WORKING CONDITIONS | -.5 |

Scale axis:

-4.0  -3.0  -2.0  VERY LOW -1.0  .LO. 0.0  .MOD +1.0 MOD  HIGH +2.0  +3.0  +4.0

CORRESPONDENCE BETWEEN OCCUPATIONAL REINFORCER PATTERNS AND MIQ SCALE VALUES FOR   DOUG   H

81 OCCUPATIONS LISTED IN DECREASING ORDER OF CORRESPONDENCE, USING D-SQUARED INDEX.
   OCCUPATIONS AT THE TOP OF THIS LIST ARE THOSE IN WHICH THIS INDIVIDUAL IS MOST LIKELY TO BE SATISFIED.
   OCCUPATIONS AT THE BOTTOM OF THE LIST ARE THOSE IN WHICH HE (SHE) IS LEAST LIKELY TO BE SATISFIED.

| OCCUPATION | CLUSTER | D-SQUARED | PREDICTION OF SATISFACTION |
|---|---|---|---|
| | | | LIKELY SATISFIED |
| LANDSCAPE GARDENER | 7 | 18.25 | LIKELY SATISFIED |
| HEAVY EQUIPMENT OPERATOR (CONSTRUCTION) | 7 | 22.84 | NOT LIKELY SATISFIED |
| AUTOMOBILE SERVICE STATION ATTENDANT | 5 | 24.21 | NOT LIKELY SATISFIED |
| RECEPTIONIST, CIVIL SERVICE | 4 | 24.90 | NOT LIKELY SATISFIED |
| TEACHER, SECONDARY SCHOOL | 4 | 24.92 | NOT LIKELY SATISFIED |
| WAITER-WAITRESS | 6 | 25.59 | NOT LIKELY SATISFIED |
| PIPEFITTER | 7 | 25.66 | NOT LIKELY SATISFIED |
| EMBALMER | 6 | 26.22 | NOT LIKELY SATISFIED |
| ORDERLY | 6 | 26.49 | NOT LIKELY SATISFIED |
| STENOGRAPHER, TECHNICAL, CIVIL SERVICE | 5 | 26.52 | NOT LIKELY SATISFIED |
| ENGINEER, MECHANICAL | 1 | 26.61 | NOT LIKELY SATISFIED |
| PUNCH-PRESS OPERATOR | 8 | 27.14 | NOT LIKELY SATISFIED |
| PAINTER-PAPERHANGER | 7 | 27.38 | NOT LIKELY SATISFIED |
| RADIOLOGIC TECHNOLOGIST | 6 | 27.57 | NOT LIKELY SATISFIED |
| SALESMAN, REAL ESTATE | 3 | 27.65 | NOT LIKELY SATISFIED |
| DRAFTSMAN, ARCHITECTURAL | 9 | 27.78 | NOT LIKELY SATISFIED |
| PRODUCTION HELPER (FOOD) | 8 | 27.86 | NOT LIKELY SATISFIED |
| POLICEMAN | | 27.98 | NOT LIKELY SATISFIED |
| BUS DRIVER | | 32.98 | NOT LIKELY SATISFIED |
| AIRPLANE STEWARDESS | | 33.00 | NOT LIKELY SATISFIED |
| CLAIM EXAMINER | | 33.20 | NOT LIKELY SATISFIED |
| CASHIER-CHECKER | 8 | 33.56 | NOT LIKELY SATISFIED |
| MEAT CUTTER | | 33.77 | NOT LIKELY SATISFIED |
| NURSE, PROFESSIONAL | | 33.98 | NOT LIKELY SATISFIED |
| SALESMAN, SECURITIES | 3 | 34.05 | NOT LIKELY SATISFIED |
| ASSEMBLER (ELECTRICAL EQUIPMENT) | 8 | 34.58 | NOT LIKELY SATISFIED |
| ENGINEER, STATIONARY | | 34.75 | NOT LIKELY SATISFIED |
| MARKER | 8 | 34.77 | NOT LIKELY SATISFIED |
| ELECTRICAL TECHNICIAN | 9 | 34.78 | NOT LIKELY SATISFIED |
| TELLER (BANKING) | | 34.87 | NOT LIKELY SATISFIED |
| SCREW-MACHINE OPERATOR, PRODUCTION | 9 | 35.28 | NOT LIKELY SATISFIED |
| INSTRUCTOR, VOCATIONAL SCHOOL | 4 | 35.64 | NOT LIKELY SATISFIED |
| PHARMACIST | | 37.11 | NOT LIKELY SATISFIED |
| OFFICE-MACHINE SERVICEMAN | 9 | 39.50 | NOT LIKELY SATISFIED |

9 OCCUPATIONAL FAMILIES LISTED IN DECREASING ORDER OF CORRESPONDENCE, USING D-SQUARED INDEX

| | | |
|---|---|---|
| CLUSTER 7 -- MANUAL OCCUPATIONS, BUILDING TRADES | 26.02 |
| CLUSTER 6 -- SERVICE OCCUPATIONS, PERSONAL | 27.01 |
| CLUSTER 1 -- TECHNICAL OCCUPATIONS, PROFESSIONAL | 28.09 |
| CLUSTER 5 -- SERVICE OCCUPATIONS, BUSINESS DETAIL | 28.54 |
| CLUSTER 2 -- TECHNICAL OCCUPATIONS, SEMI-PROFESSIONAL | 29.28 |
| CLUSTER 3 -- SALES OCCUPATIONS, SERVICE | 29.42 |
| CLUSTER 4 -- SERVICE OCCUPATIONS, SOCIAL-EDUCATIONAL | 29.45 |
| CLUSTER 8 -- MANUAL OCCUPATIONS, MANUFACTURING | 30.37 |
| CLUSTER 9 -- MANUAL OCCUPATIONS, SERVICE-MAINTENANCE | 30.48 |

Figure 9.2d. Doug's MIQ profile.
(Solid line above indicates that
items have been dropped for
reasons of space.)

225

# NCS PROFILE — STRONG VOCATIONAL INTEREST BLANK — FOR MEN

## BASIC INTEREST SCALES

| SCALE | STD. SCORE | PLOTTED SCORE |
|---|---|---|
| PUBLIC SPEAKING | 59 | |
| LAW/POLITICS | 66 | |
| BUSINESS MANAGEMENT | 52 | |
| SALES | 51 | |
| MERCHANDISING | 52 | |
| OFFICE PRACTICES | 54 | |
| MILITARY ACTIVITIES | 53 | |
| TECHNICAL SUPERVISION | 49 | |
| MATHEMATICS | 61 | |
| SCIENCE | 63 | |
| MECHANICAL | 55 | |
| NATURE | 66 | |
| AGRICULTURE | 59 | |
| ADVENTURE | 59 | |
| RECREATIONAL LEADERSHIP | 52 | |
| MEDICAL SERVICE | 68 | |
| SOCIAL SERVICE | 66 | |
| RELIGIOUS ACTIVITIES | 69 | |
| TEACHING | 72 | |
| MUSIC | 73 | |
| ART | 73 | |
| WRITING | 69 | |

DOUBLE LINE = AVERAGE SCORE FOR 650 52 YEAR OLD MEN.    SINGLE LINE = AVERAGE SCORE FOR SAME MEN WHEN 16 YEARS OLD.

## OCCUPATIONAL SCALES

| OCCUPATION | STD. SCORE | | OCCUPATION | STD. SCORE |
|---|---|---|---|---|
| I DENTIST | 19 | | VI LIBRARIAN | 41 |
| OSTEOPATH | 36 | | ARTIST | 21 |
| VETERINARIAN | 16 | | MUSICIAN PERFORMER | 38 |
| PHYSICIAN | 43 | | MUSIC TEACHER | 31 |
| PSYCHIATRIST | 46 | | VII C. P. A. OWNER | 30 |
| PSYCHOLOGIST | 32 | | VIII SENIOR C. P. A. | 23 |
| BIOLOGIST | 43 | | ACCOUNTANT | 27 |
| II ARCHITECT | 21 | | OFFICE WORKER | 22 |
| MATHEMATICIAN | 19 | | PURCHASING AGENT | 14 |
| PHYSICIST | 20 | | BANKER | 7 |
| CHEMIST | 36 | | PHARMACIST | 18 |
| ENGINEER | 25 | | FUNERAL DIRECTOR | 17 |
| III PRODUCTION MANAGER | 29 | | IX SALES MANAGER | 15 |
| ARMY OFFICER | 35 | | REAL ESTATE SALESMAN | 21 |
| AIR FORCE OFFICER | 37 | | LIFE INS. SALESMAN | 18 |
| IV CARPENTER | 10 | | X ADVERTISING MAN | 18 |
| FOREST SERVICE MAN | 28 | | LAWYER | 25 |
| FARMER | 25 | | AUTHOR-JOURNALIST | 23 |
| MATH-SCIENCE TEACHER | 33 | | XI PRESIDENT-MFG. | 9 |
| PRINTER | 17 | | | |
| POLICEMAN | 18 | | **SUPP. OCCUPATIONAL SCALES** | |
| V PERSONNEL DIRECTOR | 31 | | CREDIT MANAGER | 32 |
| PUBLIC ADMINISTRATOR | 47 | | CHAMBER OF COM. EXEC. | 38 |
| REHABILITATION COUNS. | 49 | | PHYSICAL THERAPIST | 48 |
| YMCA STAFF MEMBER | 33 | | COMPUTER PROGRAMMER | 41 |
| SOCIAL WORKER | 44 | | BUSINESS ED. TEACHER | 27 |
| SOCIAL SCIENCE TEACHER | 28 | | COMMUNITY REC. ADMIN. | 40 |
| SCHOOL SUPERINTENDENT | 32 | | | |
| MINISTER | 46 | | | |

### NON-OCCUPATIONAL SCALES

| AACH | AR | DIV | MFII | MO | OIE | OL | SL |
|---|---|---|---|---|---|---|---|
| 79 | 60 | 73 | 33 | 34 | 34 | 63 | 49 |

### ADMINISTRATIVE INDICES

| TR | UNP | FC | LP | IP | DP |
|---|---|---|---|---|---|
| 398 | 8 | 9 | 48 | 45 | ? |

SCORED BY NATIONAL COMPUTER SYSTEMS, INC., 4401 WEST 76TH ST., MINNEAPOLIS, MINN.

Figure 9.2e. Doug's SVIB profile

226

# MINNESOTA VOCATIONAL INTEREST INVENTORY

| | OCCUPATIONAL SCALES | STD. SCORE |
|---|---|---|
| 1 | BAKER | 46 |
| 2 | FOOD SERVICE MANAGER | 47 |
| 3 | MILK WAGON DRIVER | 39 |
| 4 | RETAIL SALES CLERK | 45 |
| 5 | STOCK CLERK | 48 |
| 6 | PRINTER | 56 |
| 7 | TAB. MACHINE OPERATOR | 49 |
| 8 | WAREHOUSEMAN | 34 |
| 9 | HOSPITAL ATTENDANT | 48 |
| 10 | PRESSMAN | 34 |
| 11 | CARPENTER | 24 |
| 12 | PAINTER | 49 |
| 13 | PLASTERER | 42 |
| 14 | TRUCK DRIVER | 12 |
| 15 | TRUCK MECHANIC | 07 |
| 16 | INDUSTRIAL EDUC. TEACHER | 29 |
| 17 | SHEET METAL WORKER | 24 |
| 18 | PLUMBER | 20 |
| 19 | MACHINIST | 18 |
| 20 | ELECTRICIAN | 13 |
| 21 | RADIO-TV REPAIRMAN | 36 |
| 22 | | |
| 23 | | |
| 24 | | |
| 25 | | |

a. SCORES ABOVE 60 ARE PLOTTED AS 60.
NEGATIVE SCORES ARE PLOTTED AS ZERO.

| AREA SCALES | STD. SCORE | STANDARD SCORES |
|---|---|---|
| H-1 MECHANICAL | 32 | |
| H-2 HEALTH SERVICE | 69 | |
| H-3 OFFICE WORK | 47 | |
| H-4 ELECTRONICS | 36 | |
| H-5 FOOD SERVICE | 67 | |
| H-6 CARPENTRY | 39 | |
| H-7 SALES-OFFICE | 79 | |
| H-8 "CLEAN HANDS" | 50 | |
| H-9 OUTDOORS | 33 | |

SEE OTHER SIDE FOR EXPLANATION

Figure 9.2f. Doug's MVII profile. (Reproduced by permission.
Copyright © 1965 by The Psychological Corporation, New York, N.Y.
All rights reserved.)

this young man. After reading the background sketch, I was no longer so comfortable. Here was someone who was high in intellectual stimulation but low on achievement. What do Doug's self-expressive needs mean when he does not value the mastery of skills that should accompany intellectual stimulation? I wondered whether the need for self-expression was a manifestation of a personality problem, and after what was said about the KOIS, I feel even more concern. One sees many people who manifest self-expressive values and who, more than others, are trying to find out what that self is.

## MIQ

*David Weiss:* Doug's MIQ profile shows four reinforcers "highly" or moderately important to him, with the other sixteen of "low" or "very low" importance (see Fig. 9.2d). His highest preference is for an occupation that will not conflict with his moral code (moral values). He also prefers an occupation in which the employer is likely to be fair to him (company policies), in which he can make use of his abilities (ability utilization) and in which he can try out his own ideas (creativity). He is quite decided about these four characteristics of his ideal job, since there are no error bands (dashed lines) around the scale values for these scales. This implies that his preference for these characteristics is likely to be stable. Only independence, of the remaining sixteen scales, shows no indecision associated with it. The circular triads score of 30 for the total profile also reflects an essentially stable preference system.

Because Doug has many "low" and "very low" scales, the $D^2$ index of correspondence for his profile yields few positive predictions of job satisfaction. As with Robert's profile, the counselor needs to compare further Doug's preferences with the available Occupational Reinforcer Pattern (ORP) information. Using the rankings of the eighty-one occupations given in volume I of ORPs (Borgen et al., 1968, pp. 204–243), the counselor can list those occupations high on combinations of moral values, company policies, ability utilization, and creativity (Doug's highest scales). From these lists it is possible to determine that two of Doug's highest needs might be met in occupations such as securities salesman, real estate salesman, automobile salesman, caseworker, claim adjuster, commercial artist, occupational therapist, vocational school instructor, elementary school teacher, and vocational rehabilitation counselor. These possibilities, and others derived from clinical comparisons of Doug's highest needs with the ORPs, can be used by the counselor to explore further satisfying occupational possibilities for Doug.

## SVIB

*Lenore Harmon:* My first impression after looking at the administrative indices was that Doug doesn't have any low basic interest scale scores at all. His academic achievement score is extremely high, as is his diversity of interest score (see Fig. 9.2e). The diversity of his interests may explain in part why he has not made a career choice, but I think there is more to it than that. His high scores on academic achievement and occupational level seem inconsistent with the fact that he is not achieving. This suggests some conflicts in his life. In counseling, I would want to talk about what they might be. I wonder what his family expects of him; how they and he feel about the achievements of his older siblings; and how he feels about his own masculinity. He has a low MFII score, high scores on the basic scales for music, art, and writing, and a number of college credits in music and art. Are there some reasons why he is not free to commit himself to an esthetic occupation or even a service occupation as suggested by his high scores on the basic interest scales for medical and social service, teaching, and religious activities?

On the occupational scales his service interests are most pronounced. He well may go into a service occupation once his conflicts are resolved. His aversion for the real estate business or any business is well supported by the occupational scales.

*Question:* What do you thing of his age related score?

*Dr. Harmon:* I wouldn't talk about it at all. I don't really know how to interpret high scores on the age related scale.

*Question:* How would you interpret his law/politics score?

*Dr. Harmon:* Someone else hypothesized a kind of social introversion. Occupationally, I don't see him as introverted. His OIE scale suggests he would not mind working with people. The law/politics score indicates that he is comfortable speaking to people and attempting to persuade them to change their attitudes. It does not lead me to conclude that he is going to become a lawyer because of his low scores in group X. I do place more weight on the occupational scales than on the basic scales in making predictions. However, I can see him in a persuasive or even administrative position if the general field is social service, assuming that he resolves his apparent conflicts.

## MVII-W

*Leslie Barnette:* I would like to give you my interpretations from the MVII just from my notes regardless of what everyone else has said. First, I would not have used the MVII on this man; he's a college student. Further, he grew up on a farm, and his father is in managerial work, which suggests the possibility that the home isn't particularly intellectually oriented. He's coasting, a low achiever; personal problems are probably indicated by that low achievement. He has two fairly high food scores and, knowing his background of low achievement, I questioned whether this might be a reflection of passivity. This should at least be explored. His apparent interest in art, music, and literature probably turns up in the painter-printer scores. The medical attendant score is fairly high. The area scales at the bottom of the profile list an extremely high sales-office score followed by highs on health service and food service (see Fig. 9.2f). I would suggest that he think about work in hospital administration and perhaps look over programs in this field.

*Dr. Harmon:* I think hospital administration would allow for his power orientation.

*Dr. Barnette:* Yes, it includes power, health, and food.

## Donna's Profile

BACKGROUND INFORMATION

Donna is forty-two years old, married, and the mother of two children, the younger of which is now fourteen years old. She is considering the idea of returning to college, but is in a way "certainly uncertain" of what career she would like to pursue.

Donna's husband operated a small retail business for a number of years after they were married. About five years ago, he sold the business, completed his undergraduate degree, and acquired a master's degree and a new occupation, all with her cooperation and consent. She anticipates that she will need something to do when her fourteen-year-old leaves home and she is currently planning for that event.

Donna feels that she has broad interests which complicate deciding on a field of study. While in college, she enjoyed working in the library. She began but did not complete nursing training before she was married; she has done some nursing work and in the past two years she has worked as

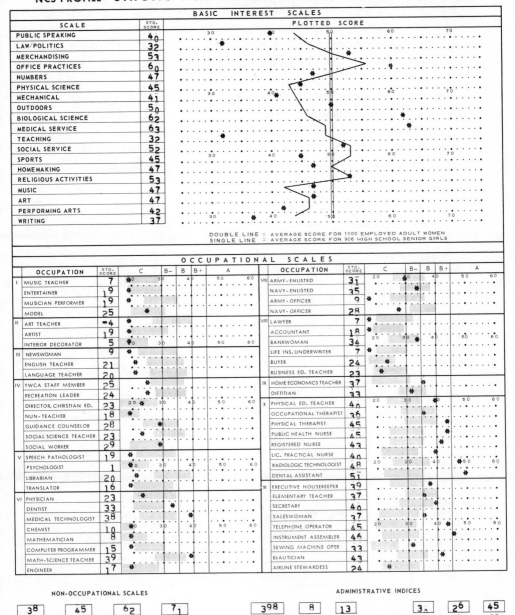

Figure 9.3a. Donna's SVIB profile

a physical therapy aide. She helped operate the store, mainly by looking after the bookwork, but she also did some selling. She has played the organ for her church and enjoys music to the extent that she has an organ in her home. She says that she thinks she likes almost everything, "except maybe teaching."

Donna questions her ability to do college work after so long an absence, and is entertaining equally the prospects of junior college technical training or completing her bachelor's degree begun so many years ago. (Because the MVII is designed expressly for men and reports mostly on occupations typically held by men, it was not administered to Donna.)

## Report of Scores — Kuder Occupational Interest Survey (Form DD)

NAME DONNA LOCATION 000-38606 DATE OF SURVEY 12-04-70

### OCCUPATIONAL SCALES, WOMEN

| Title | Score |
|---|---|
| Accountant | .57 |
| Bank Clerk | .61 |
| Beautician | .62 |
| Bookkeeper | .60 |
| Bookstore Manager | .60 |
| Computer Programmer | .53 |
| Counselor, High School | .66 |
| Dean of Women | .65 |
| Dental Assistant | .69 |
| Department Store Saleswoman | .55 |
| Dietitian, Administrative | .66 |
| Dietitian, Public School | .65 |
| Florist | .64 |
| Home Demonstration Agent | .62 |
| Home Ec Teacher, College | .68 |
| Interior Decorator | .49 |
| Lawyer | .52 |
| Librarian | .61 |
| Math Teacher, High School | .63 |
| Nurse | .69 |
| Nutritionist | .66 |
| Occupational Therapist | .64 |
| Office Clerk | .61 |
| Physical Therapist | .69 |
| Primary School Teacher | .67 |
| Psychologist | .60 |
| Psychologist, Clinical | .61 |
| Religious Education Director | .66 |
| Science Teacher, High School | .62 |
| Secretary | .64 |
| Social Caseworker | .67 |
| Social Worker, Group | .65 |
| Social Worker, Medical | .67 |
| Social Worker, Pyschiatric | .64 |
| Social Worker, School | .70 |
| Stenographer | .63 |
| X-Ray Technician | .66 |

### COLLEGE MAJOR SCALES, WOMEN

| Title | Score |
|---|---|
| Art & Art Education | .51 |
| Biological Sciences | .65 |
| Business Ed & Commerce | .55 |
| Drama | .51 |
| Elementary Education | .68 |
| English | .53 |
| Foreign Languages | .64 |
| General Social Sciences | .63 |
| Health Professions | .68 |
| History | .56 |
| Home Economics Education | .65 |
| Mathematics | .64 |
| Music & Music Education | .66 |
| Nursing | .71 |
| Physical Education | .62 |
| Political Science | .48 |
| Psychology | .59 |
| Sociology | .60 |
| Teaching Sister, Catholic | .62 |

### OCCUPATIONAL SCALES, MEN

| Title | Score |
|---|---|
| Acc't, Certified Public | |
| Architect | .38 |
| Automobile Mechanic | |
| Automobile Salesman | |
| Banker | |
| Bookkeeper | |
| Bookstore Manager | .33 |
| Bricklayer | |
| Buyer | .33 |
| Carpenter | |
| Chemist | .38 |
| Clothier, Retail | |
| Computer Programmer | .71 |
| Counselor, High School | .62 |
| County Agricultural Agent | .48 |
| Dentist | .47 |
| Electrician | |
| Engineer, Civil | .30 |
| Engineer, Electrical | |
| Engineer, Heating/Air Cond. | .38 |
| Engineer, Industrial | |
| Engineer, Mechanical | |
| Engineer, Mining & Metal | |
| Farmer | |
| Florist | |
| Forester | |
| Insurance Agent | .28 |
| Interior Decorator | |
| Journalist | .21 |
| Lawyer | |
| Librarian | |
| Machinist | |
| Mathematician | .40 |
| Math Teacher, High School | |
| Meteorologist | |
| Minister | |
| Nurseryman | .30 |
| Optometrist | .46 |
| Osteopath | |
| Painter, House | |
| Pediatrician | .53 |
| Personnel Manager | .33 |
| Pharmaceutical Salesman | |
| Pharmacist | .44 |
| Photographer | .36 |
| Physical Therapist | |
| Physician | .48 |
| Plumber | |
| Plumbing Contractor | |
| Podiatrist | |
| Policeman | |
| Postal Clerk | |
| Printer | |
| Psychiatrist | .51 |
| Psychologist, Clinical | |
| Psychologist, Counseling | |
| Psychologist, Industrial | |
| Psychology Professor | .40 |
| Radio Station Manager | |
| Real Estate Agent | .29 |
| Sales Eng, Heating/Air Cond. | |
| Science Teacher, High School | |
| School Superintendent | |
| Social Caseworker | .44 |
| Social Worker, Group | .36 |
| Social Worker, Psychiatric | |
| Statistician | .35 |
| Supv/Foreman, Industrial | |
| Travel Agent | .33 |
| Truck Driver | |
| Television Repairman | |
| University Pastor | |
| Veterinarian | .39 |
| Welder | |
| X-Ray Technician | |
| YMCA Secretary | |

### COLLEGE MAJOR SCALES, MEN

| Title | Score |
|---|---|
| Agriculture | .30 |
| Animal Husbandry | |
| Architecture | .30 |
| Art & Art Education | |
| Biological Sciences | |
| Business Acc't & Finance | |
| Business & Marketing | |
| Business Management | |
| Economics | .25 |
| Elementary Education | |
| Engineering, Chemical | .28 |
| Engineering, Civil | .26 |
| Engineering, Electrical | .29 |
| Engineering, Mechanical | .23 |
| English | |
| Foreign Languages | |
| Forestry | |
| History | |
| Law (Grad School) | |
| Mathematics | |
| Music & Music Ed | |
| Physical Education | |
| Physical Sciences | .34 |
| Political Science & Gov't | |
| Premed, Pharm & Dentistry | |
| Psychology | |
| Sociology | |
| U.S. Air Force Cadet | |
| U.S. Military Cadet | |

### Ranked summary

| OCCUPATIONAL SCALES WOMEN | Score | COLLEGE MAJOR SCALES WOMEN | Score | OCCUPATIONAL SCALES MEN | Score | COLLEGE MAJOR SCALES MEN | Score |
|---|---|---|---|---|---|---|---|
| SOC WORKR,SCHOOL | .70 | NURSING | .71 | PEDIATRICIAN | .53 | PHYSICAL SCIENCE | .34 |
| DENTAL ASSISTANT | .69 | ELEMENTARY EDUC | .68 | PSYCHIATRIST | .51 | AGRICULTURE | .30 |
| NURSE | .69 | HEALTH PROFES | .68 | PHYSICIAN | .48 | ARCHITECTURE | .30 |
| PHYS THERAPIST | .69 | MUSIC & MUSIC ED | .66 | DENTIST | .47 | ENGINEERING,ELEC | .29 |
| HOME EC TCHR,COL | .68 | BIOLOGICAL SCI | .65 | OPTOMETRIST | .46 | ENGINEERING,CHEM | .28 |
| PRIMARY SCH TCHR | .67 | | | PHARMACIST | .44 | ENGINEERNG,CIVIL | .26 |
| SOCIAL CASEWORKR | .67 | | | MATHEMATICIAN | .40 | ECONOMICS | .25 |
| SOC WORKER,MEDIC | .67 | | | PSYCHOLOGY PROF | .40 | ENGINEERING,MECH | .23 |
| COUNSELOR,HI SCH | .66 | | | VETERINARIAN | .39 | | |
| DIETITIAN, ADMIN | .66 | | | ARCHITECT | .38 | | |

V 54

| | | | |
|---|---|---|---|
| M | .34 | S | .29 |
| MBI | .18 | F | .37 |
| W | .68 | D | .64 |
| WBI | .20 | MO | .68 |

Figure 9.3b. Donna's KOIS profile. (From *Kuder Occupational Interest Survey — Form DD* by G. Frederic Kuder. Copyright © 1965, 1968, 1970, Science Research Associates, Inc. Reproduced by permission of the publisher.)

232

 **PROFILE CHART**

Date of Testing  DECEMBER 18, 1970

Grade     Age     yrs.     mos.     Sex F

**NAT**     Reference Group

<table>
<tr><td>Name</td><td>DONNA</td></tr>
<tr><td>School</td><td>IOWA ST U</td></tr>
<tr><td>Counselor</td><td></td></tr>
</table>

| Scale Number | Scale Name | Scale Score | %ile Rank | Low 1 | 2 | 3 | Average 4 | 5 | 6 | High 7 | 8 | 9 | Scale Clarity Index |
|---|---|---|---|---|---|---|---|---|---|---|---|---|---|
| 9 | NURSING | 47 | GRADE WAS NOT MARKED ON ANSWER BOOKLET | | | | | | | | | | |
| 21 | MUSIC | 42 | | | | | | | | | | | H |
| 8 | CUSTOMER SERVICE | 38 | | | | | | | | | | | H |
| 24 | MEDICAL | 37 | | | | | | | | | | | F |
| 19 | ARTISTIC | 35 | | | | | | | | | | | F |
| 22 | ENTERTAINMENT | 34 | | | | | | | | | | | F |
| 18 | MANAGEMENT | 31 | | | | | | | | | | | F |
| 4 | CARE PEOPLE-ANIM | 30 | | | | | | | | | | | F |
| 11 | TRAINING | 30 | | | | | | | | | | | F |
| 23 | TEACH-COUN-SOC W | 30 | | | | | | | | | | | F |
| 5 | CLERICAL WORK | 29 | | | | | | | | | | | H |
| 3 | PERSONAL SERVICE | 28 | | | | | | | | | | | H |
| 13 | NUMERICAL | 26 | | | | | | | | | | | F |
| 14 | APPRAISAL | 25 | | | | | | | | | | | H |
| 17 | PROMOTION-COMMU | 25 | | | | | | | | | | | H |
| 12 | LITERARY | 24 | | | | | | | | | | | H |
| 20 | SALES REPRESENT | 24 | | | | | | | | | | | H |
| 10 | SKILLED PER SERV | 23 | | | | | | | | | | | H |
| 16 | APPLIED TECH | 22 | | | | | | | | | | | H |
| 7 | CRAFTS | 20 | | | | | | | | | | | H |
| 15 | AGRICULTURE | 16 | | | | | | | | | | | H |
| 2 | MACHINE WORK | 15 | | | | | | | | | | | H |
| 6 | INSPECT-TESTING | 15 | | | | | | | | | | | H |
| 1 | MANUAL WORK | 13 | | | | | | | | | | | H |

**Student Questionnaire Information**

1. Occupational Plans

   First Choice  NURSING

   Second Choice CLERICAL WORK

2. Best Liked Subjects

   First  SCIENCES

   Second MUSIC

3. High School Program

   First  NO RESPONSE

4. Post-High School Plans

   First  NO RESPONSE

5. Interest in Vocational Programs

       NO RESPONSE

6. Vocational Program Choice

   First  NO RESPONSE

   Second NO RESPONSE

7. Local Survey Information

   A   B   C   D   E   F   G   H

   — — — — — — — —

Figure 9.3c. Donna's OVIS profile. (Reproduced from the Ohio Vocational Interest Survey Test, copyright 1969 by Harcourt Brace Jovanovich, Inc. Reproduced by special permission of the publisher.)

REPORT ON THE MINNESOTA IMPORTANCE QUESTIONNAIRE
(MIQ)
1967 REVISION

CIRCULAR TRIAD SCORE= 22
INVALID RESPONSE RANGE
BEGINS AT 255.
MIQ IS VALID.

| MIQ SCALE | ADJUSTED SCALE VALUE |
|---|---|
| ABILITY UTILIZATION ........... | 1.0 |
| ACHIEVEMENT ................... | 1.2 |
| ACTIVITY ...................... | -1.1 |
| ADVANCEMENT ................... | .4 |
| AUTHORITY ..................... | -.6 |
| COMPANY POLICIES AND PRACTICES | 1.6 |
| COMPENSATION .................. | 1.0 |
| COWORKERS ..................... | .3 |
| CREATIVITY .................... | .2 |
| INDEPENDENCE .................. | -1.1 |
| MORAL VALUES .................. | 2.4 |
| RECOGNITION ................... | .8 |
| RESPONSIBILITY ................ | 0.0 |
| SECURITY ...................... | 1.2 |
| SOCIAL SERVICE ................ | -.1 |
| SOCIAL STATUS ................. | -.8 |
| SUPERVISION--HUMAN RELATIONS . | 1.6 |
| SUPERVISION--TECHNICAL ........ | .4 |
| VARIETY ....................... | -.6 |
| WORKING CONDITIONS ............ | .6 |

VERY LOW    LO    MOD    HIGH
-4.0   -3.0   -2.0   -1.0   0.0   +1.0   +2.0   +3.0   +4.0

CORRESPONDENCE BETWEEN OCCUPATIONAL REINFORCER PATTERNS AND MIQ SCALE VALUES FOR DONNA

81 OCCUPATIONS LISTED IN DECREASING ORDER OF CORRESPONDENCE, USING D-SQUARED INDEX.
OCCUPATIONS AT THE TOP OF THIS LIST ARE THOSE IN WHICH THIS INDIVIDUAL IS MOST LIKELY TO BE SATISFIED.
OCCUPATIONS AT THE BOTTOM OF THE LIST ARE THOSE IN WHICH HE(SHE) IS LEAST LIKELY TO BE SATISFIED.

| OCCUPATION | CLUSTER | D-SQUARED | PREDICTION OF SATISFACTION |
|---|---|---|---|
| FIRE FIGHTER | - | 10.67 | LIKELY SATISFIED |
| SALESMAN, AUTOMOBILE | - | 11.00 | LIKELY SATISFIED |
| WAITER-WAITRESS | 6 | 11.92 | LIKELY SATISFIED |
| PRODUCTION HELPER (FOOD) | 8 | 12.06 | LIKELY SATISFIED |
| ACCOUNTING CLERK, MANUFACTURING | 8 | 12.09 | LIKELY SATISFIED |
| SALESPERSON, SHOE | - | 12.47 | LIKELY SATISFIED |
| SEWING-MACHINE OPERATOR, AUTOMATIC | 8 | 12.67 | LIKELY SATISFIED |
| PIPEFITTER | 7 | 12.71 | LIKELY SATISFIED |
| BAKER | 8 | 13.05 | LIKELY SATISFIED |
| ASSEMBLER, SMALL PARTS | 8 | 13.18 | LIKELY SATISFIED |
| MEAT CUTTER | 8 | 13.36 | LIKELY SATISFIED |
| MEDICAL TECHNOLOGIST | 6 | 13.54 | LIKELY SATISFIED |
| DRAFTSMAN, ARCHITECTURAL | 9 | 13.57 | LIKELY SATISFIED |
| ASSEMBLER(ELECTRICAL EQUIPMENT) | 8 | 13.65 | LIKELY SATISFIED |
| HEAVY EQUIPMENT OPERATOR(CONSTRUCTION) | 7 | 13.66 | LIKELY SATISFIED |
| PUNCH-PRESS OPERATOR | 8 | 13.80 | LIKELY SATISFIED |
| COOK(HOTEL-RESTAURANT) | - | 13.91 | LIKELY SATISFIED |
| PAINTER/PAPERHANGER | 7 | 14.04 | LIKELY SATISFIED |
| TEACHER, SECONDARY SCHOOL | 4 | 20.76 | NOT LIKELY SATISFIED |
| PHARMACIST | 4 | 20.77 | NOT LIKELY SATISFIED |
| CASEWORKER | 4 | 20.97 | NOT LIKELY SATISFIED |
| CLAIM ADJUSTER | 4 | 21.14 | NOT LIKELY SATISFIED |
| LIBRARIAN | 4 | 21.18 | NOT LIKELY SATISFIED |
| OFFICE-MACHINE SERVICEMAN | 9 | 21.71 | NOT LIKELY SATISFIED |
| NURSE, PROFESSIONAL | 4 | 21.76 | NOT LIKELY SATISFIED |
| PHYSICAL THERAPIST | 4 | 22.15 | NOT LIKELY SATISFIED |
| OCCUPATIONAL THERAPIST | 4 | 22.54 | NOT LIKELY SATISFIED |
| SALESMAN, SECURITIES | 3 | 22.61 | NOT LIKELY SATISFIED |
| RECEPTIONIST, CIVIL SERVICE | - | 22.83 | NOT LIKELY SATISFIED |
| COMMERCIAL ARTIST, ILLUSTRATING | 4 | 22.90 | NOT LIKELY SATISFIED |
| TEACHER, ELEMENTARY SCHOOL | 4 | 24.83 | NOT LIKELY SATISFIED |
| INSTRUCTOR, VOCATIONAL SCHOOL | 4 | 25.14 | NOT LIKELY SATISFIED |
| COUNSELOR, VOCATIONAL REHABILITATION | 4 | 26.51 | NOT LIKELY SATISFIED |
| COUNSELOR, SCHOOL | 4 | 27.16 | NOT LIKELY SATISFIED |

9 OCCUPATIONAL FAMILIES LISTED IN DECREASING ORDER OF CORRESPONDENCE, USING D-SQUARED INDEX

| | | | |
|---|---|---|---|
| CLUSTER 8 | -- | MANUAL OCCUPATIONS, MANUFACTURING | 12.67 |
| CLUSTER 7 | -- | MANUAL OCCUPATIONS, BUILDING TRADES | 13.90 |
| CLUSTER 6 | -- | SERVICE OCCUPATIONS, PERSONAL | 14.44 |
| CLUSTER 5 | -- | SERVICE OCCUPATIONS, BUSINESS DETAIL | 15.99 |
| CLUSTER 9 | -- | MANUAL OCCUPATIONS, SERVICE-MAINTENANCE | 16.61 |
| CLUSTER 1 | -- | TECHNICAL OCCUPATIONS, PROFESSIONAL | 18.48 |
| CLUSTER 2 | -- | TECHNICAL OCCUPATIONS, SEMI-PROFESSIONAL | 18.83 |
| CLUSTER 3 | -- | SALES OCCUPATIONS, SERVICE | 19.68 |
| CLUSTER 4 | -- | SERVICE OCCUPATIONS, SOCIAL-EDUCATIONAL | 22.92 |

Figure 9.3d. Donna's MIQ profile. (Solid line above indicates that items have been dropped for reasons of space.)

235

## SVIB

*Lenore Harmon:* The administrative indices for Donna's profile look fine so we can go ahead and interpret the profile (see Fig. 9.3a). Her scores on the basic scales for biological science and medical service as well as her scores in group X suggest paramedical occupations. She also has a high score on office practices which complements her score on the telephone operator scale. The two areas that have the greatest support from the SVIB are areas in which she has had some experience.

Whether she will acquire her training in college or at a technical level is a most important question. We know that academic achievement scores

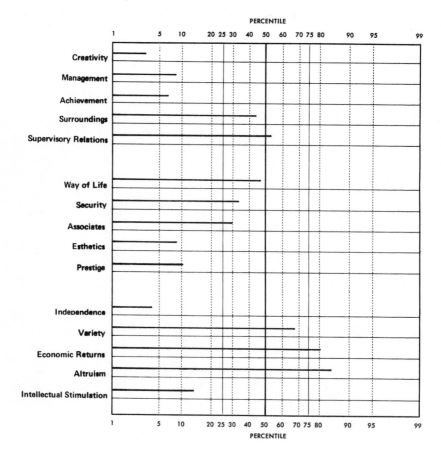

Figure 9.3e. Donna's WVI profile

236

increase with age. Yet her AACH score is 38 at age forty-two. She probably doesn't feel like finishing a college degree.

Donna appears to be quite feminine and has a high score on occupational introversion-extroversion. These scores, coupled with her low scores on law/politics and public speaking, make me suspect that she would not even like to take a bachelor's degree in nursing. Nurses with college degrees are usually placed in administrative positions, such as head nurse or team leader, and I don't think she would like that. I would talk with her about choosing a health-related occupation such as X-ray technology for which she would be trained at a technical level.

## KOIS

*Donald Zytowski:* It doesn't seem illogical to follow the discussion of the SVIB because my conclusions from the KOIS are somewhat similar to Dr. Harmon's. Donna's validity score is quite high; therefore there is no doubt that her profile is valid. The level of her W score, 68, is quite high (see Fig. 9.3b). There is no exact interpretation of this level, but it means she has a lot in common with some hypothetical women-in-general group. It is substantially higher than the M score, so we can assume that she has no difficulties accepting women's interests and the roles they generate. I would observe tentatively that her interests are not as mature as her chronological age, owing to the similarity between her Mo and D scores.

Having such a high W score elevates the general level of her occupational and college major scales. They run as high as 70. In my experience, this level is gained more often by women than by men and by older people than by younger. The moderate level of aspiration manifests itself in the elevation of the dental assistant, nurse, and physical therapist scales in the occupational ranks and nursing in the college major rank. College teacher and social worker scales are intermingled with these also, which makes it more difficult for Donna to decide what level is the most appropriate for her. Perhaps it is the influence of the interpretation from the SVIB, but I take the high ranks on health professions among the men's occupations as indicative of medically related interests. Nevertheless because these scores are more than .06 from the highest women's scales, their level should not be used as an indicator. By themselves they are interpretable, but in comparison with the women's scales they add little. Since Donna has much in common with women, she would necessarily have much less in common occupationally with men, especially on the college major scales. In summary, I would suggest that she explore the health service training opportunities available to her in the area in which she lives. What she finally does might depend more on what training opportunities are accessible than on a strong commitment to one occupation or another.

## OVIS

*Ayres D'Costa:* What the other two interest inventories report is consistent with the OVIS profile. There are no norms at present for adults, and therefore no percentiles or stanines are given. The current questionnaire section in OVIS is relevant to high school students only — hence the blanks or no responses in Donna's profile. Interpretation must therefore proceed mainly from the raw scores. The high interest scales turn out to be nursing, customer service, and medical (see Fig. 9.3c). I am skipping music because it is known that music is presently an avocation with her. Donna is very clearly interested in working with people and seems to dislike working with things.

Note the least like interest scales. Notice that the scale clarity index associated with medical is not H but F. This could mean that she likes the people-involvement in the medical scale but would dislike the use of machines or instruments. Generally, Donna is people oriented in the sense that she enjoys attending to people rather than being a mentor or being closely involved with them. She is specifically oriented toward medical work.

Donna needs vocational counseling to explore how she can prepare for a job. The scale clarity indices are high at the two extremes in the list of interest areas, which suggests maturity in vocational development. Thus, this is an easily interpreted profile. Her main concern is how to pursue her vocational interests and plans.

## MIQ

*David Weiss:* Donna appears consistent in her stated preferences, as indicated by the circular triads score of 32; it is likely, therefore, that her preferences will not change much unless she is exposed to occupational experiences different from what she has known in the past. Her highest need is on the moral values scale — it is important to her that her job not conflict with her ethical beliefs (see Fig. 9.3d). Her preferences are moderately high for company policies and practices, security, supervision — human relations, and, to some extent, recognition. These are all "extrinsic" reinforcers, indicating that much of her satisfaction in an occupation is likely to derive from the conditions of work rather than from the work itself. Only ability utilization and achievement, of the intrinsic (work itself) reinforcers, are in the moderate range.

Comparison of her MIQ profile with the ORP profiles for eighty-one occupations shows a wide range of jobs in which she is predicted to be "likely satisfied." These include a number of manual and personal service occupations in which extrinsic rewards predominate. Her needs are least likely to be met in technical and sales occupations, with predictions of "not likely satisfied" for occupations in which intrinsic rewards predominate. These include teaching and other professional-service types of occupations. The MIQ results seem to imply that her leanings toward technical training are more likely to be satisfied (in those occupations with primarily extrinsic rewards) than those toward the majority of college-trained occupations which depend on satisfaction with the intrinsic characteristics of the work.

## WVI

*Donald Super:* Donna's high scores are on altruism and on economic returns, which are in the human relations and materials areas. Looking at her low scores, we find a rather large number, including creativity, management, achievement, prestige, esthetics, independence, and intellectual stimulation (see Fig. 9.3e). Some of the values that fit into the human relations area, such as associates and supervisory relations, are neither high nor low. The profile isn't altogether a consistent one until her present status and history are taken into consideration. People tend not to value so much that which they have always known. Her domestic situation is such that apparently she is secure economically, so evidently her interest in making money, in being economically productive, is for the sake of income rather than for the sake of security. The high altruism fits in with some of the other inventories and with what she says about herself, and it is apparently valid even though it is one of the scales that can be easily faked. The fact that she is not high on achievement, creativity, or intellectual stimulation made me wonder, from the profile alone, whether she has any substantive or intrinsic interests. She is a woman who has been primarily a career homemaker. Although recognizing that after her child grows up she may need something to do, she hasn't had driving interests in any particular area that have led her to do anything in addition to being a homemaker. I do not mean to imply that homemaking is not doing anything — it is in fact doing everything; what I mean is interest in one special kind of work. This picture from the WVI seems to fit in with some of the accompanying information: broad interests, though comparatively shallow, perhaps. It supports the notion of relatively short-term training in medical services rather than in biological science.

My thoughts about counseling with Donna, before hearing what others had to say on the basis of other inventories, were that she might look for an area involving relatively short-term training in which she could work with people and be economically productive. The particular outlet should be dependent upon training and employment opportunities rather than on what would be particularly meaningful and challenging to her. What we have learned from the SVIB, the KOIS, and OVIS fits in well with the interpretations one would make from the WVI, and these other inventories further pinpoint some specific occupations which meet the specification that I think I see in the WVI.

*Question:* What effect do you think college norms would have: would they change the profile?

*Dr. Super:* That's a good question. Here we are using twelfth-grade norms and not college or adult norms. The fact that there is relatively little change from grade 10 to 12 leads me to use the twelfth-grade norms with her with a fair amount of confidence. But there is some indication that people who have not been in the labor force answer work values inventories somewhat differently from people who have had regular work experience. I think it is not so much age that influences work values, but actual employment experience. We might thus see some change in Donna's profile after she has worked for a while. Change is not so much dependent upon age as it is upon knowing the realities of working.

*Question:* Do you think mature women have a lot of self-doubts that are hard to handle if they have not been working and are about to resume work?

*Dr. Super:* Yes, we do see this often in women who are thinking about returning to the labor force. They recognize work has demands that are different from those they have been used to meeting at home and in the neighborhood. I'm not sure that I see that in Donna's profile. I think that if she were particularly threatened by the prospect of returning to work, she would have valued security and achievement more highly than she does. Therefore she is not fearful that she is unqualified to reenter the labor market.

## *Summary*

It is appropriate to comment on the discussants' remarks to illuminate similarities and differences in how they managed the information the inventories yielded. It should also be pointed out how some of the features of the inventories themselves influenced the data from which the participants drew their inferences and suggestions.

Many of the distinctive features of the inventories are discussed in chapter 1: differences in conceptualizations of interests and values, in item content and response format, in keying or scoring procedures, and in types of scales.

Some of the inventories are not appropriate in certain situations for a variety of reasons. The MVII is not useful for women or college students; the SVIB should not be given to persons much under the level of a high school senior; and the OVIS, because of its lack of norms, should not be administered to persons too far beyond high school. The applicability of other inventories in certain situations is a more subtle matter. For the MIQ and KOIS it is discovered after the person has taken the inventory that his interests are not sufficiently crystallized to yield meaningful information; thus a cautious interpretation is required. In addition, Super suggests from his clinical experience with the WVI profile that it might have been inappropriately assigned in Robert's case, because of his apparent lack of crystallization of self-concept.

As one reads the interpretations and comments by each of the members of the panel, a striking concept emerges: consistency. Each commentator makes mention of where there is and is not consistency. Some of the inventories provide the data for this judgment within each scale by means of error bands or scale clarity indices; in other inventories consistent responses are weighted more heavily than inconsistent ones. Consistency was also sought among sets of highest and lowest scoring scales. Occasionally a high-scored scale was judged inconsistent with its company — several scales known to go together. The ability to make judgments of this kind is dependent upon knowledge of the intercorrelations of the scales. Scales that are completely independent or correlated near zero among themselves will not support any judgments of consistency, but scales that are moderately correlated may. This is usually expressed as "people who tend to score high on x scale will also score high on y and z." Sometimes the phrase "ought to" appears in place of "will also," suggesting that the interpreter is using clinical insight or intuition rather than data from the inventory manual. Consistency at this level is valued too; inconsistencies among high or low scores are mentioned together with suggestions for further counseling or exploration.

Finally, several commentators remark on the consistency of the profile data and the person's expressed choice. It is usually assumed that an expressed choice of occupational plans is reliable until it is rejected as invalid, and that inventoried interests should be consistent with it. When a person's inventoried interests do not agree with his expressed choice, as is seen in Doug's KOIS profile, the counselor is reluctant to insist that the inventory results ought to be considered more strongly than his expressed choice. For normative inventories the assessment of consistency with expressed choice is easy; for the homogeneously scaled interest and value inventories the judgment of consistency is more open to error, depending upon how well informed the interpreter is about the kinds of interests or values that are appropriate to a given expressed choice.

It should be mentioned that all the interpreters at one point said or implied that inventory results were not sufficient by themselves for career planning. Additional exploration and counseling were suggested to resolve the conflict between inventoried and expressed interests or to clear up what might be some confusion in self-definition and perception. Although no personality scales are offered by the inventories, the tendency on the part of some of the interpreters to make judgments about personality or adjustment was strong. Although it is widely assumed that personality and vocational interests and values are interrelated, solid empirical support for this supposition is lacking, and such inferences should be approached circumspectly.

The interpretations of the commentators also reveal that most of the inventories yield more information than can be processed in one look. Each remarks on how he looks for the highest and/or lowest scores first or for patterns within the profiles. The OVIS and the MIQ even do this automatically by means of their computer-produced profiles. After highs and lows are discussed, the interpretation typically proceeds to scales that relate to expressed choices. Scales that had scores at an intermediate level and were not relevant to an expressed choice received little attention from

242

the commentators. For inventories that are scored for many scales, this represents a considerable loss, since the cost of generating information is significant. A further troublesome aspect is that there are areas of interests and occupations for which no scales exist. Attending only to high or low scores on any homogeneously scaled inventory will not yield the suggestion that a client try for a career as a professional athlete, for example. Many important occupations in our society are absent from the profiles of the normative inventories — diplomat, fireman, chef, fisherman, machine operator in a manufacturing plant, to name a few — and therefore would not receive attention from the interpreter whose scope is only as broad as the profile's.

The way in which levels of scale scores were interpreted varied. To begin with, a variety of standardized scores are employed: raw scores, T scores, stanines, lambda coefficients, percentiles, and $D^2$. It is the unusual counselor, much less client, who can make his way among these varied forms of information and understand the peculiarities of each. All the inventories require a different vocabulary with which to communicate scores and results: "high ranking," "most similar to," "greater than x percent of . . . ," or "not likely to be satisfied in. . . ."

There was also significant variation in whether real predictions were made. Some of the discussants were willing to say a given occupation would or would not be suitable. Much more of the interpretation was concerned with confirming what the person said about himself or with providing a description of the person's types or areas of interests.

The inventories and their interpretations were in moderately good agreement for Robert. There was sound support for his expressed interest in business enterprise as well as agreement that his relative youth made it difficult to form normative comparisons and that he had many low scores on homogeneous scales. Interpretation of Doug's profile indicated a lack of agreement on the potential avenues of his career development. Yet a number of interpretators, for different reasons, suggested that more counseling with Doug would be appropriate. Donna's inventory results attracted the most positive support. Possibly this is the consequence of Donna's age and former work experience; her expressions of interests and values are based on real experience rather than on projections made at age sixteen or during the college years. Since taking the inventories, Donna has enrolled in a two-year course at a nearby community college designed to secure her registration as a nurse. It must be understood that this does

243

not necessarily validate the inventories. It may be only a self-fulfilling prophecy, since the results of the inventories were interpreted to Donna as a part of the agreement that she would take them. But had she not inventoried her interests and simply acted on her expressed choice, that would have been self-fulfilling prophecy too. At least she began her preparation to reenter the world of work with more conviction and is likely to remain in her career with more than ordinary fulfillment and satisfaction.

## Reference

Borgen, F. H., D. J. Weiss, H. E. A. Tinsley, R. V. Dawis, and L. H. Lofquist. Occupational reinforcer patterns. *Minnesota Studies in Vocational Rehabilitation*, 1968, 24.

*Index*
▼▼▼

# Index

247